Chinese Corporate Identity

Chinese Corporate Identity represents the first study of economic restructuring in reform era China to apply the concepts of identity and corporate space, both of which have become increasingly relevant as foreign invested and Chinese ventures face complex operational and societal issues in the wake of globalization.

Peverelli uses his own theoretical framework to examine and detect multiple identities of Chinese enterprises within a larger, comprehensive organization theory. A host of practical case studies taken from Peverelli's portfolio as a consultant help to illustrate this original theory, while providing a practical reference to the modern Chinese economy and Chinese management.

Chinese Corporate Identity will prove a valuable resource to academics working in organization theory, cultural anthropology, sociology, and business and economics. In addition, its supporting case studies will be of interest to consulting firms, foreign embassies and consulates in China.

Peter J. Peverelli is a lecturer in the Department of Management and Organization at the Free University, Amsterdam, the Netherlands.

Routledge advances in Asia-Pacific business

Chinese Corporate Identity

Peter J. Peverelli

Routledge
Taylor & Francis Group

LONDON AND NEW YORK

First published 2006
by Routledge
2 Park Square, Milton Park, Abingdon, Oxon OX14 4RN

Simultaneously published in the USA and Canada
by Routledge
270 Madison Ave, New York, NY 10016

Routledge is an imprint of the Taylor & Francis Group

Transferred to Digital Printing 2009

© 2006 Peter J. Peverelli

Typeset in Times by Wearset Ltd, Boldon, Tyne and Wear

British Library Cataloguing in Publication Data
A catalogue record for this book is available from the British Library

Library of Congress Cataloging in Publication Data
A catalog record for this book has been requested

ISBN10: 0-415-37208-9 (hbk)
ISBN10: 0-415-54676-1 (pbk)

ISBN13: 978-0-415-37208-4 (hbk)
ISBN13: 978-0-415-54676-8 (pbk)

Contents

Preface

This study was conceived exactly ten years ago. In the rapidly changing competitive environment a genuine vogue for corporate identity emerged among Chinese enterprises. It struck me as an exciting topic for a study, but once I started collecting and analysing identity statements by Chinese companies, I found that I lacked a proper framework to observe and analyse.

My quest for a workable theory brought me in contact with Henk van Dongen and his group of researchers at Erasmus University Rotterdam. His model, which combined Karl Weick's model of organizing, Paul Watzlawick's theory of communication and elements of postmodern thinking from philosophers like Michel Foucault and Jacques Derrida, appealed to me and I first started applying it to my consulting practice, which consisted of helping my European clients co-operate better with their Chinese partners, to put it simply.

While working with the theory and its methodology, I also added some elements of my own, in particular the concept of 'mental space' introduced by the psycholinguist Gilles Fauconnier. My linguistic training in a previous life proved useful after all. The synergy created by theoretical work and consulting practice resulting in my book *Cognitive Space* (Peverelli 2000), with which I finally had the theoretical foundation to return to my favourite subject, which is the topic of this study.

This is an elusive text. In the beginning it may not be what you expect it to be, but after a while it may not be what you thought it to be in the beginning. Further on it may appear to you that you are reading the same thing over and over again, while yet further the repeated stories may strike you as different each time. By that time, I hope that you will start to realize that it is not my text that is elusive, but the processes in which Chinese corporate identity is constructed. This study is written in the way Chinese enterprises construct their identities. I hope that it will help academics as well as professionals regularly dealing with Chinese companies understand why they found it so hard to understand those companies. It explains how Chinese enterprises are products of more general Chinese modes of organizing and offers simple but highly effective methods to observe and understand those processes.

Although as a category this book is an academic study, it has been written like a story. Try to appreciate it in both ways simultaneously, while reading it.

A number of people have contributed to this study. I would first like to thank Henk van Dongen for his support, which was as elusive as this text. I guess I inherited this trait from him. Second in line are my clients. I have already mentioned them in the preface of Peverelli (2000), but they remain my most challenging discussion partners. I thank my wife for keeping up with me for more than two decades, in particular for enduring another period of writing. Although we have not known one another that long, I would like to mention Chan Kwok Bun here as well. We always have very limited time for our meetings, as we live on different parts of the globe, but I experience them as extremely inspiring. Some of the authors cited in this study have been suggested by him.

Peter J. Peverelli,
Delft, May 2005

Introduction
Chinese corporate identity

Rethinking identity

This is not a psychological study, but as one of the key terms, identity, of my subject matter is derived from psychology, I want to make a very short walk through the definitions of this term in mainstream social psychological literature.

According to my dictionary of psychology (Bergsma and van Petersen 2000), identity is the perception of personal unity, the conviction to remain unchanged and essentially the same. This definition depicts the formation of identity as one-way traffic. Identity seems to originate from within the person. This strikes me as highly unsatisfactory, as it would only make sense for us to construct an identity to distinguish us from 'the others'. In other words, identity should have three aspects: how I perceive myself, how others perceive me and the interaction between those two.

Social psychology includes studies into the formation of identity of persons vis-à-vis social groups. These studies are generally referred to as 'social identity theory' (Hogg and Vaughn 1995: 328 ff.; Ashforth and Mael 1989). Such groups can be large groups such as nations or religions, or smaller groups like associations. Such groups provide members with a social identity:

> a definition of who one is and a description and evaluation of what this entails. Social identities not only describe members but prescribe appropriate behaviour (that is, norms) for members.
>
> (Hogg and Vaughn 1995: 329)

This definition seems to approach identity from exactly the opposite direction to my dictionary of psychology. Hogg and Vaughn seem to understand identity as bestowed onto the individual by the social group. It is one-way traffic once more. Ashforth and Mael show some awareness towards the bidirectionality of social identity by pointing out that it also provides a means to define others.

Haslam's approach seems to make a serious effort in defining social identity in terms of two-way traffic (Haslam 2001: 27). According to Haslam,

> Social identity theory was originally developed in an attempt to understand the psychological basis of intergroup discrimination. Why do group members malign other groups and what makes people so often believe that their own group is better than others?

(p. 27)

However, in the remainder of his chapter, Haslam does not go beyond describing how the identity formation of one group is dependent on the perception of the relation between that group and other groups. That process is still understood as taking place with that particular group. The 'others' are part of the sense-making process, but in the end it is still one-way traffic.

McCall and Simmons (1966) is an early attempt to define identity as a bidirectional process. They link identity of an actor to the role that actor develops vis-à-vis other actors as a result of social interaction (op. cit.: 142). Interaction is defined earlier in the book as:

> Whenever a relationship of deterministic influence between two events cannot be resolved into a simple function of one but instead must be treated as a joint function, as a mutual or reciprocal influence, we have a case of interaction.

(op. cit.: 47)

My main problem with McCall and Simmons' concept of identity is that in the end it still seems to be something actors 'have'. It may be an outcome of interaction (as other such outcomes of interaction treated in this seminal study), but once identity has been constructed, it seems to be something static, something that is apart from the interaction. I seem to prefer a model of identity that can explain identity as a process, or, closer to the terminology used by McCall and Simmons: identity as part of the interaction instead of its result.

The first definition of identity construction that adopts a bidirectional process approach is Hatch and Schulz (2002). Although this is an article on organizational identity, the authors point out that there is no fundamental difference in the ways individuals and organizations construct their identities. Hatch and Schultz reason that the identity constructs of organizations as expressed through business cards, brochures, dressing style, etc., leave impressions on others. In a similar fashion, the identity constructs of other related parties will leave an impression on the own identity of an organization. They then conclude that:

organizational identity occurs as the result of a set of processes that continuously cycle within and between cultural self-understandings and images formed by organizational 'others'.

(p. 390)

This definition is indeed much more dynamic than any definition of identify proposed before. However, it still seems to depart from individual identity constructs. Organizations (individuals) construct their own identity, while the individual identity constructs of others can affect the own identity process.

I believe that the main problem causing this one-way traffic type of definitions is that psychologists have so far regarded identity as an entity, something that exists out there. It seems that we can obtain a much richer definition of identity if we start perceiving it as an interactional process, i.e. identity as the construction of identity by the holder of the identity and the social-cognitive environment of which the holder is a member. Such a definition is richer in two directions:

1 it comprises the three aspects of identity: the holder of the identity, the environment in which the identity is constructed and the construction process;
2 it allows for a multiple definition of identity: an individual can be perceived has having multiple identities in multiple contexts.

Such a theoretical framework exists and I will introduce it further in this chapter. We first have to deal with one more core topic: 'corporate identity'.

Rethinking corporate identity

Mainstream thinking on the subject of corporate identity seems to approximate the definition of identity as presented in my dictionary of psychology: the presumptions of an enterprise on what it is and how it wishes to be perceived by others. It is one-way traffic once more: the enterprise first constructs an 'identity' and then devises a strategy to promote it to its stakeholders. Moreover, a considerable part of the corporate identity writings is devoted to the material, visual, part of the identity like designing logos, writing promotional publications, etc. (e.g. Olins 1978; Albert and Whetten 1985).

The most frequently quoted definition of corporate identity is that proposed by Birkigt and Stadler in 1986:

Corporate Identity ist die strategisch geplante und operativ eingesetzte Selbstdarstellung und Verhaltensweise eines Unternehmens nach innen und nach aussen auf Basis einer festgelegten

Unternehmensphilosophie, einer langfristigen Unternehmenszielsetzung und eines definierten (Soll)-Images – mit dem Willen, alle Hand-
lungsinstrumente des Unternehmens in einheitlichem Rahmen nach
innen und aussen zur Darstellung zu bringen.

(Leu 1994: 14; van Riel 1996: 41)

All core terms in this definition evoke one-way traffic thinking: *Selbstdarstellung, Unternehmensphilosophie, Unternehmenszielsetzung*: it is the
company that devises its identity. Moreover, it is a singular definition (*in
einheitlichem Rahmen*) in the sense that it presumes that an enterprise has
one identity that it wishes to promote in all contexts. Finally, it is a static
definition. Once the identity of a company has been conceived, it exists
and is promoted as an unchanging fact.

This definition does not work for me. Referring to my tentative definition of identity above, I miss two aspects in the definition by Birkigt and
Stadler: the environment in which the identity is constructed and the
process by which the identity is constructed by the enterprise in its interaction with the environment.

It is the aim of this study to formulate an entirely novel way of looking
at the identity of enterprises. I intend to formulate a definition of corporate identity as a process of identity construction during the continuous
interaction between the company and its social-cognitive context. I will
show how corporate identity emerges from what the company wished to
be and what its environment wishes it to be. Moreover, I will demonstrate
that an enterprise develops multiple identities in multiple social-cognitive
contexts.

Corporate identity in a theory of organizing

I believe that the main reason why the context of identity construction has
been slighted in the mainstream literature on corporate identity is that the
topic has been approached as a separate problem, as a field of academic
research by itself. In this study I propose to perceive corporate identity as
part of, and embedded in, a comprehensive theory of organizing. I have
already used the term (social-cognitive) context a number of times in this
introduction. Chapter 1 of this study will be devoted to the introduction of
a theory of organizing in which this term is one of the core concepts.

Enterprises are organizations, they are constructed and continuously
reconstructed in ongoing social interaction. In this sense, enterprises have
no special status compared with other types of organizations. Instead of
corporate identity, we may very well speak of organizational identity. Such
a term would comprise corporate identity. However, we might even take
this line of thinking one step further and presume that the identity is the
organization. Organizations can be regarded as social-cognitive structures
that only exist in that they are perceived as existing by a group of actors.

However, this introduction is not the proper place to go into this matter in detail. The main point I wish to state here is that we would be able to obtain a much more useful definition of corporate identity if we would cease to regard corporate identity as a separate field of study and would instead consider it part of a more general study of human organizing processes.

Chinese corporate identity

If we wish to study corporate identity, we need something to study. We need a corpus of enterprises and observe the processes that construct their identities. I have chosen Chinese enterprises as the sources for my cases in this study. This decision is motivated in two ways. One is a very obvious one. I have been advising Western companies in their co-operation with Chinese counterparts for almost two decades and have therefore accumulated a huge knowledge base regarding Chinese enterprises. I have described Chinese organizing processes before in previous publications (Peverelli 2000).

A more convincing reason for selecting Chinese corporate identity construction is that the concept of corporate identity has only been recently discovered in China. A number of developments in the Chinese economy of the past two decades have led to the 'discovery' of the notion of corporate identity:

1 As part of the gradual transition from a planned economy to a market economy, the large state-owned enterprises (SOEs), still the backbone of the economy, were gradually made responsible for their own profit and loss. The role of the State and its local representative organizations was changed from manager to owner. The leaders of SOEs were upgraded from agents of the State to real managers.
2 The smaller collective enterprises, enterprises established by local governments, underwent a similar change.
3 Several new types of enterprises appeared, including privately owned ones. Because of the recent establishment, these enterprises were managed in a more 'managerial' way than the older types from the start (for a thorough introduction of the current situation in this respect see Tang and Ward 2003: 132 ff.).

One consequence of these developments, that was especially hard to cope with by the leaders of the SOEs, was competition. Formerly, the economic planners of a city like Beijing would estimate the number of shoes needed annually in their own region and make sure that sufficient shoe-making capacity was available. Suppose that at the beginning of the planned economy three standard shoe factories were deemed necessary for meeting the shoe demand in Beijing, these would be spread evenly over the urban area and named Beijing Nr 1 Shoe Factory, Beijing Nr 2 Shoe Factory and Beijing Nr 3 Shoe Factory. With the increase of the population, another factory would be needed at a certain point. This would be built and named ... All shoes would be purchased by a state trading company, which took care of the distribution of the products to the state-owned retailers.

In the new competitive environment, the leaders, now managers, of these enterprises suddenly realized that they needed to attract buyers, now referred to as consumers, to their particular shoes. The director of the Beijing Nr 1 Shoe Factory faced the problem of having to persuade those consumers to buy their shoes, rather than those of Nr 2.

While this problem involved a number of realms, such as marketing and strategy that were all rather new for the managers from the planned economy era, one aspect that is especially interesting is the discovery of corporate image as a means to distinguish, not only the products, but the entire enterprise, from its competitors. Not only the bureaucrats turned managers, but also the new generation of managers of companies established after the beginning of the economic reforms felt that 'selecting' (many of them literally spoke of 'selecting' an identity) a corporate identity was the foundation for long-term survival.

By the mid-1990s, the interest in corporate identity had grown into a genuine corporate identity vogue. Companies would use their identity in advertisements; national newspapers carried columns in which major corporations explained their CI (these Latin letters appeared in Chinese texts), etc.

Many of these stories seem quite similar at first sight, but closer inspection reveals a broad variety in cues, occasions, symbols, etc., that are used as building blocks of Chinese corporate sense-making. To mention only a few examples: some enterprises select features of the region in which they are situated, thus profiling themselves as being part of the local culture. Other companies use the story of the enterprise's establishment as the main constituent of its culture. Yet others try to derive their identity from the type of technology used by the company.

A major impediment for Chinese companies trying to make sense of their identity, as well as for Western researchers attempting the same, is that they all try to craft singular, one-way traffic type, definitions of those identities. In imitation of mainstream Western corporate identity thinking, Chinese companies are trying to 'design', by themselves or with the aid of corporate identity specialists, identities of their own, spending considerable effort on the material corporate image, including logo, corporate colours, etc.

However, this type of identity does not provide information as to what the company is for its home region, its employees, its clients, etc. I contend that what a company believes itself to be is equally important for a complete understanding as what the company's environment believes it to be.

The company('s management) may wish to profile itself in a certain way in a certain context, but other parties in that context also hold certain beliefs as to what the company is to them. I argue that neither is the identity of that company, but that the interaction between those two sets of beliefs constructs the identity. I would like to take this even one step further and propose that the interaction itself is part of the identity. Corporate identity is a process of constructing and continuously reconstructing the identity of an enterprise in a specific social-cognitive context.

In order to work out this tentative definition into a model of corporate identity, I will first introduce the more comprehensive organizing model in which this corporate identity definition should become an inextricable part.

1 Corporate identity in a theory of organizing

Identity in context

This text intends to study the identity of enterprises from an organizing perspective. In this chapter, I intend to show how a more useful definition of corporate identity can be reached by trying to craft such a definition as an organic part of a comprehensive model of human organizing processes. This model is based on social integration theory as formulated in Peverelli (2000) and regards an enterprise as a social-cognitive structure, produced and continuously reproduced in ongoing social interaction. It has a social element, the actors connected to the enterprise, and a cognitive element, the ideas, perceptions, causal models, ways of doing things, etc., shared by those actors in relation to the enterprise. This coarse formulation will probably be more confusing than clarifying, but I will introduce the model in more detail further in this chapter. The gist in this paragraph is to clarify that I regard an enterprise as a product, a construct, of social interaction. The enterprise is a story, told and continuously retold by the actors involved. These actors include people working for the enterprise, but also comprise other actors, usually referred to as stakeholders in mainstream management literature. The analysis of such stories will therefore be an important methodology employed in this study.

There are more of such social-cognitive structures than enterprises. The city of London is one and so is the province of Limburg in the Netherlands. FIFA is yet another example, but also a street gang making a certain neighbourhood of Chicago unsafe for a nocturnal stroll. Even your family is one. To summarize, all our social institutions, organizations, etc., can be regarded as stories that are continuously narrated by a certain group of actors.

Those stories consist of a main theme, a plot, various sub-themes, a certain perception of reality, particular symbols, etc. The actors pertaining to the structure tell their story to give themselves a place to exist, to specify the role they play, recognizable for actors not belonging to that particular structure. I have coined the term cognitive space to refer to such structures. This term is inspired by the dual meaning of the notion of space. On one hand it provides a location, and on the other hand it puts a fence around that location, indicating what does and what does not belong to the location. In other words, the term space simultaneously refers to the location and its limits.

Now I am already coming closer to the link between my model of organizing and the topic of this study: corporate identity. I propose that the identity of a social-cognitive structure like an enterprise is the whole of the cognitive element. It is the cognitive element that creates coherence in the social element and at the same time makes the structure recognizable for actors not belonging to it.

If this was it, discussing corporate identity would be a simple matter. We actually may conclude that we do not need to discern a separate notion of corporate identity, as we already can refer to it as the cognitive element of the enterprise as a social-cognitive structure. However, the attempt to arrive at a definition of corporate identity we have initiated above already reveals that the identity of an enterprise is not only embedded in the cognitive element of that enterprise. It is also part of the cognitive elements of other social-cognitive structures. If we observe that the identity of an enterprise is not only recognized by its own actors, but also by those belonging to other such structures, we conclude that the identity is co-constructed by the latter. Identity is a bidirectional thing. Identity is apparently something that exceeds the limits of its owner. Your identity is useless unless it is also recognized by me and vice versa. Your identity is also part of mine and mine of yours. Apparently, identities of social-cognitive structures are created in a social-cognitive structure that is higher, or broader, than the individual structures. For the time being, I will refer to such a higher structure as a 'context'. The identity of a social-cognitive structure, in our case an enterprise, is constructed in a certain context, which is itself also a social-cognitive structure, of which the enterprise acts as if it were an individual actor.

Adding the notion of context greatly enhances the descriptive power of the definition of corporate identity. We can now envision a particular enterprise as being part of a number of different contexts. In each context a different identity will be constructed. In other words, enterprises develop multiple identities in multiple contexts. Albert and Whetten's seminal article (Albert and Whetten 1985) does speak of multiple identities, but fails to provide a proper definition of the different contexts in which such multiple identities are created. Moreover, Albert and Whetten are still defining the construction of organizational identity as a deliberate process.

The differences between various identity constructs do not have to be large, but even subtle differences can create confusion, or even conflicts, if the nature of the differences is not recognized by the actors involved. For example, Philips is based in Eindhoven, the capital of the province of Noord-Brabant of the Netherlands. When the company published its intent to move the corporate head office to Amsterdam, this met with severe resistance, from the staff as well as other parties in Eindhoven, including the municipal government. The identities of Philips and Eindhoven were apparently so intertwined that moving the head office to Amsterdam was almost regarded as treason. The Board of Philips, however, consisting of people from various regions of the Netherlands or even beyond, failed to recognize this identity construct. In my model of organizing the Board is a social-cognitive structure of its own, referred to as social-cognitive configuration or simply: configuration (this term will be further defined below). Apparently, the regional aspect of the corporate identity of Philips as constructed by the Board was 'the Netherlands' rather than 'Eindhoven'. The Board therefore wished to move the head office to Amsterdam, the nation's capital, which is better known internationally than Eindhoven.

Summarizing, enterprises are social-cognitive constructs consisting of a social element and a cognitive element. The identity of an enterprise is the whole of the cognitive element with which the actors give themselves a place in society. It is also part of the cognitive element of other enterprises that are part of the same higher social-cognitive structure, called context. An individual enterprise can have multiple identities in multiple contexts. These are not yet hypotheses. In order to formulate hypotheses, I first need to formalize the above casual introduction of the organizing theory that I will use in the remainder of this text to study the various aspects of corporate identity.

A theory of social integration

Social integration theory draws heavily from the organizing theory of Karl Weick (Weick 1979, 1995, 2001). The central theme in Weick's theory is that of sense-making. Actors constantly encounter situations that are multiply interpretable. They try to make sense of such situations by reducing the equivocality to one single interpretation. This reduction process takes place in social interaction between several actors. Actors will exchange information regarding a specific topic until they have reached a certain level of agreement. In this respect, Weick's definition of interaction is close to the one proposed by McCall and Simmons (1966) quoted earlier. The achievement of this purpose is reflected by the degree to which the actors' behaviour becomes interlocked. The interlocking of behaviour of actors in continuous social interaction is the basic definition of organizing in Weick's theory.

Weick further observes that actors perform this interpretation retroactively. Actors first act [enactment] on previous experience, until they encounter an equivocal situation. At that moment, the process to reduce equivocality starts until a sufficient degree of non-equivocality has been attained.

Moreover, actors do not search for the best (most realistic, most true,

etc.) interpretation of that situation, but for the most plausible interpretation, i.e. the interpretation that suits the current context (the moment the
interpretation takes place) of the actors best, is selected [selection].

As a result of the reduction, some possible meanings of the equivocal
data will be rejected and some will be retained [retention]. The actors will
then continue to act based on that interpretation, until more equivocality
is met. This cycle of enactment → selection → retention is repeated end-
lessly. Actors build up a certain view of what the world is like based on the
continuous process of sense-making. Weick refers to these views as cause
maps. In the course of his sense-making, actor A may observe event Y and
judge that it has been caused by event X. The next time event X occurs, A
will presume (retroactive sense-making) that Y will follow. Consequently,
if A wants to prevent Y from happening, A will try to avoid X. This will
continue until something happens that runs counter to this part of A's
cause map (e.g. an event X happens without causing an event Y), at which
moment A will revise this map.

Another key theme in Weick's thinking is the notion of double interact,
which was proposed to describe the sense-making process by actors in
ongoing interaction. Actors who have to co-operate in performing a certain
task will at first hold different interpretations of various aspects related to
that task (equivocality). This equivocality will impede them to interlock
their behaviour. During their initial interaction, the actors will exchange
these interpretations and mutually adapt them until a common interpretation (regarding aspects essential to perform the task successfully) has been
attained. If we wish to understand such interaction, it is insufficient to
observe how B reacts to A. We also have to observe A's reaction to B's
reaction to A. When actor A makes a statement to actor B, B can either
affirm or deny A's statement. Subsequently, A can accept or reject B's
reaction. This results in four possibilities as represented in Table 1.1.

Simple interacts are insufficient to assess the relation between A and B.
If we know that B rejects A, we only know exactly that. However, if we
also know that A in turn rejects B's rejection, we know that the relation
between A and B on that particular issue is one of independence. If A had
accepted B's rejection, the relation would have been one of conformity.
Different outcomes of the double interact have different consequences for

Table 1.1 Types of double interact

Act	Interact	Double interact	Type of influence
A	A	A	Uniformity
A	A	B	Anticonformity
A	B	A	Independence
A	B	B	Conformity

Source: Adapted from Weick 1979, p. 115.

the continuation of the interaction between A and B. Moreover, the double interact is also indispensable for the construction of identity of both A and B, i.e. what A is to B and B to A. Again, Weick's analysis of interaction approaches the one drawn up by McCall and Simmons (1966). However, where McCall and Simmons stop at stating that interaction is 'a *joint* function, as a mutual or reciprocal influence' (McCall and Simmons 1966: 47), Weick elaborates on this concept by defining the double interact as the basic building block of social interaction.

Social interaction is an endless repetition of double interacts between actors. In the course of social interaction, actors will adjust their behaviour to their fellow actors, resulting in interlocked behaviour. Several consecutive cycles of interlocked behaviour constitute a collective structure, a pattern of collective behaviour, like regularly repeated activities in a company. A typical example of such a structure are the employees of a company who leave home every weekday to go to the place of work they share to do the things they do every working day, etc. Their collective sense-making of the world has crystallized in a number of shared daily routines, symbols of which they make sense of in similar ways, etc. That they do not have to make sense of what to do and why to do it every single workday makes life a lot easier for them and allows them to make more efficient use of their limited span of attention to make sense of whatever is not compliant with their expectations.

The last key notion from Weick's theory to be mentioned is 'partial inclusion'. Each actor will be part of several groups of actors with interlocked behaviours. The formation of such groups is a continuous process; groups form and disband. Actors enter groups, while others leave them. During an effort to stabilize his inclusion in a certain group, an individual actor may be forced to integrate more of himself into that group. This notion of inclusion seems to bear great importance to organizing processes, however it is not very well elaborated by Weick.

It was especially this aspect that H.J. Van Dongen and his associates have used as a starting point to enrich Weick's theory. The most complete theoretical statement of their framework can be found in Van Dongen *et al.* (1996). The core theoretical notion of Van Dongen *et al.* is that of configuration. Configurations are groups of actors who, during continuous social interaction, have attained a similar interpretation of reality (compare Weick's interlocked behaviour). This definition reflects the two aspects of configurations:

1   a social aspect: frequent, organized, social interaction (e.g. work-related meetings);
2   a cognitive aspect: similar interpretation of reality.

Reality is understood as having a constructed nature. Actors construct their (version of) reality via an ongoing process of social interaction. These definitions of reality are never comprehensive theories comprising all aspects of reality. Actors only possess a limited span of attention. They will use this span to cover that part of reality that is essential; that which comes to the fore in the present context. Complex phenomena are reduced to simple, comprehensible, treatable facts (compare Weick's reduction of equivocality). Reality is constructed using a set of construction rules. Actors apply these rules in a continuous process of reconstruction of reality.

Following Weick, Van Dongen *et al.* recognize that actors are simultaneously included in several configurations. However, they replace Weick's term of 'partial inclusion' with the notion of 'multiple inclusion'. Weick's term seems to reflect the perception that actors divided their attention over a number of inclusions and is therefore never totally included in any one structure. Van Dongen's term 'multiple inclusion' emphasizes that actors are included in several, theoretically indefinite, configurations. In each concrete occasion of social interaction, actors will tighten a shared inclusion, but they will also have access to other inclusions.

Van Dongen *et al.* regard Weick's double interact as a useful tool in describing the interaction between two actors. However, its shortcoming is that it presupposes a dyadic relationship. This may explain why Weick has problems in elaborating his concept of partial inclusion. Van Dongen *et al.* introduce a third party into the relationship between two actors. Instead of dyadic relationships, they look at the relationship between actors as being tertial. This third refers to other inclusions of actors. During social interaction within a certain configuration, actors can bring elements of their other inclusions into that interaction. A particular actor can use a certain definition of reality in one context (configuration), but use another one in another context (configuration). Actors can draw from a multitude of inclusions and the nature of their relationship is different for each different third party.

The framework of Van Dongen *et al.* still has a number of shortcomings. The main issue could be called the macro–micro problem. A configuration is defined as a relatively small number of actors who frequently interact on a very specific subject. The problem is that it is virtually impossible (and probably undesirable) to define a set of criteria to determine when a group of actors is too large to be called a configuration. Actors form groups in various ways and of various sizes. Some of these groups, for example a national political party, can be quite large. Such a national political party consists of a relatively large number of people who do not all frequently interact. There are conventions, but these tend to be large and not all conventions are attended by all members. However, they are bound together by cognitive matter comparable with the cognitive element of a configuration. That cognitive matter is constructed in more or less the same fashion as is the case in a configuration. For example, a political party usually has its own magazine in which members exchange ideas.

One possible solution would be to expand the definition of configuration, but that would lead to such a broad definition that its explanatory power to clarify organizing processes would be harmed. We would like to have a notion akin to that of configuration that could be applied to the social aggregates described above.

Another conceptual flaw of the Van Dongen *et al.* model that is revealed in the political party example is that cognitive matter is not only constructed by actors in social interaction, but that social interaction between actors can also be stimulated by cognitive matter. To use an American example: Democrats from New York and those from San Francisco share some cognitive matter related to being Democrats, but may (and will) differ in the way New Yorkers differ in their world outlook from San Franciscans. New York Democrats may convene because they are Democrats, but seen from another perspective (third party) such a convention is also one of New Yorkers. To solve this problem I proposed the concept of cognitive space defined as: an association of any number of actors bound by a certain shared cognitive element. This definition may seem excessively complicated, as it could be simplified to: any number of actors bound by a certain shared cognitive element. However, such a definition seems to state that a cognitive space is 'a number of actors' with a certain attribute: 'with a shared cognitive element'. By defining it as an association of a social element and a cognitive element the equal importance of both is better expressed.

As indicated in the introductory section of this chapter, I like the term space, because it refers to something that confines, but is broader than the notion of configuration. Space touches upon time as well as place, it refers to space in which interaction can take place, but simultaneously to the socially constructed limitations (impediments) of the interaction. Within a certain space, activities proceed according to the rules that hold in that space. It is like Weick's bracketing: actors are unable to comprehend all cues that come to them from their environment and construct their version of reality using a selection of cues (Weick 1979: 113). Actors give meaning to their activities and agree on rules prescribing the ways how to act or not to act during interaction and consequently start regarding those meanings and rules as existing confinements of their actions (reification). However, contrary to the framework of Van Dongen *et al.*, we believe that this not only holds for social cognitive configurations, but also for larger groups of actors, which we are now referring to as spaces. The cognitive element (cause maps, construction rules, etc.) of such spaces are less specific than within configurations. Moreover, spaces differ in their degree of specificity. Larger, more diffuse, spaces can comprise smaller, more specific, spaces, which will inherit the traits of the larger space, while adding some specific traits of their own. California is a space. San Francisco is a more specific version of the California space. In this framework, configurations are in fact very similar to spaces. This could be defined as small group of actors with frequent social interaction evolving around a strong specific cognitive element. As a special type of sub-space, configurations will inherit the cognitive and social traits of the space in which they are constructed and will add more specific ones pertaining to their particular configurations.

Spaces can also be regarded as potential triggers of organizing processes. We cannot only observe ongoing social interaction within a space, but once we understand the cognitive element of a particular space, we may attempt to predict possible social interaction that may take place, or could have taken place, as a consequence of the cognitive element of that space, including the way(s) such interaction could be initiated and developed. Such insight will be valuable for an in-depth understanding of organizing processes by organization theorists, social psychologists, sociologists, etc., but will also serve a number of practical purposes, such as analysis of and intervention in organizational problems, marketing research and feasibility studies. I will not elaborate this topic here, but will illustrate several uses of spaces as potentialities at several places in this study. My notion of space is also an excellent tool for tackling one of the core unsolved problems in the theory of social integration: the nature of what are called 'organizations' in everyday parlance (enterprises, associations, government institutions, etc.). Following Weick, Van Dongen *et al.* are weary of using nouns like 'enterprise', 'association', etc., because they refer to entities and easily lead to reification, the belief that enterprises, associations, etc., exist. They prefer the use of verbs, like 'organizing', which refer to processes. However, human language is not that well suited for 'reification-free' discourse. We are not only used to speak of 'enterprises' as if they exist, the structure of the Western languages forces us to refer to such products of social-cognitive interaction with nouns.

With our methodological tool of space, we now have a simple and elegant solution for this problem. Enterprises, associations, institutions, unions, clubs, etc., are spaces. An enterprise comprises a number of actors (the employees) who continuously reconstruct the enterprise in their (work) daily routines. An enterprise also has a distinct cognitive aspect. Through the frequent social interaction employees of an enterprise share a certain cause map. Employees do certain activities in certain prescribed ways (construction rules). An important activity in enterprise spaces is the production of texts (brochures of the enterprise itself, or its products, magazines, annual reports, advertisements, etc.). Such texts serve a dual purpose: they present the space to the outside world and provide instructional material for the socialization of new employees.

Although I have described a space as having both a cognitive and a social element and have stated that those elements are mutually influencing, the cognitive element is stronger in a space than the social element. As sense-making, the reduction of equivocality, is the basic motor for human organizing processes, the influence of the cognitive element on the social element is stronger than the opposite. Once social activity has been set off, it can in turn influence cognitive activity, which can again affect social activity, in a continuous double-helix-like process. Moreover, when we observe structures of large spaces comprising one or more sub-spaces, the former seem to have a strong cognitive element, while the social element is quite weak. Information, meanings, etc., are easy to spread to a high number of people through the various means of communication. However, within a large space, such as a province, opportunities for common intensive social activities diminish. Seen from this angle, we could put space and configuration on a sliding scale. On one end of that scale there are very large spaces, which are almost purely cognitive spaces (nation spaces may be tentatively taken as examples of such spaces). When we proceed to the other end of the scale, spaces get smaller in terms of numbers of actors and the social element becomes more elaborate. At a certain moment, not too far from the other end, we encounter spaces like enterprise spaces. Arriving at the opposite end, we find the social-cognitive configurations, or for short, configurations. There, the cognitive and the social element are equally strong.

The notion of (multiple) inclusion can be applied to cognitive space as it was applied to configurations by Van Dongen *et al.* A particular instance of social interaction will always take place in a specific social-cognitive context (space), but actors can access the cognitive elements of other spaces through their multiple inclusions (a graphic convention for clarifying spaces and multiple inclusions of actors in those spaces can be found in Peverelli 2000). Organizational researchers can employ a number of methods to detect cognitive spaces. Some of them will be introduced later in this chapter in a section that will be entirely dedicated to one method: narrative analysis.

Back to contexts of identity

Armed with the social integration model I can now try to formulate my main theses regarding (corporate) identity:

1   The identity of actors or an aggregate of actors is the way those actors or aggregate of actors make sense of themselves in interaction with other actors or aggregate of actors.
2   In the course of that interaction the identity of the other actors or aggregate of actors will also be constructed simultaneously.
3   As a social construct, the identity of an actor or aggregate of actors will be different in each different social-cognitive context.
4   As an aggregate of actors, an enterprise will obtain a different identity in each different social-cognitive context.

In the remainder of this study I will examine the social-cognitive contexts, the cognitive spaces in which enterprises operate and observe the different processes of identity construction in those contexts. Such research can be initiated from two points of view:

- individual enterprises;
- types of contexts.

We can take an individual enterprise and look at the different identities it obtains in various contexts and we can take one type of context and observe the recurring aspects of corporate identity construction within that particular context. In this study I will do both, often using combination to emphasize the matrix nature of corporate identity.

Narratology as methodology

The most important research tool adopted in this study is the collection of a large number of stories related to a particular company and sort them in various ways according to different types of cognitive space. Stories are here used in the broadest possible meaning of the word and refer to company brochures, press releases, stories told within the company, newspaper articles, etc.

Stories give sense to people, their activities and the social institutions that are the products of their activities. When we would like to get to know a person better, we will ask him for his story. Facts and figures are often insufficient to explain a complicated matter, learning the story behind it will be far more explicative. For each of the case chapters (Chapters 3–7) I have constructed a corpus of texts. These texts can be searched with specialized software. A simple, but very useful tool is a concordance, a list of all contexts of a particular word, such as the name of the core company of that chapter. Once such a list has been created, we can observe the different ways in which that company is making sense in different social-cognitive contexts.

Story telling goes a long way back. Primitive cultures used stories to maintain contact with their ancestors and forge relations between the present and past generations, lacking a writing system and the proper media to retain hard copies of events. Identities of nations, cities, organizations, etc., are expressed in the form of stories (Boje *et al.* 2001: 132). In fact, organizations are so closely linked to their stories, that, from a constructionalist point of view, we could even state that our organizations are stories (see also Parker 2000: 81 ff.).

Stories tell us who were and are important in organizations, what people do and why they do so. Stories inspire, motivate, explain causal relations between events as perceived within a particular context. In other words, stories are a powerful tool for the socialization of new members of an organization. This makes the analysis of stories an important part of the research methodology of social integration theory.

Organizational stories are also linked to actors outside their organization of origin. Such stories tell as much about the 'them' as they do about 'us', hence we may look upon organizational stories as mirrors reflecting the relationship between the organization and other organizations and actors. Moreover, stories do not stand alone. Each story is linked to a number of other stories, which are in turn linked to yet other ones, thus forming a network of related stories.

In line with the basic theoretical consideration explained above, stories should not be judged as being true or false. All stories express realities as constructed in the social-cognitive environment from which they originated. Stories can be functional and dysfunctional in the sense that functional stories facilitate social interaction, while dysfunctional stories discourage and sometimes even obstruct interaction.

In view of the above, it is not surprising that narrative analysis, the critical study of organizational stories, is more and more recognized as a valuable addition to our repertoire of tools for organizational research. A considerable part of the current writings on narrative analysis draws heavily from Derrida's concept of deconstruction (Derrida 1976). Deconstructive reading of a story looks at the symbols embedded in the text and attempts to link them to what they represent in the perception of the author. It also tries to point out the opposite, that which is deliberately not represented in the story. Without assuming to provide an exhaustive treatment of deconstruction techniques, I will list a number of important aspects of deconstructive reading.

Bipolar terms

Bipolar terms, dichotomies, etc. are important objects of narrative research (Boje 2001: 23 ff.). Such bipolar terms are co-genetic (Van Dongen 1991: 50), one cannot be understood when separated from the other. A word like 'correct' can only be interpreted in comparison with its antonym 'incorrect'. Moreover, the border between 'correct' and 'incorrect' is also constructed in each individual context. An action considered as 'correct' in one context, can be regarded as 'incorrect' in another. Whenever we encounter the term 'correct' in a narrative, we need to link it with 'incorrect' and we need to establish the location of the border between those bipolar terms in each of the contexts relevant to that particular narrative.

Contextual links

Stories are teeming with symbols referring to cognitive spaces relevant to the content of the story. Although a particular story will be the product of a specific social-cognitive context, it may (and will) contain a number of links to other contexts. They are contexts in which the authors of the story are included, but when such a symbol is hit by readers who are also included in those contexts, those readers will recognize it intuitively. Moreover, readers may perceive certain symbols in a text as links to inclusions that are not shared by the authors of the story. Each time a story is read by a particular reader, it becomes a different story in the sense that the reader will interpret it from his/her own set of inclusions. In this respect the researcher is also a reader, who will be wary of not confusing his/her own inclusions with those of the author. The researcher of story telling will therefore have to discern three types of (references to) inclusions:

* those of the author(s);
* those of various intended readers;
* the researcher's own inclusions.

The other voice

Stories can sometimes only be understood properly if we identify parties involved that are not specifically mentioned in the story. I will refer to such parties as the other voice, or in Boje's terms, the rebel voice (2001: 25). For example, a company's brochure may contain several strong statements regarding the company's commitment to a clean environment. This could indicate that that particular company has been under attack from environmental organizations (administrative ones, pressure groups, etc.). Although those organizations may not be specifically mentioned in the brochure, they do play an important background role, as they could be envisioned by the corporate authors of the brochure as an important audience. The relation between the company and the external organization has thus influenced the production of the brochure. The other voice is embedded in the authors' line of reasoning, choice of words, etc. I have included a Chinese example of such a hidden other voice in Peverelli (2001).

Variation is meaningful

Reduction is probably one of the greatest sins of modernist scholarship and one of the most frequent occasions for reduction is regarding various different forms of a term as being the same. For example, John, John Doe and Mr Doe are taken to refer to the same person. However, we can envision that John Doe would be the proper way of reference in one context, while Mr Doe would be more appropriate in another one. The choice to select one variety rather than another is significant.

This aspect is especially important for the study of the identity construction of Chinese enterprises. As will become clear in the following chapters, many Chinese companies adopt a number of different names in different contexts. For example, Chinese enterprises tend to include the name of their home location in their company name. A fruit juice manufacturer located in Sanmenxia (a city in Henan province) called Hubin often calls itself Sanmenxia Hubin Fruit Juice Co. On some occasions, it also adds its home province to its name: Henan Sanmenxia Hubin Fruit Juice Co. However, Hubin Fruit Juice Co., or even simply Hubin are also possible. We should be extremely wary of presuming that all these names refer to the same company. Different names may be used in different cognitive spaces, which in our ontological position would mean that they refer to different identities of the company. Variations of the name of a company, or similar variations of what seems to be the same term, should be regarded as different terms, until evidence is found for the opposite.

This example of including geographic names in the names of companies is especially important, as different geographic names refer to different cognitive spaces. An enterprise may, and usually will, have different identities in different geographic cognitive spaces, which has considerable consequences for the relation of the enterprise with the government of that particular space (for an analysis of the various geographic identities of a Chinese enterprise also see Peverelli 2000: 90–95).

Corus – geopolitical identities of a steel maker

I will present one small example in this section: the Dutch branch of the Anglo-Dutch steel manufacturer Corus, known as Hoogovens, before the merger with British Steel in 1999. To prepare for a lecture on corporate identity, I have collected a random number of texts related to the Dutch Corus plant at Ijmuiden, an old port town in the province of Noord-Holland. I sorted the stories according to three geopolitical levels:

- the town: Ijmuiden;
- province: Noord-Holland;
- the state: the Netherlands.

Subsequently, I scanned the stories for recurrent themes. No statistical methods were used, as the number of stories was too small to generate reliable statistical indicators. In this methodology, we are looking for themes that are conspicuously recurrent. It seemed that most stories related to Corus as a company in Ijmuiden (town level) had 'employment/ labour' and 'environment' as their main themes. Stories related to the provincial level also frequently discussed environmental problems, but also regularly introduced Corus as one of the major enterprises in the province; a source of pride. The latter, the 'major enterprise' theme, was the single most important topic in the stories about Corus related to the Netherlands (national level). Table 1.2 summarizes these findings.

There is also a special context: Corus is frequently associated with 'steam'. The former use of steam technique frequently occurs in stories issued by Corus and the company sponsors the only steam engine museum in the Netherlands.

Table 1.2 Main themes associated with Corus in different geographic spaces

Space	Employment/ labour	Environment	Major enterprise
Ijmuiden	X	X	
Noord-Holland		X	X
The Netherlands			X

The emerging of those particular identities of Corus in those spaces can be explained in terms of the cognitive elements of the various spaces. The employees of Corus will be for the greater part drawn from the local work force. Entire families partly or completely depend on the monthly salaries earned in exchange for labour at Corus. Corus is therefore first of all regarded as an employer. The employment situation in the company is a major concern for the local community. Lay-offs will not only affect those whose source of income will disappear, but also various administrative agencies, like those overseeing social security whose work load will increase, the local police force, which may be facing more social unrest, the local retail sector whose turnover will decrease, etc.

Environment is a concern of all administrative levels in the Netherlands, but local governments have been granted ample freedom to issue special regional legislation. As the state is often too large for specific legislation and the municipality too small, the provincial government has gradually been developed into the most important administrative level for environment-related activities. This is an excellent example of a social construction process itself. Municipalities often have to co-ordinate their environmental matters, as rivers, protected landscapes, etc. usually do not stop at municipal borders. The province is then the level where broad national legislation is specified into local regulations. Although the province has not been designated as the administrative level to deal with environmental policies by law, it has gradually been given the function in the course of ongoing social interaction. As Corus' business has a significant impact on the environment, it is easy to understand why environmental issues make up the bulk of Corus stories related to the province.

The environment is a town issue as well, but in a different way. The local community is directly affected by Corus' impact on the environment. The stench and water and air pollution are daily reminders of the presence of a major smelter. On the other hand, on the Ijmuiden level the employer identity may be conflicting with the polluter identity for employees of Corus. As an employee who lives within 'smelling distance' of the company, you may complain about occasional stench, but your complaints will not easily lead to calls for closing the plant down. I will not go into this matter here, in this simple example of multiple corporate identities, but if we wished to make an in-depth study, we would have to account for this conflict and may find it necessary to discern several identities at the town level linked to different configurations of actors.

Being a major enterprise in the Netherlands is the main identity at the national level. It is also important at the provincial level, but at the national level Corus is a genuine source of pride. Lay-offs, even large ones, tend to be perceived at the national level as temporary measures to safeguard the continuation of the enterprise and do not affect the image of Corus as a major Dutch enterprise. Here it is also interesting to see that the merger with British Steel (so far) does not seem to have changed the perception of Corus as 'Dutch'. However, this is another detail of corporate identity construction that I will work out later in this study.

How then could this insight into the corporate identities of Corus be utilized in practical management? I will again present one example and restrict the depth of my argument. Suppose that the merger between Hoogovens and British Steel is not yet a fact. The two sides are already on speaking terms, but are afraid of possible resistance from a number of parties. The future partners decide to present the intended merger. We could pose ourselves as consultants and advise that, when talking to parties on the lowest level, the town, the merger should be presented as the best guarantee for continued employment. Other issues, like the environment, should not be shunned, but employment should be the core theme.

A different presentation should be crafted for the provincial government. There the environment, in particular the corporate concern for the environment, should be the central theme. Finally, the presentation team would need to move on to The Hague to present their plans to the relevant ministries and other national organizations. During that presentation, the representatives should clarify that the merger would not negatively affect Hoogovens as a source of national pride. Several successful Anglo-Dutch corporations, like Unilever and Shell, can be cited as examples. Above, I already mentioned that this has actually happened: Corus is still perceived as a Dutch company.

This may strike many readers as rather Machiavellian at first sight. However, it does not have to be so. Real Machiavellian presentations would miss their objectives, as they would lack credibility. My argument is that three (or perhaps more; this example is not exhaustive) slightly different presentations would need to be crafted, each touching on all relevant issues, but with a different set of emphases for different audiences.

Seen from another angle, the identity construction process of the new company would already start before the merger agreement had been signed. Our advice would help the representatives of Hoogovens and British Steel to interact better within the various social-cognitive contexts the new company would be operating in. Formal presentations would have to be followed by sufficient time for informal questions and answers, which would be a valuable occasion for sense-making in social interaction.

2 The enterprise in the People's Republic of China

Danwei the basic 'unit' of socialist society

Danwei is a term that originates from the military as the Chinese equivalent of the English concept of unit. The Communist Party of China and the People's Liberation Army, although theoretically separate entities, have always been extremely closely organized. During the revolutionary years in which the Communists gradually expanded their territory they established 'revolutionary bases'. Those bases were governed by local military leaders and all social organizations like farms, schools, enterprises, etc., were referred to as units (*danwei*). Each citizen of a revolutionary base belonged to a certain unit (Dutton 1998: 53). This unit provided a salary, housing, food and clothing, etc. Moreover, a person's unit was responsible for keeping a file of that person's course of life, including family members, friends, associates, social behaviour, membership of organizations, political reliability, etc. Such a file became known as a person's dossier (*dang'an*). Many people had access to your dossier (your superiors, their superiors, the police, etc.), however you yourself were not allowed to know its contents. When you were moved from one unit to another, your dossier was moved as well. Seen from a political angle, the unit system was the ideal form of social control.

After the establishment of the People's Republic of China (PRC) the unit system was adopted and developed as the basic form of (re)organizing society. The unit was a centre of power or right. It had 'the right to engage in propaganda, make regulations, perform administration, engage in economic activities, etc.' (Zhou and Yang 2000: 3). It was also regarded as a means to protect the system of public ownership. The constitution of the People's Republic of China guaranteed public ownership as the highest form of ownership and the *danwei* was the basic social unit to manage (*guanli*; Zhou and Yang 2000: 3) people employed within the system of public ownership.

Young people leaving the educational system were not required to go out looking for a job themselves. A position would be assigned to them by special government-run labour offices. As unemployment was regarded as incompatible with socialism, all youngsters leaving middle school or some form of tertiary education were assigned to a work unit. Sometimes a unit needed extra staff, but often units would be allocated new staff, even though they had no vacancies at that particular moment. On the other hand, young people entering the labour system would not necessarily be allocated a job in congruence with their education. The public need was supposed to be more important than private needs and wishes. For the same reasons, you would not necessarily be assigned to a unit in your own home region. Once assigned to a certain unit, it was extremely difficult to move on to another one. Most switches of unit were decided by officials of the government organization supervising your unit. Such switches were again made for public needs, rather than based on application by the employee involved.

In the early years following 1949, the unit system was mainly regarded as pertaining to the urban population and to distinguish it from the rural population that mainly consisted of independent farmers (Zhou and Yang 2000: 3). This aspect of the initial stage of the unit system casts a new light on the gradual attempts to collectivize the Chinese countryside, starting with the establishment of 'mutual help groups' in the mid-1950s, to the People' Communes some years later. From the angle of political administration, we could reformulate this development as an attempt to bring the Chinese farmers, the vast majority of the Chinese population, into the unit system. If successful, every Chinese citizen would have belonged to a unit.

In the basic unit system there was no fundamental difference between commercial enterprises and government organizations. In political parlance, some distinctions were made between:

- non-productive units or government agencies (*zhengfu danwei*); ministries, police, etc.;
- non-profit productive units (*shiye danwei*); electricity companies, educational organizations, etc.;
- profit generating productive units or enterprises (*qiye danwei*).

However, people working for a ministry, a primary school or a state-owned steel factory all had the same relation with their unit. It housed them, fed them, gave them permission to marry and, consecutively, a window to produce a baby, picked up their medical bills, etc.

Although the unit system has been affected by the numerous political and economic upheavals in the short history of the PRC, its basic system is still intact. As this is not a study of the nature and history of the unit system, I will restrict the remainder of this chapter to the enterprises (*qiye danwei*, or for short: *qiye*). I will first take a look at the 'traditional' socialist Chinese typology of enterprises and then continue with more recent types. For each type in each period, I will dwell on the particularities of that type of enterprise as a *danwei*.

Chinese enterprises: the early typology

In the early years of socialist China, three main types of enterprises were distinguished, based on the form of ownership:

1   state-operated enterprises (*guoying qiye*), also referred to as enterprises 'owned by the entire people';
2   collective enterprises (*jiti qiye*); this term is slightly misleading as it is not completely comparable with collective enterprises as those in the former Yugoslavia, it refers to enterprises owned by lower level governments;
3   private enterprises (*siying qiye*); these were privately owned enterprises established before the proclamation of the PRC.

The unit status of the private enterprises is unclear. According the definitions provided by Zhou and Yang's seminal study (seminal in the sense that it is the first comprehensive study of the history, nature, flaws, etc., of the unit system ever published in China) cited above, the private enterprises already existing during the establishment of the PRC should not be regarded as *danwei*, as they were not part of the public ownership system. However, the central government soon launched a campaign to merge the private enterprises in the unit system by establishing a system of 'public–private joint operation (*gongsi heying*)', followed by a complete takeover by the State. By the time that the collectivization of the agricultural production started, the old private enterprises were virtually all nationalized. Only a number of family-run enterprises, mainly handicraft, remained in the countryside.

The main difference between the state-operated enterprises and all other types was that the former were able to offer complete social security from cradle to grave (Lu and Perry 1997). Once you were assigned to such an enterprise, housing, medical care and an old age free of financial problems would be more or less secured. State enterprises would build apartment blocks for their employees, which would be distributed according to seniority, marital status, etc. They would sign collective contracts with a hospital which would then be the designated hospital providing health care to its employees.

Collective enterprises lacked the means for such a generous treatment of their employees. Their primary function was to provide employment. As stated above, unemployment was considered incompatible with the socialist system. Low level government, which could be as local as neighbourhood committees in the urban areas, would establish small factories or mere workshops to manufacture products or offer services needed in the daily lives of local people. They thus served a dual purpose: they provided a unit for people who would otherwise fall outside the system and they fulfilled some of the daily needs of the local population. The government organization that was in charge of the enterprise would be considered responsible for the needs of its employees, but would regularly rely on other administrative organizations to provide, for example housing, which was a scarce commodity in China until recent years.

The few privately employed people, as well as young people who were not yet assigned jobs (the so-called 'youth waiting for work' (*daiye qing-nian*), another euphemism to avoid the word 'unemployed'), were attached to the lowest level administrative organization, usually the neighbourhood committee, which was then considered their unit.

Contexts of the early industrial units

In this section, I will look further into the organizational contexts in which enterprises in this period were operating. The task in this, still introductory, chapter will be to make an inventory of the main types of contexts. I will not go into the identity construction process in those contexts. That will be the subject matter of the remainder of this study.

Even though I have referred to the early unit system as rather 'simple', when we start making an inventory of the various contexts in which enterprises, in particular state enterprises, were interacting, we meet with surprising complexity. The complexity itself should not be surprising, as complexity is an essential trait of human organizing. The surprising aspect of the organizational properties of the early PRC enterprises is that the nature of the contexts is often strikingly different from those that we are familiar with in Europe.

An important type of context, which still persists today, is the industrial sector. Chinese economy is divided into a number of industries, headed by a central ministry or organization with ministerial status in Beijing. Each province and autonomous region has a Department (*ting*) corresponding with the central organization. Lower administrative regions have, again corresponding, Bureaus (*ju*). According to the official parlance, a state enterprise is the property of the entire people, but the central administrative organization of its industrial sector has been given the power to manage the enterprise in the name of the people. The central organization will then delegate that power to its corresponding lower level organization (also see Steinfeld 1998: 48–49). An example will help clarify the situation: paint manufacturing is regarded as chemical industry in China. A state paint factory located in Suzhou, Jiangsu province, will therefore be typically managed by the municipal Chemical Industry Bureau, which will report to the provincial Chemical Industry Department, which operates under the Ministry of Chemical Industry in Beijing. As already mentioned in Chapter 1, the main locus of control for our paint factory could be placed at different administrative levels according to its importance in the sector. This would be reflected in the enterprise's official name, as hung besides the main entrance. If the official name is Suzhou Paint Factory, its main locus of control is in the municipal Chemical Industry Bureau. If it were managed at the provincial level, the official name would more likely be Jiangsu Suzhou Paint Factory or Jiangsu Paint Factory.

If the same administrative level operated more than one enterprise in the same business, they would be distinguished with numbers. The number would indicate the relative importance of that enterprise within its home region. For example, if our paint factory was called Suzhou Nr 2 Paint Factory, we may conclude that it was managed at city level and that it was the second most important paint factory in that city. The top manufacturer in the city would be designated by 'Nr 1', 'General', or without any indication of rank.

Which types of paint would be produced and in what quantities would be stipulated by the Chemical Industry authorities according to a national plan. Each individual enterprise would be given a production plan each year. The enterprise would be required to fulfil the plan and only that. It might happen that a certain factory was unable to fulfil it completely. However, it happened more frequently that an enterprise would accomplish its quota before the end of the year, at which moment it would switch off the machines and send the workers home, until the new quota came in.

Another type of context relevant for the operation of enterprises in the early unit system was that of managerial function. An area strongly affected by this was personnel management (Zhou and Yang 2000: 40 ff.). As pointed out above, providing employment was one of the central functions of a unit. The most fundamental precept of social organization (and social control) in the initial stage of the PRC was that ideally each Chinese citizen would belong to a unit. That unit would then manage all aspects of the citizen's life, for as long as they lived. Employment-related matters were therefore referred to as 'people matter' (*renshi*), controlled by a central ministry of its own: the Ministry of Personnel (*Renshibu*). This ministry had its corresponding organizations in various lower levels of the administrative system as introduced above. Returning to our example of the paint factory in Suzhou, the person heading its Personnel Department would not only be responsible to the management of the enterprise, but also to the municipal Personnel Bureau. The latter would regularly relay directives from the Ministry to the personnel officers in organizations in its home region and those personnel officers would be obliged to follow them up as strictly as possible.

This created a potential source of conflicts between the personnel policy of the enterprise and that of the government. In the case of such a conflict, the government policy would usually prevail over that of the leadership of an organization. The degree of influence of these government agencies on the day-to-day management of a Chinese enterprise is reflected by the term that is regularly used to refer to those agencies in everyday speech: mothers-in-law (*popo*). The relation between a married woman and her mother-in-law has always been fraught with conflicts in

Chinese society. Apparently Chinese enterprises, in particular the state enterprises, felt like the daughters-in-law of their supervising government agency.

Another sector that directly affected the operation of enterprises was Internal Trade, which was responsible for the distribution of goods in China. Analogous to the planned production of goods, the distribution of those goods via a system of wholesale companies to the retail outlets was also centrally planned. The ministry responsible for this aspect of the economy was the Ministry of Internal Trade (*Neimaobu*). After our paint producer had produced tin after tin of paint, the goods would be stored in the warehouse. The factory itself would not engage in sales and marketing activities, as the destination of its products was part of an overall distribution plan. The Internal Trade system would pick the paint up and send it to various wholesale companies and retail outlets, e.g. for construction materials. Our paint factory would have a Sales Department, but it would not consist of adroit sales people set to fulfil their sales targets, but of clerks filling in forms of what goods have left the factory in what quantities at what date. In case some readers may think I have forgotten about price negotiations: prices were fixed by the state as well; no negotiation was needed. The head of the Sales Department, like his colleague in the Personnel Department, was responsible to the local Internal Trade Bureau as well as the enterprise management and in the case of conflicts, the government's interest would have priority to that of the enterprise.

Yet another external organization that greatly affected the operation of an enterprise was the Communist Party (I will refer to the Communist Party as the Party in the remainder of this text). As the voice of the lowest classes 'the Party was in charge of everything'. Apart from its own organization, each unit had a 'party organization' of its own. This term became so common that the word 'organization' (*zuzhi*) began to be used in reference to the Party organization. The Party members in our paint factory would constitute its Party organization, headed by the Party Secretary. The main task of the Party organization was to make sure that the enterprise's behaviour complied with the policy of the Party in all respects. The Party Secretary would be an employee of the factory, but his work for the Party would be a full-time job. As we saw before for the production and distribution of goods and the personnel management, the Party Secretary would be responsible to the local Party organization. In this respect, the Party Secretary was even more detached from the enterprise, as he was not responsible to top management of the enterprise. In order to avoid the easily imaginable conflicts between the Party Secretary and the CEO, in most enterprises the CEO simultaneously fulfilled (and still fulfils) the position of Party Secretary.

Organizations comparable with, though less influential than, the Party were:

1   the *Communist Youth League*; an incubator for Party members;
2   the *All China Women's Federation*; aimed to protect the rights of women in a traditionally male-oriented society;
3   the *Labour Union*; more in charge of workers' welfare than fighting for their interest (striking was and is forbidden in China);
4   *Public Security*, the Chinese Police; units have a task in maintaining public order and assist Public Security personnel in solving crimes. Our factory's Security Department would have regular contacts with the local Public Security Office.

For more on these types of organizations and their relation to enterprises see Tang and Ward (2003: 102) and Beamish and Speiss (1993: 174).

Apart from its specific 'mother organization', the general municipal government also constituted a context for our paint factory and as Suzhou municipality fell under Jiangsu province, the province was yet another context. The influence of each of these contexts would depend on the importance of the enterprise, and would be visible from its official name as indicated earlier in this section.

I have so far introduced some of the more important formal contexts. However, the number of informal ones is probably still larger. Suppose that the CEO (probably also the Party Secretary) of our paint factory were a brother of the mayor of Suzhou. This would be a potentially influential configuration in any culture, but certainly in the Chinese context, where using the power that comes with the job for private purposes is common practice.

As the number of such informal contexts is theoretically infinite, I will refrain from bringing up more examples in this section. The actual cases in the remaining chapters of this study will provide ample examples. Before turning to the case studies, I first need to examine the current situation.

The post-reform situation

Chinese enterprises have undergone numerous, at times quite radical, changes since the start of the economic reforms around 1980. As I do not intend to write a history of the Chinese enterprise, but a study on Chinese corporate identity construction in current times, this section will explain the changes in the types of enterprises introduced earlier in this chapter and the major new types that have been developed during recent years, without paying attention to their historical order of appearance.

State-owned enterprises

The state-owned enterprises, still the backbone of the Chinese economy, are now theoretically detached from their supervising administrative organization. In current parlance, the State owns the enterprise, but no longer participates in its management. From the description earlier in this chapter it should be obvious that it is easier for the central government to proclaim such a policy than to implement it in practice. A more suitable formulation of the official phraseology in view of the current practice would be that state-owned enterprises are currently engaged in a process of acquiring full independence in management from government agencies. The fact that the word mother-in-law is still used when referring to those supervising agencies is noteworthy in this respect.

The process of the State taking its hands off the daily management of state enterprises even created a new type of 'mother-in-law', in the form of asset-management companies. These can purchase bad debts of selected enterprises from the banks and in exchange receive shares in the firms responsible for the debts (Tang and Ward 2003: 46–48). Apart from the financial complications created by this, still rather new, development the new asset-management companies have a potential of evolving into a new type of mother-in-law in the Chinese cultural context. I will investigate this problem later in this study.

Another type of relation that has changed dramatically is that between the (state) enterprises and their banks. In the old command economy, the enterprises would hand over their profits to the State in return for an annual allowance based on the budgeted needs for the next year period. At present, the enterprises pay corporate income tax to the tax authorities and retain the remainder of the profits. Again in theory, they are responsible for their own profit and loss. If an enterprise is not able to finance a certain investment by itself, it will have to take a loan from a bank. This will make banks influential parties in the operating of enterprises, as they are elsewhere in the world. However, as most of the banks are still state-owned enterprises themselves, being the debtor of a certain bank may put a Chinese enterprise in a daughter-in-law type of position in, once more, the Chinese cultural context.

On paper, the central government intends gradually to rid itself of most state-owned enterprises. The plan is to retain about 1000 major corporations and sell the remaining ones. However, it will take considerable time to realize such a plan, because the employees of state-owned companies will be afraid of losing their traditional benefits.

Collective enterprises

The old collective enterprises, those set up by low level administrative organizations, continue to exist. Some of them have been able to use the opportunities offered by the new situation to develop into major enterprises. The appearance of the limited company, especially, has offered interesting prospects for collective enterprises with a vision. One option collective enterprises have for growth is to form strategic alliances with larger state-owned enterprises. The case studies in the remainder of this study will show that this can lead to interesting multiple corporate identities.

A special, and frequently studied, sub-type of collective enterprises are the Town and Village Enterprises (TVE; *xiangzhen qiye*). This is an umbrella term for a broad range of enterprises established in China's rural areas. Some of them are the descendants of enterprises set up by the old communes that were abolished in 1984, while others are established by local governments. The impact of TVEs on the national economy has experienced a dramatic growth. An important factor behind this success is the relative freedom they enjoy in enterprise management. Quite a number of TVEs are known to violate intellectual property rights and virtually all of them engage in creative bookkeeping in order to pay as little tax as possible. While this is common knowledge in China (it is reported in published studies on TVEs; a seminal study is still Wong *et al.* 1995), the authorities so far seem to be in no hurry to deal with these phenomena. The main reason for this inertia is that TVEs have been and still are the driving force behind the increase in the standard of living in the Chinese countryside. Because they provide jobs (or units) for surplus labour in the countryside, TVEs are considered a pillar for social stability and maintaining social stability is the primary objective of the current Chinese government. TVEs will be investigated in a separate chapter in this study.

Private enterprises

The number of private enterprises and their impact on the Chinese economy has increased as well during the past decade and a half. However, their status has experienced fluctuations related to similar fluctuations in the national policy with regard to private enterprises. Most of the time, private enterprises are said to have a place of their own, but every now and then voices are heard that their influence on the total Chinese economy should be limited, as too large a share of the private sector in the national economy would change its socialist nature. One way of dealing with the ever imminent danger of obstruction from various government agencies is to attach a private enterprise to such an agency. While actually operating as a private enterprise, such companies are then legally regarded as collective enterprises and enjoy protection from the government agency for a fee. This practice is known in China as donning a 'red cap' (*hong maozi*). The percentage of this type of hidden private enterprise among the collective enterprises can be quite large, varying from an average of one third in small towns to more than half in some rural areas. The motivation these private entrepreneurs give for their eagerness to buy a collective status can be narrowed down to three categories:

1   they prefer to belong to a 'mother-in-law';
2   collective enterprises have a better average reputation than private ones;
3   some regional governments prohibit access to certain industries to private enterprise (Huang 1996: 103–111).

It is interesting to observe that, while the state-owned enterprises are struggling to rid themselves of their mothers-in-law, these private entrepreneurs are actively seeking one, for protection. In terms of my theoretical framework, we could conclude that the mother-in-law function of government agencies in China is reconstructed by this practice. Being 'in charge' of enterprises is apparently a very basic element of the identity of such government organizations. Now that their old daughters-in-law are running away from home through the front door, new ones are knocking on the back door. This newly constructed mother/daughter-in-law relation is different from that of the old days, but similar enough to continue the basic administrative structure. I will leave this, highly interesting, topic for what it is in this introductory section and revert to it further in this study.

Private enterprises are still relatively small. This can be partly explained by the fact that they are still relatively controversial and small companies are easier to hide than large ones. Another impediment in the development of private enterprises in China is that the bulk of them are family enterprises. A typical procedure is that a man establishes a company and from the start, or once it has developed to a certain extent, also takes on his wife as an employee. Brothers and sisters and even parents are next in line. Children leaving the educational system are also common candidates. Family enterprises are conflict prone in two respects. In spite of the fact that the family plays such a pivotal role in Chinese culture, quarrels among relatives are as common in China as anywhere else. A conflict with a business partner is much more complicated when that person is simultaneously your relative (Redding 1993: 143–182).

Family relations also frequently complicate other types of enterprises, in particular the People-Operated Enterprises. If the researcher turned entrepreneur in the example I introduced above appointed his wife as the accountant of the company, the two of them would constitute a powerful configuration within the company. While this does not necessarily have to lead to conflicts, it will often do so, once again in a Chinese context. My case studies will include the demise of one of China's leading manufacturers of household appliances, a People-Operated Enterprise, in which this type of problem added a family business identity to the other identities of that company.

Groups/conglomerates

Another new type of enterprise in China is the group (*jituan*). From a legal point of view, the group is not a legal entity. It is a conglomerate of companies with one enterprise, usually a larger, more successful, one as the core enterprise (*hexin qiye*). A number of other companies from the same or related industries can form a group around such a core enterprise. The other companies remain independent legal entities, but voluntarily give the core company the authority to interfere in their management. The core company will receive a management fee from the other group members. Group members are often divided into close members and loose members, according to the degree of involvement of the core company in their management (Keister 2000; 81 ff.). The establishment of groups is sometimes a voluntary act, but more often a policy decision by local governments as a means to save small underperforming enterprises by linking them to a profitable one. Core companies are often state-owned enterprises, while many of the other members are collective ones.

The reason for the appearance of the group company in China is the large number of small enterprises in the same industry. This tendency to set up a large number of small plants rather than making use of the economy of scale, as is the practice in most other regions in the world, often astonishes foreign companies during the first stage of their entry into the Chinese market. As this theme is important for the understanding of Chinese corporate identity construction, I will devote some space here to the various mechanisms that have led to the highly dispersed character of so many Chinese industries.

The first mechanism is Chinese federalism. Although the Chinese are known for their strong national feelings, China should be regarded as a de facto federal state. The main geographic regions, consisting of provinces, autonomous regions and four independent municipal areas, act economically (and culturally, politically, etc.) as if they were states in a fashion partly comparable with that of the USA. One consequence of this self-perception of the regions is that all of them would like to produce everything within their own borders. For some products this is physically impossible, because the climate is unsuitable, no raw materials are available, etc., however this propensity for regional independence is so strong that some provinces are willing to support the importation of raw materials from far away regions to establish at least one manufacturer of a certain product in the home region.

The second mechanism is that of copying what others (seem to) do well. Copying is an inherent part of Far Eastern culture in general and of Chinese culture in particular. When a company is reported to be successful by producing and marketing a certain product, it is only a matter of time before more companies in its vicinity will start manufacturing the same product. Sometimes even special enterprises are established for this purpose.

The third mechanism is a preference for small scale in Chinese culture. Traditional Chinese culture advocates harmony and one of the ways to create and maintain harmony is making sure that one company is not much better, larger, etc., than others. Chinese politics through the ages has been affected by this. People who were rich were obliged to share their riches with their community, either through taxes or through good deeds like funding a local school. Consequently, it was better to hide some of your riches, to avoid being called upon for money too often. In more modern times, this practice has continued for larger enterprises. Such a company was (and is) often regarded as a money machine and was also regularly requested to give financial support for various good deeds. One way to cover up some of the apparent wealth within a company is to establish another company as a means to grow, instead of expanding the existing company. A large company in a city can, for example, set up a smaller plant in a suburban town producing the same product. Although they are separate legal entities, from an organizational point of view, the two plants can be regarded as one company. In practice, certainly in the context of a desk study, it will be hard to impossible to determine whether different plants belong to the same company or not, but is important to understand this principle.

The fourth mechanism is more practical: tax. Chinese enterprises can be divided into different groups according to ownership. The type of ownership is indicated for most of the enterprises in our list. State-owned enterprises are large enterprises officially owned by the entire Chinese people, whose management is performed by an appropriate local government organization. Collective enterprises are set up and managed by low level government. Private enterprises are owned by natural persons. Joint stock enterprises are a new type of legal person owned by a number of legal and/or natural persons. Finally, foreign-funded enterprises are (partly) owned by foreign legal or natural persons. The income tax differs for all these types of enterprises. State-owned enterprises pay 55 per cent income tax, while collective enterprises only pay 20 per cent. The other types pay about 30–35 per cent. This is almost an invitation for state-owned enterprises to set up a small company somewhere disguised as a collective enterprise run by the local government. Again, it will be hard to impossible to determine this is the case in any individual situation, but it is important to know the principle. In some locations we can see a state-owned enterprise and a foreign-funded enterprise. In that case the latter has probably been set up in co-operation with the state-owned enterprise. It will be interesting to see how recent changes in the Chinese taxation system will treat this practice.

The fifth mechanism is the rigid division of the Chinese economy into sectors. From the establishment of the People's Republic of China, society has been divided into a number of sectors such as Light Industry, Education, Agricultural, Metallurgy, Aviation, etc. These sectors are headed by central ministries or organizations on the same level as a ministry, situated in Beijing. However, the link between a certain industry and a certain hierarchical sector is not strictly implemented. The food industry is a good example. Food is primarily a matter of Light Industry, but some food manufacturers operate in the hierarchies of Agriculture and Internal Trade. Large state farms (= Agriculture) can set up factories, which then automatically are part of the Agriculture hierarchy. A typical food sector with strong links to Internal Trade is cereal processing. Cereal products, unprocessed like rice or processed like flour, used to be distributed using a coupon system. As the distribution of goods was the typical task of Internal Trade, cereal processing also became the business of this sector. Even after the abolition of the coupon system in the early years of the economic reforms, a large number of cereal processing companies (including animal feed) remained linked to the Internal Trade organization of their local government. This can lead to interesting differences in identity construction. In my case studies I will introduce a county in which the dairy industry is divided into three sectors: Light Industry, Internal Trade and Agriculture. These different sector affiliations significantly affect the formation of strategic alliances in the local dairy industry.

Limited companies

Another development that should have a major effect on the identities of a Chinese enterprise (state owned and others) is the appearance of limited companies. Legal and natural persons can buy shares in a limited company, or contribute capital to the establishment of a new one, thus becoming stakeholders of that company. Enterprises of all ownership types can be reorganized into limited companies. A major incentive for Chinese enterprises to make such a step is that it is a necessary step on the route to a listing on one of the country's two stock exchanges (Shanghai and Shenzhen).

The appearance of the limited company as a legal type of enterprise has given rise to the birth of a variety of enterprises with mixed ownership (Tang and Ward 2003: 132 ff.). For example, a researcher employed by a research institute (in terms of unit: a non-profit productive unit, *shiye danwei*) has made an invention he believes to be a potential money maker. However the institute is not equipped to develop the invention into a product, let alone produce and market it. The institute could theoretically craft a marketing plan and apply for a bank loan, but does not perceive itself as a future manufacturing company. The researcher can then make a deal with his employer and a number of other legal (including the local government) and natural persons (colleagues, relatives, friends) to accumulate the capital necessary for establishing a company around his invention. Hundreds of companies have already been established in this way in recent years. Quite a number of them fail, but some of them have already developed into major corporations. Especially in the realm of high-tech markets this process has created a number of successes (Tang and Ward 2003: 137). The Chinese term for these companies with mixed ownership structure is 'People Operated' (*minying*).

Most newly established enterprises in China are limited companies. The bulk of the smaller state-owned enterprises are sold to private or legal persons, or a combination both, changing their legal status to limited company as well. This type can therefore be expected to develop into the main type of enterprise in the medium to long term. Especially for state-owned enterprises, the transformation into a limited company provides the possibility to decrease the ownership of the State to less than 100 per cent. On one hand such a development would reduce the State's influence on the operations of the enterprise, but on the other would also decrease the responsibility of the respective state organization (mother-in-law) for ill-managed enterprises. The establishment of limited companies allows the State to retain a 100 per cent stake in selected key enterprises and discard some or all of its stake in others.

Foreign-invested enterprises

The appearance of enterprises wholly or partly owned by foreign investors may very well be the most significant development of the economic reforms. Foreign investment had been virtually banned in China since the establishment of the PRC, but the first Chinese leaders after the end of the Cultural Revolution period (1976) were faced with what they perceived as an immense technology gap between China and the developed countries. Even if the fledgling education system could be shaped up within reasonable time, the total time needed to bridge that technology gap was beyond estimation. The Chinese government decided to speed up the development by allowing foreign enterprises to team up with Chinese counterparts and form joint ventures. The rules for such joint ventures were laid down in a law promulgated in 1979. The event became known in Chinese parlance as Reform and Opening (*gaige kaifang*). This term was given almost as much political importance as the establishment of the PRC. The latter is known as Liberation (*jiefang*) and people speak of events 'before' and 'after' Liberation. In a similar fashion, Chinese speak of the situation 'before' and 'after' Reform and Opening.

For this topic as well I will refrain from an extensive historic treatment of foreign investment in China. Useful texts concerning the development and problems in this respect are: Beamish and Speiss (1993), Han and Xu (1997), Xing (1998), Yan (2000) and Peverelli (2000). Here we are once more primarily concerned with the various modes of participation in Chinese enterprises currently available to foreign investors. Such modes are:

1   *Joint ventures*; foreign companies can link up with Chinese counterparts to form joint ventures in much the same way as elsewhere in the world. The Chinese law distinguishes equity joint ventures in which the partners invest a certain share of the capital with a minimum

foreign investment of 25 per cent and co-operative joint ventures in which the partners simply agree to co-operation in certain business with fewer restrictions on the terms.

2   *Wholly owned companies*; 100 per cent owned by the foreign investor(s), without Chinese participation.

It is also possible for foreign investors to buy shares of listed Chinese limited companies, but the percentage of shares is so far limited to 5 per cent. It is therefore hard to speak of 'foreign-invested enterprises' in this respect.

From one point of view foreign-invested enterprises can be regarded as limited companies. Legally they are Chinese legal persons, but because of the many special laws and regulations related to foreign-invested enterprises, they need to be treated as a separate category. The case studies should show whether the fact that they are partly or wholly owned by foreign investors is significant for their identity construction. However, from the point of view of my theoretical framework the very fact that they are regarded as a separate type of enterprise in Chinese law, Chinese statistical publications, the perception of most Chinese people, etc., constructs them as a separate category. We will then have to study how their sense-making differs in various contexts.

Seen from yet another angle, the study of Chinese corporate identity is interesting to (potential) foreign investors in joint ventures as a means to gain insight into their existing or intended partner organizations. One of the main theses in Peverelli (2000) was that the majority of foreign partners in Sino-foreign joint ventures have at best superficial insight into who their partners are, how the joint venture makes sense to the partners in different contexts, how the joint venture makes sense to other parties in different contexts, etc.

The structure of the remainder of the study

The amount of data produced by my ongoing investigation into the nature and identity of enterprises in China is already overwhelming. An important objective of this study is to provide insight into the multiplicity of corporate identity constructions. One way to achieve this goal would be to examine the various identities of a number of individual enterprises. However, in order to create maximum insight, I would need to present a large number of enterprises. These cases would contain considerable overlap, which would not only not contribute to the objective, but could even obscure the common features in the processes of identity construction of the various cases.

Therefore, I have opted to look at the identity construction of only a selected number of Chinese enterprises. I will observe the identity construction of each case in great detail, from a multitude of perspectives.

The selection of the cases was based on the objective to have maximum variation on important aspects. A major aspect is type of ownership. We would like to be able to compare state-owned enterprises with private ones, etc., to observe how this parameter affects the construction of identity. It would also be useful to compare cases of old, established enterprises, and companies set up after the beginning of the economic reforms. Both parameters can be studied through separate case studies of enterprises with different types of ownership, etc., but it is also possible to incorporate them in one single case study. For example, in a study of a state-owned enterprise we could include a comparison with a collective one in the same industry and the same region. My experience is that the latter method usually offers better insight. Such companies (same business, same region, etc.) are often regarded as competitors and competitive relationships are an important context in the construction of identity.

The case chapters will be structured in a fashion that I would like to refer to as incident-driven case studies. An efficient way to observe various aspects of an enterprise is picking out an incident in which those aspects suddenly come to the foreground. The case description starts with a general description of the company, its business and its unique position in the business.

The second part of the case study describes the company in terms of the main topic of research, which in this study is the construction of corporate identities. In this part I will introduce a number of identity constructs specific to the core enterprise of each chapter, but a number of identities will recur in more than one chapter. A typical example of such an identity is the region. Region is an important source of identity for organizations in any culture, but for the rather chauvinist Chinese, the impact of regional identities on identity constructs of organizations in that region is huge. Instead of devoting a special chapter to 'regional identity', incorporating it in virtually every chapter will provide a much deeper insight into this phenomenon. Other examples of recurrent themes are administrative level, industrial sector, mothers-in-law, etc.

The third part is the incident, a moment in the history of the company that calls for a heightened level of sense-making. Such an incident is an excellent occasion to study any aspect of organizing. Actors will then move from a state of enactment to a state of selection (Weick 1979: 130–132), which will provide an opportunity for researchers to observe their construction rules (see Chapter 1) and all other aspects of organizing. It is always interesting to study a major corporation like Hp. However, if you wish to test some of your hypotheses about Hp, the merger between Hp and Compaq, or more recently, the dismissal of Carly Fiorina, are more interesting periods to concentrate on. Either of these events could serve as the 'incident' in a case study about Hp.

The following cases and major themes have been selected.

Chapter 3: Mothers-in-law

The leading role in this chapter will be played by a large state-owned enterprise in the pharmaceutical industry. The main theme of the chapter will be to investigate the variety of mothers-in-law that the enterprise has to please and the ways they affect the management of the company. Moreover, as some of these mothers-in-law are divided into several administrative layers, this case chapter will also provide insight in the ways mothers-in-law of the same hierarchy influence the operation of the enterprise in different ways. I will pay particular attention to the way such an enterprise is embedded in and affected by the Communist Party organization. The incident in this chapter is a conflict between the enterprise's CEO and the General-Manager of a subsidiary over who has the final say in the day-to-day operation of that subsidiary. When the conflict seems hard to solve within the company, the General-Manager of the subsidiary seeks a solution through another inclusion. However, the CEO follows suit and comes out as the winner.

Chapter 4: Administrative layers

For this theme I have selected two dairy companies in a central Chinese province. Both are physically situated in the provincial capital, but one enterprise is linked to the provincial government, while the other is operated by a municipal organization. I will show how these two companies are on one hand operating in distinct cognitive spaces in the same geographic space, but on the other hand also share inclusions through the multiple inclusions of key actors. Moreover, this case illustrates how Dutch investors active in that industry in that region fail to make sense of the local dairy market, owing to a lack of understanding of the nature of differences between these two companies. The 'incident' in this chapter is more subtle than the straightforward conflict in Chapter 3. The incident is related to the arrival of the Dutch, government subsidized, investment. The foreigners came to the region through the provincial organization and throughout their five-year operation, their strong inclusion in the cognitive space of their partner decreased their ability to see that there was another local dairy world, co-existing with theirs. The actual incident is the evaluation research by a Dutch consultant commissioned by the Dutch Ministry of Economic Affairs that had subsidized part of the project. This evaluation took place during the last week of the project, but produced more insight into the project and its environment than was accumulated during the five years of its duration.

Chapter 5: Industrial sectors

As already indicated above, the Chinese economy is divided into a number of industrial sectors. Each sector operates under a central ministry, or ministry-like organization, in the capital, with corresponding organizations in the lower administrative levels. The relation between products and sectors is not always strictly one to one. Enterprises involved with a certain product, or product group, are in some instances distributed over a number of sectors. Comparing manufacturers of the same product operating in different sectors will provide valuable insight in the way that sector identity can influence the operation of a Chinese firm. This chapter will once more examine a number of Chinese dairy companies operating in different sectors. The core enterprise is a dairy company from Inner Mongolia, which is probably China's fastest growing corporation of the past decade. It is located in the region's capital, which is also the home of what until recently was China's largest dairy company. These two had been engaged in fierce competition even before the case enterprise was officially operating. This chapter therefore also provides insight into the mechanisms of competition, Chinese style. Without giving away too many clues, I can reveal here that this Chinese-style competition includes a certain degree of interference from the local government. The incident in this chapter is the way these two enterprises create one another's identities in their home region and then reconstruct a similar relation in their competition in another region in China.

Chapter 6: Conglomerates

The formation of group companies (*jituan*) seems to be a major trend in the organization of the Chinese economy and therefore deserves to be studied in a separate chapter. Moreover, such groups increasingly incorporate member companies in different parts of China. In view of the strong ties Chinese and Chinese organizations have with their home region, it should be interesting to see how the expansion of a group over various provinces affects the identity of the group as a whole. The core enterprise in this chapter is China's largest brewer, based in the national capital Beijing. Although only established at the beginning of the economic reforms, it expanded quickly to reach the number one position in 1995. A special feature of the identity constructs of this case company is the enormous symbolic power of its name, which is a synonym for Beijing. This means that we can transpose the meanings of the word 'Beijing' as a symbol to this company metaphorically and then use this as a tool to investigate further how some of the identities of Beijing can be applied to the sense-making of this company. I will show that Beijing's meaning of 'central government' can indeed be applied, giving the brewery a far-reaching political identity. The incident in this chapter is the less than smooth route of this company's expansion drive from Beijing to the South of China. The general trend of the acquisition activities of this group is from its home region, Beijing, to the rich Southern province of Guangdong. However, the road to the South is full of hurdles and each hurdle is an occasion for intensified identity construction.

Chapter 7: Foreign-funded enterprises

Foreign investment has been allowed in China since the end of the 1970s. Although, since then, interest in China from international investors has shown ups and downs, the general trend has been upward and when this study is finalized, direct foreign investment in China will be higher than ever before. Foreign companies are now even allowed to establish wholly owned subsidiaries in China and foreign investment is still restricted in only very few sectors of the economy. However, discussions regarding the extent of foreign influence that China should allow in its economy is an ongoing issue. Discussion on this topic often includes warnings for the weakening of China's 'national safety', which shows how sensitive this subject still is. The case enterprise in this chapter is an experiment in the sense that it is an organization-like entity that would not be recognized as an 'organization' by most organization theorists: a trade fair. I will not go into my motivation for including it here, but refer the reader to the chapter itself. The trade fair is organized by the Dutch subsidiary of a British company, in co-operation with the Chinese joint venture of a Hong Kong based subsidiary of the same British mother company. The Dutch organizer used to work with a Chinese partner, but after the mother organization had set up its own Chinese company, the latter replaced the original partner, who then continued on its own with a competitive trade fair. This is a scenario for a complicated set of identity constructs. It will be especially interesting to see how the Dutch and the Chinese organizers, who belong to the same multinational, make sense of the trade fair in strikingly different ways, with dramatic consequences for the coupling of their behaviour. The incidence in this final case chapter is the most recent edition of the trade fair, held in March 2005. In this year the foreign trade fair that is the core of this chapter and its Chinese competitive trade fair have begun to resemble one another so much that it is difficult to distinguish them. The key question for the foreign investor is then how its own trade fair can survive. My reply will be challenging.

Chapter 8: Summary and integration

The findings of the case studies will be summarized in the concluding Chapter 8. In this chapter I will start building a model of Chinese corporate identity construction.

3 Lukang

The construction of a state-owned enterprise

Intermezzo

As announced in the previous chapter, the main theme of this chapter will be to look at the variety of mothers-in-law that a large Chinese state-owned enterprise has to please and the ways they affect the management of that company. From among those organizations, I will pay particular attention to the way such an enterprise is embedded in the Communist Party organization. The role of the Party has always intrigued Western observers, academically and otherwise, but an in-depth study of its relation with a present-day Chinese enterprise has so far been obstructed by the lack of a proper organizational model. In this chapter I will attempt to describe this relation in terms of Social Integration theory.

The company selected for this chapter is called Lukang. Lukang is a large Chinese manufacturer of antibiotics, located in Ji'ning, a city in Shandong province. Armed with the concept of cognitive spaces introduced in the theoretical chapters, the little information provided in this sentence already allows us to make several deductions concerning this enterprise:

Lukang = pharmaceutical industry

In this chapter, and all following ones, I will use the X = Y convention to indicate space inclusions.

Industrial sectors are strong space constructors. They have their own typical ways of doing things, typical legislation, professional associations and periodicals, trade fairs, etc. When we learn that a certain enterprise is a pharmaceutical company, we know that a major part of its identity will derive from the pharmaceutical industry space.

One typical feature of the pharmaceuticals business, regardless of the nationality of the enterprise concerned, is that the manufacturing, trading and application of the products are much more strictly controlled than is usual in most other industries. R&D to produce a new pharmaceutical requires more time and capital and before such a product is allowed to be sold to patients, a lengthy application procedure has to be followed, often including years of clinical trials.

The Chinese pharmaceutical industry is supervised by the State Drug Administration (SDA), formerly known as the State Pharmaceutical Administration of China (SPAC), a ministry-level central organization, obviously located in the national capital Beijing. This organization has branches in all major administrative regions, including the Shandong Pharmaceutical Administration Bureau (SPAB). The latter has the same responsibilities as its national mother organization within Shandong province. In practice, the national SDA will delegate its tasks concerning Shandong to SPAB, unless a particular situation requires otherwise. Without any additional information other than that Lukang is a pharmaceutical enterprise in Shandong, we can already presume that SPAB will have considerable influence on the operation of Lukang.

Lukang = Shandong

The Shandong space is a geographical space. Shandong is considered a relatively rich province of China. It is an important agricultural region and famous for its food and beverage industry, whose turnover in 2002 represented 14 per cent of the total Chinese turnover in that sector. Shandong has a long stretch of coast and therefore a number of port cities. Qingdao is one of China's main international ports, but Yantai, Rizhao, Weihai and more recently Longkou are also growing in importance. Rizhao is vying with Lianyungang in Jiangsu as the east end of the Eurasian Continental Bridge, a conceived railway link between the East China coast and European port cities of Rotterdam and Antwerp. Shandong people are regarded as simple, straightforward and honest by Chinese from other regions. They do not easily get exited, but once they start at something, they will spare no effort making it into a success. Shandong people live by the laws and regulations as promulgated by the authorities. They do take part in reforms and innovations, but will not easily go beyond the limits set by the (current) law. Foreign influence has been strong on the construction of the Shandong space. When the Western powers divided China's coastal cities for concession areas, Germany received part of eastern Shandong, known as the Jiaodong Peninsula, including the port city of Qingdao. The German influence is still very visible in the German-style buildings in Qingdao and other cities in the area. Another vestige of German influence is that one of China's oldest breweries, the Qingdao Brewery, is located in that region. The Riesling grape (Leisiling in Chinese), brought to the region by German missionaries, is still growing there and producing Qingdao Riesling. However, the foreigners have always been a minority in Shandong, and Chinese and foreigners have always lived in harmony there. Many fewer horror stories about living in China seem to be heard from the foreign expatriates in various places in Shandong than from those stationed in other Chinese regions.

Lukang = Ji'ning

The Ji'ning space is another geographic space, but being a municipal space it is a much more restricted one than the Shandong space. Most Chinese from different parts of China will be readily able to describe what Shandong is about. Most of them will know Ji'ning, but will probably not know anything about it. Ji'ning is not a location of much historic fame. It is situated along the Grand Canal, dug during the Sui Dynasty (581–618), that connected Hangzhou, the current capital of Zhejiang province, with Beijing. When the Grand Canal was the main transportation channel for Southern goods to the Capital, Ji'ning was one of the key landing places. Within Shandong, Ji'ning is less favourably located in its mountainous Western part, while most of the fertile soil is concentrated in the Eastern part. The city started developing as an industrial centre after the 1980s.

I will revert to these three identities later in this chapter. The above intermezzo is presented to show how the mere knowledge that Lukang is a pharmaceutical enterprise located in Ji'ning, Shandong is already extremely rich in information on the various identities of this enterprise. The concept of cognitive space enables the researcher to identify these multiple identities. I will now first present a short historic overview of Lukang. This case story draws heavily from Peverelli (2000).

Lukang – past and present

Establishment

Lukang was first established as the Third Branch of the Shandong Xinhua Pharmaceutical Factory (Zibo, Shandong) in 1966. The link with its parent was severed in 1970 and the factory was reformed into an independent enterprise belonging to the Ji'ning Chemical Industry Bureau. At that time, the pharmaceutical industry was still regarded as part of the chemical industry in the Chinese division of industrial sectors. The company was renamed: Shandong Ji'ning Xinhua Pharmaceutical Factory.

The enterprise grew steadily and the ownership was transferred to the provincial authorities in 1980, when it was attached to the Shandong Provincial Pharmaceutical Co. (the pharmaceutical industry had already been separated off as an independent industrial sector). Along with this change, the company was renamed once more as the Ji'ning Antibiotics Factory. In 1984, the current CEO, Mr Zhang Jianhui, was appointed as Director and the enterprise was included in an experimental programme placing the main responsibility for enterprise management at the CEO. The factory was given the designation 'National Second Class Enterprise' in 1989. The basic requirement to attain that status was an annual turnover exceeding RMB 50 million.

From factory to company

Ji'ning Antibiotics Factory established the Shandong Lukang Pharmaceutical Group Co., Ltd in 1992, a conglomerate with itself as the core enterprise. *Lu* is the literary designation of Shandong and *kang* is an abbreviation of the Chinese word for antibiotics (*kangjunsu*). This move enabled the company to raise capital from a number of private and institutional investors. Two years later, Lukang changed its name to the current one, Shandong Lukang Pharmaceutical Co., Ltd. During the first half of the 1990s Lukang accomplished a number of provincial key products, all in the field of antibiotics, firmly establishing Lukang as one of China's foremost manufacturers of antibiotics.

During that period, Lukang also started expanding through strategic alliances and acquisitions, then newly emerging business opportunities in China. It established a joint venture company with the State Raw Materials Investment Co. in 1992, called Lukang Raw Pharmaceutical Co.

Lukang further acquired the bankrupt Ji'ning Nr 1 and Nr 2 Pharmaceutical Factories in 1994, by taking over all their debts. Although no details regarding these acquisitions have been published, the little information we do have already suffices to analyse the situation. These two enterprises were designated as 'factories', which indicates that they were state-owned enterprises managed by a municipal administrative organization. They still were named with numbers (see Chapter 1) rather than individual names, even in 1994, which is a sign that they had not been able to establish more individual identities as separate independent commercial enterprises. We may then presume that the Ji'ning authorities have approached Ji'ning Antibiotics, a successful local state-owned enterprise, to 'take care' of these fledgling sister enterprises.

Lukang was approached by the government of Heze, a city in West Shandong, and the leadership of the local pharmaceutical factory with the request to take over that factory in 1997. Once more, these few details are more than sufficient to see another state-owned pharmaceutical enterprise looking for support from a large company in its vicinity.

An important milestone in Lukang's history was its listing on the Shanghai Stock Exchange on 23 January 1997, again utilizing new possibilities to expand and diversify its business activities. Lukang attracted RMB 488 million with this first issue.

1000 t Penicillin project

The main event of the following years was the accomplishment of the already existing plan to expand the penicillin fermentation capacity to

1000 t p.a. The then Ji'ning Antibiotics Factory had conceived an ambitious plan to expand the production of the beta-lactam range of antibiotics, which includes penicillins and cephalosporins. As the increase of the crude penicillin output to 1000 t p.a. was the core of the project, it became known as the '1000 t penicillin project'. At first, the company sought cooperation with an international manufacturer. One major multinational started a dialogue and visited Ji'ning to inspect the current conditions in the spring of 1990. However, Ji'ning was not regarded as a favourable location for expatriates and the negotiations were discontinued at an early stage. Lukang had to initiate the project by itself and a revised project plan was approved by the State Planning Commission in November 1994 and further by the State Council, China's cabinet, in March 1995. A month later, in April 1995, the Shandong provincial government ranked the 1000 t penicillin project among the province's top 100 projects. The construction work for the project was finally started with an official ceremony in December 1995. This ceremony was attended by dignitaries representing national and provincial authorities, including the State Planning Commission and its Shandong affiliate organization, the State Pharmaceutical Administration of China and its Shandong branch and the Shandong Construction Commission. No progress reports have been published since.

Fraud or no fraud

So far, Lukang's story has been one of success and gradual expansion. However, the company experienced a serious set back in December 2002 and the first months of 2003, when it was accused of falsification of documents in order to obtain permission for a second issue of shares.

The beginning of these problems goes back to August 2000. At that moment the national government started a campaign to remove the direct links between administrative bodies and commercial enterprises. The Shandong Pharmaceutical Administration Bureau operated a pharmaceutical trading company called Lingzhi Pharmaceutical Co., Ltd. This company has been established in 1953 as the Shandong Ji'ning Pharmaceutical Purchasing & Sales Station and was reorganized as a limited stock company under the Lingzhi name in 1993. The State has a 61 per cent share in the company. Lingzhi was a highly successful company, fully licensed to trade in all types of pharmaceuticals. When the Bureau had to sever its direct links with Lingzhi, it moved the ownership of the state assets in Lingzhi to Lukang. This decision made sense, as Lukang was a pharmaceutical manufacturer with no licence to engage in trading. Lukang and Lingzhi's respective businesses were therefore complementary. However, instead of treating Lingzhi as one of its daughter companies, Lukang gradually started to move the businesses of Lingzhi to other companies within the Lukang group, eventually leaving Lingzhi as an empty shell.

This angered the original leaders of Lingzhi. When a Lukang delegation was in Beijing to handle the application procedure for a second issue of shares in December 2002, two of Lingzhi's top managers, the CEO Mr Wu and a manager originally hired for preparing Lingzhi for listing on the Shanghai Stock Exchange, turned to the National Securities Supervisory Commission (also in Beijing) accusing Lukang of exaggerating financial figures. Lukang's application procedure was immediately frozen to give the Securities Supervisory Commission time to investigate the accusation. Mr Wu returned to Ji'ning and the other manager to his own home town Wuhan. Mr Wu was arrested by the Ji'ning procurator general for questioning on 15 January 2003. He was locked up in a hotel room by the procurator and questioned for several days by the Lukang Party Commission. He was finally transported to jail on 22 January to be released shortly before Chinese New Year. During the period of his imprisonment, Mr Wu's wife received threatening telephone calls and windows of their apartments were smashed by stones.

Officials from the State Securities Supervisory Commission came from Beijing to visit their branch in Ji'ning, but had to return to Beijing without being able to carry out any investigation, as they were not allowed to have contact with their main witness, Mr Wu, who was then already in jail.

Although the top management of Lukang have done the utmost to deny the accusations, this entire issue, including the treatment of Mr Wu, has been elaborately reported in the national press. In March 2003 the State Securities Supervisory Commission came out with the verdict that it had not found any evidence to sustain the accusations against Lukang, hence the company could start the procedure for a second issue of shares once more.

CEO

The CEO of Lukang, Mr Zhang Jianhui, was born in Zhejiang province in 1945. He studied chemistry at Zhejiang University, where he graduated in 1968. After working at the North-China Pharmaceutical Factory (Shijiazhuang, Hebei; now called North-China Pharmaceutical Co.) for six years, he was transferred to Ji'ning in 1974. His promotion was rapid and he was appointed Director of what was then called the Ji'ning Antibiotics Factory in 1984. Mr Zhang received a Provincial Advanced Manager award in 1988 and a Provincial Excellent Manager award in 1990. After the establishment of Lukang, Mr Zhang retained the position of CEO. After the listing of Lukang on the Shanghai Stock Exchange, as a result of which the top managers have to be elected by the owners, Mr Zhang was still voted Chairman of the Board. A report dated September 2001 states that Mr Zhang then owned 13 000 shares of Lukang with a value of RMB 104 260.

From the day he was made Director of the Ji'ning Antibiotics Factory up to the present date, Mr Zhang combines the function of CEO with that of Party Secretary, the most senior rank in the Party organization within Lukang.

The above is only a concise history of Lukang. I have concentrated this narration on the institutional aspects: ownership, type of enterprise, alliances and acquisitions, etc. I have highlighted two recent events. The penicillin project is an essential part of Lukang's long-term strategy to sustain its identity as one of China's top manufacturers of antibiotics and provides an opportunity to observe the relations between Lukang and the various mothers-in-law involved. The most interesting aspect of the problems around the second issue of shares is that it shows that an enterprise like Lukang in not only controlled by its mothers-in-law, but that it can also derive considerable power from those relations. In the remainder of this chapter, I will first select a number of important organizations that affect Lukang's operations and than pick one, the Communist Party of China, for a more detailed investigation.

Mothers-in-law

As explained in Chapter 1, narratology was the main research tool used to uncover the identity formation processes in this study. The methodology used to investigate the relation between Lukang and the various administrative organizations started with collecting a large corpus of texts. Such texts can be newspaper articles, articles in professional periodicals, advertisements, company communications like press releases, personal communications, industrial yearbooks, etc. The texts used for this chapter span a period of time from the mid-1980s to the present. Moreover, I have had personal contacts with Lukang (then still known as the Ji'ning Antibiotics Factory), including a two-day visit to Ji'ning in 1991.

Pharmaceutical industry

The first category of mother-in-law I will discuss in detail is the industrial sector in which Lukang is operating: the pharmaceutical industry. The strict division of the Chinese economy in sectors is a product of the unit system (see Chapter 2). The unit is conceived as the source of the person's income (employer), it is responsible for that person's housing, providing health care, etc. At the time this system was conceived, it was considered the best guarantee for a fair distribution of scarce goods, as well as the most effective way of exercising social control. Although a single unit could be used to regulate a considerable number of people, the number of units needed to control the entire Chinese population was still enormous. The units themselves had to be arranged in some sort of a hierarchy as well. Such a hierarchy was established with the type of economic activity as the main divider. Hospitals, clinics, first aid centres, etc., could be easily grouped together under the common denominator of 'Health Care'. Such a group of units was then given a leading unit, in this case named 'Ministry of Public Health'. Such a central ministry, which would always be located in the capital, would establish branch organizations in all provinces, major cities, etc. Hebei province has its 'Public Health Department'; Shanghai its 'Public Health Bureau', etc. In every day parlance, such a hierarchy is often referred to as a 'system' (*xitong*).

While most sectors were given a ministry (*bu*) as its top organ, a minority of activities, perceived as more related to controlling other sectors, like drawing up economic plans, were placed under a 'commission' (*wei*). Both terms were soon linked together, coining the term *buwei*, which can be translated as 'central authorities.' The column *buwei xinxi*, 'news from the central authorities', is still an inalienable item in the Communist Party's official organ, the *People's Daily*. A hierarchical system was created in which, for example, Doctor Li belonged to the Number Four General Hospital of Shanghai (his unit), which was controlled by the Shanghai Public Health Bureau, which had to report to the Ministry of Public Health in Beijing.

In the Intermezzo at the beginning of this chapter, I have already enumerated a number of aspects of the pharmaceutical industry and its organization in China. The pharmaceutical industry is a separate industrial sector in China. This means that it is controlled by a ministry or organization with ministerial status located in the capital. In the case of the pharmaceutical industry its leading organization is the State Drug Administration (SDA). This organization has been affected by the reorganization of the central government that has been going on for a number of years and is still in progress. The SDA was known as the State Pharmaceutical Administration of China (SPAC) until 1998 and is currently (July 2003) being transformed into the State Food & Drug Administration, modelled after the American FDA. Although its name does not contain the word 'ministry', the SDA has in practice a similar authority as a real ministry. It is located in a high-rise building adjacent to Beijing's Xizhimen interchange, referred to by insiders as the 'pharmaceutical building'. Although regulations issued in the late 1990s prohibit such organizations from taking part in commercial activities, the SDA operates a number of enterprises. It officially does not participate in their day-to-day management (this is not allowed any more; see Chapter 2), but at the end of the day, those enterprises are a main source of income for the SDA organization. Responsibilities of the SDA include: handling the registration procedures of new medicines, issuing licences to manufacture and distribute pharmaceuticals, inspecting the production facilities of pharmaceutical manufacturers, organizing trade fairs in China and Chinese delegations to trade fairs abroad and advising the central government. Other ministries and organizations with ministry status have similar responsibilities, but a typical feature of the pharmaceutical industry is that the central control on the production and distribution of pharmaceuticals is significantly stricter than in most other industries. For example, to obtain a licence to produce a new type of pastry it suffices to hand in to the proper authorities a recipe, a concise description of the product and quality specifications of the finished product. Authorities will not require the pastry to be consumed by a number of people during a certain period of time to test for potential side effects. The latter is the case with new pharmaceuticals for which an extensive test procedure, including years of clinical trials, are usually required, before the inventor can start commercial production. As a result, pharmaceutical manufacturers, like Lukang, will have more and more intense interactions with the pharmaceutical administrative organizations.

The SDA has branch organizations in each province, autonomous region and city with provincial status. The regional SDAs have more or less the same responsibilities as their national mother organization, except that there authority is restricted to the home region. In practice, the national SDA will delegate its tasks related to a particular region to the local branch, unless a particular situation requires otherwise. Such an occasion could be a project that has been included in a national development programme. In that case the SDA in Beijing will at least be involved in the approval procedure and will send a representative to attend such events as the official start of the construction of such a project, the official start of production, etc. This means that in the case of Lukang, which ranks among China's largest pharmaceutical conglomerates, we should expect to observe a more than average interaction with the national SDA. In the following sections, I will first investigate Lukang's interactions with the national SDA, followed by an analysis of the company's dealings with the SDA's Shandong branch.

Lukang as a national pharmaceutical company

Before looking at specific interactions between Lukang and the national SDA, it will be useful to see how Lukang generally makes sense in the national pharmaceutical context:

> Lukang = 3rd antibiotics manufacturer of China; one of the three giants (Lukang, Harbin Pharmaceutical Co., North China Pharmaceutical Co.)
> Lukang = the largest pharmaceutical project within the ninth five-year-plan
> Lukang = the largest pharmaceutical project since the establishment of the PRC
> Lukang = first ISO9001 certified pharmaceutical company of China
> Lukang = one of the first listed Chinese pharmaceutical companies

This relation between the three top antibiotics manufacturers is also a highly interesting matter in the construction of Lukang's identity in the national pharmaceutical space. It is a useful example of how competition is defined in present-day China. While competition is now not only allowed but even stimulated by the government, a certain level of co-ordination is also applied by the central authorities, especially where strategically important industries are concerned. Although Lukang is praised for standing tall in the fierce national and international competition, the three giants, Lukang, North-China Pharmaceutical Corporation (NCPC) and the Harbin Pharmaceutical Co., held a joint conference in October 1995. The three companies agreed to co-ordinate their activities on the global market to avoid undesirable competition. There exists a special relation between Lukang's CEO, Mr Zhang Jianhui, and NCPC. Before his transfer to Lukang, he held a position at NCPC. At the time Zhang was transferred to Ji'ning, jobs were still assigned in China. Therefore, this transferral between competitors could very well be a kind of state-orchestrated control. Chinese employees, especially those with managerial functions, tend to maintain a certain tie with previous employers. The people who engineered Zhang's transfer knew that this would create a bond between Lukang and NCPC. This situation affects the identity of Lukang. Within the context of the Chinese pharmaceutical industry, Lukang is one of the main competitors of Harbin and NCPC, while in the context of international trade Lukang is part of the 'Chinese antibiotics industry', which profiles itself as an entity competing with other multinational market players.

The remarks on the technological project both refer to the '1000 t penicillin project' introduced in the historical overview. Lukang used to be regularly mentioned in the national pharmaceutical press for reaching record levels of penicillin in the fermentation broth. Increase in the production of antibiotics is not (only) attained through investing in more equipment, but especially by producing more using the same equipment, by making the mould secrete ever more antibiotic. The latter is considered as a real technological advance in fermentation processes. In my corpus of texts on Lukang, such reports regarding Lukang's penicillin production appeared on the following dates: 7/2/91, 4/4/91, 28/11/95, 12/3/96, 20/2/97 and 3/4/97. Similar reports are also published for the other major penicillin manufacturers, but Lukang is most frequently mentioned. This constructs Lukang as a symbol of technological progress of Chinese penicillin production. It is interesting to observe that references to such technical matters significantly decreased since mid-1997. This coincided with the listing of Lukang on the Shanghai Stock Exchange. Apparently, financial indicators like turnover and profit became more important to judge the performance of an enterprise like Lukang than the technological accomplishments. In terms of identity construction, the identity of Lukang as a technologically advanced manufacturer of penicillin was constructed within the context of the pharmaceutical industry. Once Lukang obtained its listing at the Shanghai Stock Exchange, it entered the context of financial speculation, in which (perceived) profitability prevailed over technology.

Now we are ready to look at some of the occasions in which Lukang interacts with the national SDA (or its predecessor SPAC; to avoid confusion, I will exclusively use the acronym SDA to refer to this organization).

- Vice-director of SDA attended start ceremony of the penicillin project;
- Vice-director attended handing over of grant Lukang to Shenyang Pharmaceutical University (under SDA);
- Vice-director of SDA attended national bridge contest in the Great Hall of the People co-sponsored by Lukang;
- Certification Centre of SDA sets up a team to inspect the penicillin workshop of Lukang for General Manufacturing Practice (GMP) certification accompanied by people from the provincial and municipal SDA branches;
- Team of SDA experts inspects Lukang's penicillin production line and finds it compliant with GMP specifications;
- Managers of Lingzhi report fraud by Lukang to SDA.

SDA involvement with the penicillin project is quite straightforward, as it is a project defined on a national level. In terms of cognitive space, the '1000 t penicillin project' is constructed in the national pharmaceutical space. Lukang is one of the 'big three antibiotics manufacturers' of China, another national metaphor. It is therefore a matter of course that it is controlled by the national pharmaceutical administrative organization. The fact that a vice-director was sent indicates that the SDA regarded this event as quite important.

Although the Shenyang Pharmaceutical University (SPU) is located in Shenyang, the capital of the Northeastern province of Liaoning, Lukang has special ties with this institution. The General Manager, Mr Lin Yongbin, is a graduate of that university and so is Lukang's Chief Engineer. It would be good Chinese tradition that these ex-alumni would want to do something to express their gratitude to their alma mater. SPU is directly operating under the national SDA. When such a nationally renowned company like Lukang offers a grant to such an equally well known university in their own sector, it is highly likely that the SDA would send a representative to attend the ceremony. Note that once more a vice-director was delegated.

Sponsoring intellectual games like bridge or go is a way in which Lukang wants to profile itself on a national scale as an enterprise interested in more than just generating profit. A national bridge contest sponsored by Lukang would be incomplete without a senior representative from the SDA. Again a vice-director was delegated. The Great Hall of the People, the home of the People's Congress, is probably the most luxurious (and conspicuous) location one can find in China for such an occasion.

General Manufacturing Practice (GMP) is a set of internationally recognized procedures to guarantee the safe production of pharmaceuticals. To obtain GMP certification, a manufacturer is required to let its facilities be inspected by a specially licensed organization. In China, this is one of the typical tasks of the SDA. However, as I will show later, such tasks can, and often will, be delegated to SDA branches in the home region of the pharmaceutical company to be certified. However, the penicillin project was a project of state-level importance. An SDA representative had earlier attended the official start of the construction work for the project. For the GMP certification of this workshop, the inspection team was composed by the national SDA. The actual inspection activities were conducted in co-operation with its provincial and municipal branch organizations.

So far, the interactions between the national SDA and Lukang introduced here have been neutral to positive in nature. They ensue from the nature of both organizations, Lukang being a pharmaceutical manufacturer and the SDA being the government organization supervising pharmaceutical production in China. The last item on the list, however, is related to the recent problems Lukang has experienced with its second issue of shares. Mr Wu and his colleague did not only lodge their accusations at the National Securities Supervisory Commission, but also at the SDA. Most of the texts regarding this incident mention the reaction of the National Securities Supervisory Commission: halting Lukang's application for a second issue. However, the decision also to involve the SDA may have been a grave error. The National Securities Supervisory Commission did not reveal the identities of the accusers to Lukang, to protect their safety. However, Lukang still discovered that Mr Wu was the main culprit jeopardizing the new share issue and Lukang's good name, thereby endangering the company's financial position and credibility. It seems likely that this information had been passed on to Lukang by the SDA. As one of China's leading pharmaceutical groups, the SDA can be expected (and should have been expected by Mr Wu) to protect the company against any kind of peril. The SDA does not have the authority to discharge the accusations of fraud, but it can try to interfere with the investigations of the National Securities Supervisory Commission by revealing the identity of the person(s) that filed the accusation. I will devote more space on the problems related to the second share issue in the section on the identity of Lukang in the Party context.

From the above account of Lukang's activities within the context of the national pharmaceutical sector, the following identity construct becomes apparent. Lukang is regarded as a major Chinese pharmaceutical manufacturer and in particular one of the top three antibiotics producers. As such it enjoys intensive support from the national SDA. This is a two-way interaction. The SDA sends representatives to important events related to Lukang (e.g. the ceremonial start of the construction work on the penicillin project), but Lukang also makes sure it invites dignitaries from the SDA for such promotional events as the go contest. Moreover, the SDA's support to Lukang not only takes place at formal occasions, but is also enacted in less formal ones, like the protection of Lukang from attacks by vindictive employees.

The top three antibiotics manufacturers constitute a smaller space within the national pharmaceutical cognitive space. Representatives of the three convene regularly and Lukang's CEO, Mr Zhang, used to work for another member, NCPC. Such amicable contacts between competitors are another result of the influence of the national SDA on Lukang. One of the tasks of Chinese ministries, or ministry-like organizations, is to contain excessive competition between manufacturers of similar products, as this can easily damage China's position in the global market for those products. A certain level of co-operation or exchange of information can, on the contrary, strengthen that position. Formulated differently, Lukang is also an element of the Chinese antibiotics industry, profiling itself globally as an organic whole.

Lukang as a Shandong pharmaceutical company

The entire Chapter 4 will be dedicated to the difference in sense-making of a Chinese enterprise in the different administrative levels. I will try to restrict this section to a treatment of Lukang in the Shandong pharmaceutical context as much as possible and avoid references to Lukang as a Shandong enterprise in general. As I did earlier in this chapter, I will start with a number of general metaphors used to describe Lukang vis-à-vis the Shandong pharmaceutical industry:

> Lukang = reform pioneer among Shandong's pharmaceutical state-owned enterprises
> Lukang = end of Shandong not having its own antibiotics manufacturing
> Lukang = provider of 50 per cent of Shandong's pharmaceutical export income
> Lukang = winner of Gold award in the Shandong Pharmaceutical Construction Cup

With the exception of the last one, these metaphors all refer to honour brought to Shandong by Lukang. As mentioned earlier, in 1984, Lukang was included in an experimental programme to 'place the main responsibility for enterprise management at the CEO'. This coincided with the year that Mr Zhang was promoted to the position of CEO of the Ji'ning Antibiotics Factory. His efforts have contributed to Lukang's identity as 'reform pioneer'.

The reference to Shandong not having its own antibiotics industry will strike most readers who are not familiar with Chinese regional chauvinism as rather odd. The production of antibiotics is a typical economy of scale.

A small number of large players control the entire global market. However, antibiotics are currently manufactured in virtually all main administrative regions of China and even the fact that one single country, however large, has three main penicillin producers seems to defy the basic concepts of economy.

An important constructor of provincial space in China is interprovincial political and economic strife. Economic reporting in the Chinese media is often oriented around the provinces. Each province, autonomous region or city province aims to be independent of other regions for such major strategic goods as cars, pharmaceuticals, etc. (Studwell 2002: 63–68). The result of this tendency towards provincial autonomy is that each of the main administrative regions has its own antibiotics manufacturer. When a certain Chinese province or region of comparable level lacks a manufacturer of a product that is considered strategically important, this will be regarded as a weakness and repairing the deficiency will be top priority in the regional economic construction programme. The fact that certain regions may be less suitable for a certain industry usually does not play a role in this matter. When the predecessor of Lukang was established in 1966, its only product was Terramycin, a type of antibiotic. Being the first antibiotics manufacturer in Shandong was still an occasion of sense-making 30 years later.

Generating hard currency is an important source of political clout for a Chinese enterprise. With an inconvertible national currency, China relies heavily on export earnings to finance the import of basic products like cereals or strategic goods like fighter planes. Hard currency earnings of an individual Chinese enterprise are divided between the State, the organization(s) managing the enterprise and the enterprise itself. A detailed description of this system and its development during the past decades falls outside the scope of this study. What is interesting is that the identity of Lukang as a hard currency earner seems to be strongly linked to the province. In the texts scanned for this study, one remark can be found concerning Lukang as a hard currency earner of Ji'ning, but the reports on Lukang's interactions with foreign companies seem to be concentrated on the provincial level. Narrowed down to the Shandong pharmaceutical sector, we are even told that Lukang is responsible for half of the total hard currency earnings of the provincial pharmaceutical industry. This is almost like stating that Lukang is the most influential pharmaceutical company in Shandong.

Winning the first prize in the Shandong Pharmaceutical Construction Cup is not entirely an achievement by Lukang. The award was given for the construction work on the 1000 t penicillin project, the design of which had been contracted out to the Shanghai Pharmaceutical Design Institute (SPDI), one of China's top industrial design institutes. It was Lukang's vision to invest in the services of an ace designer, instead of saving costs and using a locally based institute.

Again following the structure adopted earlier in this chapter, I will now look at the interactions between Lukang and the Shandong SDA (SSDA) as reported in the corpus of texts.

- Director of SSDA attended start of Lukang's penicillin project in December 1995;
- SSDA prohibited Lingzhi's listing in 1997;
- SSDA managed Lingzhi until August 2000 when Lingzhi was transferred to Lukang;
- SSDA approves changing Lingzhi from a shareholding company into a limited company in October 2002.

As a pharmaceutical enterprise in Shandong province, it is a matter of course that a representative of SSDA attend the ceremonial start of the construction work for the penicillin project. While the national SDA delegated a vice-director, SSDA's director attended this event in person. This should not lead to the conclusion that Lukang is more strongly included in the Shandong pharmaceutical space than in the national one. A vice-director of the SDA would still outrank the director of a provincial branch. The fact that the national SDA still sent a representative of such high rank marks the important position of Lukang nationally. For SSDA Lukang was its number one company and delegating anyone else but the director would have been an insult to Lukang, which outsiders would probably interpret as the result of a major conflict between Lukang and SSDA. While the national SDA sends people to Lukang's events in Shandong, no SSDA attendance of Lukang's activities outside Shandong can be found in the corpus.

When SSDA deterred Lingzhi from seeking listing on the Shanghai Stock Exchange, this company was not yet a part of Lukang. However, as Lukang is also 'managed' by SSDA, the transferral of the state-owned equity in Lingzhi to Lukang can be regarded as a merely cosmetic act. From one point of view we can say that SSDA moved the state-owned assets it operated to a (partly) state-owned enterprise. At the time of the transfer, 61 per cent of the equity of Lingzhi was state owned, while the stake of the state in Lukang was almost 40 per cent. The state, through the management by Lukang, remained a major stakeholder. The main difference between the old and the new situation was that SSDA did (on paper at least) not interfere with the daily management of Lukang.

The people who were most radically affected by this move were the leaders of Lingzhi, whose position changed from the managers of a rather successful state-owned enterprise to the managers of a daughter company of a conglomerate. Although the CEO of Lukang had promised not to interfere with the management of Lingzhi after it became a part of the Lukang group, he almost immediately sent a CEO from among Lukang's top managers and consequently transferred Lingzhi's most valuable assets, its licences to trade in all types of pharmaceuticals, to other daughter companies of Lukang. Lingzhi was stripped to the bone. The former CEO of Lingzhi, Mr Wu, ended up as a minor manager of a nearly empty shell. Finally, SSDA approved Lukang's application to change the ownership type of Lingzhi from stockholding company to limited company, even though a compensation programme for the shareholders had still not been decided on.

Although this course of events has been extensively reported, even in the national press, SSDA has never interfered and we may presume that SSDA at least condoned Lukang's treatment of Lingzhi. However, knowing the position of Lukang as the single most important generator of hard currency in the Shandong pharmaceutical sector, it is very well possible that SSDA would not have been in the position to stop Lukang, even if it did not agree with Lukang's treatment of Lingzhi.

When we attempt to summarize Lukang's identity in the Shandong pharmaceutical sector, we see quite a different type of company. While in the national pharmaceutical sector Lukang has an important, though not a leading, position, the company seems to be almost in charge of the pharmaceutical industry of Shandong. Both according to its legal authority as in its general behaviour, SSDA is the government organization that is in charge of the provincial pharmaceutical sector. However, in a number of practical incidents SSDA does not seem to interfere in actions by Lukang that strike many observers, including reporters of national publications, as improper. Although it is never said verbatim, the management of Lukang is aware that it is backed up by the national SDA. In that respect it is one of the very few Shandong pharmaceutical companies that enjoys such national support. In terms of identity construction, the support of the national SDA provides Lukang with a 'national SDA' identity (Lukang = SDA). Seen from this angle, Lukang becomes a local agent of the national SDA's authority, which overrides that of SSDA. On the other hand, SSDA will treat Lukang with a level of respect close or even similar to that with which it will approach the national SDA.

In terms of Social Integration theory, Lukang is included in the large Chinese pharmaceutical space and also in the Shandong pharmaceutical space, a sub-space of the former. Lukang's inclusion in the national space seems to be stronger than that in the Shandong space. Lukang is more a Chinese enterprise than a Shandong enterprise. During interactions in the Shandong space, Lukang can introduce its national identity into that interaction and can derive considerable political clout from it.

Lukang as a Ji'ning pharmaceutical company

After observing that Lukang's identity as a Shandong pharmaceutical enterprise is weaker than that as a national pharmaceutical enterprise, it will not be a surprise to observe that the company's identity as a Ji'ning pharmaceutical company is even more limited. As a Ji'ning enterprise in general, various texts in the corpus tell us that Lukang ranks among the city's largest companies, that it is a big tax payer and that it has made a major contribution to the city's development. However, identity construction in different administrative levels will be the main theme of the next chapter. Here I intend to restrict my observations exclusively to Lukang as a Ji'ning pharmaceutical enterprise.

Only two interactions are reported between Lukang and the municipal SDA:

- The national SDA takes representatives of its provincial and municipal branches along during the inspection of the new penicillin plant mentioned earlier in this chapter;
- Ji'ning SDA inspects GMP conditions of three workshops for the production of finished antibiotics.

In the first event, the national SDA is the active party and the regional and local branches are permitted to join in. The '1000 t penicillin project' is ostensibly a national project, rather than a provincial or a municipal one.

Although the inspection of finished pharmaceuticals involves stricter GMP regulation than that of bulk pharmaceutical products, their production does not contain any element of national pride. It is a routine activity that can be perfectly well performed by the lowest level SDA, the municipal one. It is no job for SSDA, let alone the national parent.

I have already observed some interference with Lukang by the Ji'ning pharmaceutical industry in the historical section of this chapter. Lukang took over the Ji'ning Nr 1 and Nr 2 Pharmaceutical Factories in 1994. The names of these enterprises contain two indications regarding their enterprise status. The fact that these enterprises were registered as factories (*chang*), rather than companies (*gongsi*), indicates that they were directly managed by an administrative organization. At that time, state-owned companies that were believed to be able to take responsibility for their own profit and loss were one by one transformed into companies. They were still state owned (*guoyou*), but no longer state operated (*guoying*). Although the consulted literature does not indicate so verbatim, from the fact that their names contained the geographic name Ji'ning we can conclude that this organization was the Ji'ning SDA. Although the notion of bankruptcy started to cease to be a taboo word in China at that time, experimenting with actually letting state-owned enterprises go bankrupt was still only considered, rather than executed. The major deterrent was that the government still had no way of dealing with the employees of bankrupt enterprises. Unemployed citizens are a major cause for social unrest and social unrest is the single worst nightmare for the Chinese authorities. One way of dealing with enterprises that a local government deem to be incapable of continuing to operate independently is to 'ask' a local enterprise that is performing well to take it over. The quotations here indicate that there is very little room for the latter to refuse such a request. Again, although the texts do not report any details regarding this transaction, the fact that two of these factories were 'acquired' by Lukang in one deal, by taking care of the enterprises' debts, strongly indicates that Lukang was at least not the active party in this case.

There is an interesting difference between the transfer of Lingzhi to Lukang by SSDA and Lukang's acquisition of the Ji'ning Nr 1/2 Pharmaceutical Factories. The reporting on the former elaborately explains that SSDA had to make this move in the background of new national policy regarding severing of direct relations between administrative organizations and enterprises. The latter deal is simply reported as such, without revealing any details. SSDA had a well performing company to give away and selected Lukang as the recipient. The municipal government of Ji'ning found itself confronted with two problem enterprises and approached Lukang to take over this burden. Formulated in terms of benefit, SSDA did Lukang a favour with Lingzhi, while Lukang did the Ji'ning government a favour with the Nr 1 and Nr 2 pharmaceutical factories.

From the point of view of identity, Lukang was approached by SSDA as a major pharmaceutical company, for which Lingzhi would make a valuable resource. The Ji'ning government, on the other hand, approached Lukang as one of the city's best performing enterprises, one that would be able to handle the financial burden brought on by the takeover. The interaction between SSDA and Lukang constructs a primary pharmaceutical identity. The interaction between the Ji'ning authorities and Lukang constructs a primary strong enterprise identity. With this observation I am not stating that Lukang does not have a pharmaceutical identity in the Ji'ning context. Lukang has multiple identities in the Ji'ning space, including a pharmaceutical one. However, for the Ji'ning government, Lukang is first of all a successful enterprise and one of the region's major employers. As such it contributes to the local social stability and therefore is a strong pillar of the municipal government, regardless of what its business actually is. In the following section on the way the Party organization affects the operation of Lukang, in particular when analysing another takeover, I will revert to this identity and bring on additional evidence to corroborate this conclusion.

Lukang as a pharmaceutical company

When we look back on the previous section analysing the identity of Lukang as a pharmaceutical company at different administrative levels, we can conclude that the strongest pharmaceutical identity of Lukang is constructed at the national level. For the national pharmaceutical world, Lukang is one of China's major companies, in particular one of the top manufacturers of antibiotics. Lukang's pharmaceutical identity plays a role at the provincial level as well, but much less prominent. Lukang has more identities at that level that seem to be at least as important as its pharmaceutical identity.

At the municipal level, the fact that Lukang is a pharmaceutical manufacturer does not seem to play a significant role. Lukang is a major employer and as such a pillar for local social stability.

The Communist Party organization

Political parties are a sensitive subject in China. There is *the* party, the Communist Party of China (CPC) and that party does not tolerate any other party besides itself. Remnants of a small number of political parties established in the first half of the twentieth century still exist under the, ominous, name of 'democratic parties', but the first rule of their articles of association is that they support the leading role of the CPC. The CPC is the ideological motor of the People's Republic of China. All units comprise a number of party members, who constitute that unit's Party Group. The leadership of the Party Group is called the Party Committee, which is headed by the Party Secretary. The latter is such an important function in the unit that this person is usually simply referred to as the unit's Secretary.

CPC membership is an important source of multiple inclusions in China. Important decisions in a Chinese enterprise need to be stamped by that enterprise's Party Group. If the Party Group has a problem with the plan, it has the power to order changes or to discard it altogether. Moreover, if the Party Group suspects that a certain plan is ideologically incorrect, it can consult other Party Groups, in particular the Party Group of the mother organization of its own organization. If, for example, a shoe factory in Suzhou, Jiangsu province, which is owned by the Suzhou Light Industry Bureau, intends to apply for a large bank loan to invest in new equipment and the Party Group of the factory is in doubt whether such a huge investment is appropriate, it can contact the Party Group of the Suzhou Light Industry Bureau, without notifying the factory's leadership. This situation has led to an interesting practice in a large number of state-owned enterprises: the administrative CEO is very often simultaneously the Party Secretary. The multiple inclusion of that person is believed to facilitate decision making.

An important practice in the CPC space is secrecy. Although CPC membership is not an official secret, party members are not supposed to exhibit their membership status publicly. Chinese also rarely inquire after each other's Party membership status. It is a question that can easily lead to loss of face, when a Party member is put in the embarrassing position of being circumspect about it. Party Group meetings are also supposed to be a secret. Such meetings are held irregularly, when deemed necessary by the Party Committee. The date for the meeting is conveyed by word of mouth, or on memory pad-like scraps of paper that would not easily arouse suspicion of non-members.

The role of the Party cell in a Chinese enterprise has been affected by the economic reforms of past decades. In the past one of their tasks was to carry out the political battles between Party factions at the grass-roots level. While such battles continue, as they are an inherent part of the Party space, the daily operations of enterprises are no longer affected by 'struggle meetings' to expose the followers of 'erroneous Party lines' (You 1998, cited in Tang and Ward 2003: 68–69). However, the Party organization within a Chinese enterprise continues to be a major base for organizations in the external environment of the enterprise to control that enterprise's activities. Tang and Ward (2003: 68–75) offer an interesting account of the way the Party organizations function in present-day Chinese enterprises, but their description concentrates on the internal affairs of enterprises. In this section, I will analyse a number of instances in which the CPC organization outside the company has affected Lukang.

Before turning my attention to those events, I need to stress a very peculiar aspect of the Party organization. The main theme of this chapter is to analyse the identity construction processes of a state-owned enterprise like Lukang through its interactions with its various mothers-in-law. However, the CPC is strictly speaking itself not a mother-in-law. All mothers-in-law of Lukang, as Lukang itself, have a Party group of their own. A mother-in-law like the municipal government of Ji'ning can interfere directly with the operations of Lukang, for example by issuing new enterprise safety regulations. Ji'ning Municipality, as a unit, will have a Party group of its own. This Party group has the authority to interfere with the internal affairs of Lukang through Lukang's Party group, whenever the former feels there is need to do so. In such a case, the municipal Party group will usually contact its sister organization within Lukang. However, most members of both Party groups will also hold administrative functions in their respective units. For example, the Party Secretary of Lukang, Mr Zhang Jianhui, is also its Chairman of the Board. This means that for each instance of interaction between a Chinese enterprise and one of its mothers-in-law, it could be a contact between an enterprise and an administrative organization, or between the Party groups of both units. Such information is often lacking, however sometimes it is possible to find cues that may point at possible Party involvement. One of the more conspicuous cues is the way actors are named. Mr Zhang Jianhui can be referred to as Chairman Zhang (*Zhang dongshizhang*) which would refer to his identity as Chairman of the Board. He can also be introduced as Secretary Zhang (*Zhang shuji*), a designation pointing at his identity as Party Secretary. Interesting evidence for the importance of titles is that the corpus of texts on Lukang includes one reference to the same person as 'Mr Zhang' (*Zhang xiansheng*). The word *xiansheng* used to be the regular form of address for male persons, before the Communists replaced it with the gender neutral term comrade (*tongzhi*). Its use was then restricted to foreign men. The word has returned in everyday parlance during the years of reforms and is especially preferred in a business context. This designation for Mr Zhang was used in a report on the official presentation of the annual account of Lukang during a shareholder meeting. The stock market and everything that has to do with it is perceived as something that is not really a part of socialism, even though it is sanctioned by the CPC. Rather, it is a concept imported from abroad. In this context, *dongshizhang* as a form of address seems to carry a slightly old-fashioned feeling. Mr Zhang is therefore introduced as 'the Chairman of Lukang, Mr Zhang Jianhui'. *Dongshizhang* is then used as in most Western languages, as the designation of a profession, while the person himself is politely addressed with *xiansheng*.

Lukang and the national Party organization

Scanning the corpus of narratives on Lukang for direct influences from the national Party organization on the operation of Lukang, there is hardly anything worth mentioning. The only event that may be interpreted as such is the fact that second-level Party leaders received training at the Central Party School in Beijing. However, this can hardly be called 'influence' on Lukang's management.

The Lukang Party organization regularly organizes political study meetings to discuss important national political events like Party congresses. The national Party leadership may, for example, launch a campaign against corruption (it regularly does). Corruption, however, is an extremely broad concept and the Party group of each individual unit needs to study its own particular situation and try to find out if, and how, the current national anti-corruption campaign applies to the local situation. This may lead to a number of people within the unit being accused of corruption or behaviour that verges on corruption. This in turn may lead to warnings, or even stronger penalties, meted out to the culprits.

However, even if the outcomes of such study meetings were to have certain repercussions on the management of Lukang, for example if top managers were accused of corruption, it would still be an indirect type of influence, as it would be the result of the localized interpretation of the national policy. It would not be a deliberate act of *the* national Party organization to penalize that particular manager of that particular company.

Lukang and the provincial Party organization

The corpus contains three instances of direct interactions between the provincial Party organization and Lukang. Two of them are related to the same topic: the promotion of fair government (*lianzheng*); the third one concerns a subsidiary of Lukang in Heze, a city in the most western part of Shandong.

The fair government campaigns that are regularly launched by the CPC seem to be yet another example of national political decrees that have to be localized by the Party committees in individual units. However, the sources clearly state that the notion of fair government is simply discussed by the enterprise Party organization, not that there are actual interactions between provincial Party organizations and that of Lukang. The study meetings are held on the premises of Lukang. Lukang Party sections mentioned are the Party committee itself and the Company Disciplinary Department; on the province's side we find the Disciplinary Department, the Organization Department and the Propaganda Department. The Disciplinary Department is the section of a Party group that has the authority to mete out punishments to Party members. Occasions for doing so can be violations of national laws, or behaviour not becoming a Party member.

The Organization Department is more or less the general management department of a Party group. It co-ordinates the way the Party organization is embedded in the host organization and is in charge of the interaction between Party groups of different units. The tasks of the Propaganda Department are more obvious. However, the sense of the term 'propaganda' in this case is broader than that of the English term. It can comprise virtually all forms of publication of the unit, including press releases, internal news bulletins, the nomination of model employees, etc.

Each of these Party departments can interact with a sister department in a related unit. For example, the Organization Department of the municipal police can interact with that of the municipal government to co-ordinate regular communication between the two units. In a similar way, the Propaganda Department of the same police unit can interact with that of the local daily newspaper to ensure that the paper reports on local police activities in a proper fashion. Such interactions can run parallel with interaction on the same topics between the leaders of the units involved. To stick to the same examples, the Chief of Police of our police unit can discuss the matter of regular communication between their units at the same time that their respective Party organizations discuss the same matter. In such a situation, the Chief of Police and the Mayor would decide on the matter, with their Party organizations making sure that the decision did not violate the current Party line. However, it can, and frequently does, happen that the decision makers first check with the Party people, before making their final decision.

The occasion of interaction between Lukang and the Party organization at the provincial level that is not related to the fair government issue is the acquisition by Lukang of the Heze Nr 2 Pharmaceutical Factory. According to the official news report, the Heze municipal government and the Heze Nr 2 Pharmaceutical Factory approached Lukang in April 1997 with the request that Lukang take over the fledgling Heze Nr 2. The acquisition agreement was signed in August of the same year. The factory was incorporated into the Lukang Group as its Heze Branch. Four years later, the provincial Party secretary paid the Heze Branch an official visit. During that visit he was accompanied by Lukang's vice-Party secretary, who was also the company's General Manager, the Party secretary of Heze Municipality and the Mayor of Heze. When we try to analyse the case of Lukang's Heze Branch using the cues in the texts, the first thing that attracts attention is the enterprise's original name: Heze Nr 2 Pharmaceutical Factory. Exactly like the two Ji'ning pharmaceutical factories acquired by Lukang (see above), this name is composed in the command economic way of the geographic name followed by a number. This indicates that it was an enterprise established and owned by the Heze government. Moreover, the enterprise had still not been given a more modern designation as late as 1997. Apparently the enterprise and its owner organization has failed to make sense of the new competitive environment. Closing it down was not an option. It was still extremely hard, in spite of the parlance of the national government, to actually let enterprises go bankrupt. Moreover, such a shut down would generate a number of unemployed people in the Heze region, for which the Heze government would be held responsible. The step to find a healthy company to take over Heze Nr 2 was a logical decision and Lukang was the nearest candidate. The fact that the parties involved were represented by their leading Party members (secretaries and vice-secretaries) indicates that the Party organizations in the units involved (Heze Nr 2, Heze Municipality, Lukang, Shandong Province) have at least been instrumental in cooking up this deal.

The conclusion of this section is then that the provincial Party organization can exercise considerable influence on a large enterprise like Lukang. In terms of identity, the identity of Lukang in relation to the fair government campaign is that of one of the larger units of Shandong, which implies that Lukang's Party organization is also one of the province's largest single Party organizations. This makes it an important vehicle for the propagation of Party policies. In the case of the Heze Branch, the identity of Lukang is that of a major local enterprise in the same industrial sector as that of the fledgling Heze Nr 2. The leaders of the respective Party organizations will simultaneously hold leading positions in their own organizations. Heze Nr 2, with the aid of their municipal government, can access the leadership of Lukang through its Party apparatus.

Lukang and the municipal Party organization

My corpus contains five instances of interactions between the Party organization of Lukang and its sister organization of Ji'ning Municipality. Apparently, the interactions between an enterprise and the Party organization are more frequent with those of lower level units. The national Party organization does not really interact with Lukang. The provincial Party organization occasionally exercises influence. Interactions on the municipal level are much more frequent and concern a wide range of activities.

General inspection of Lukang

A delegation from Ji'ning Municipality visited Lukang for a general inspection of the status quo, demonstrating the government's concern for local industry. This type of visit takes place regularly. The delegation consisted of the following persons:

* Ji'ning Municipality's Vice-Party Secretary;
* The Deputy Mayor;
* A Vice-Mayor;
* A Vice-Secretary of Ji'ning Municipality;
* The Director of the Municipal Economic Committee.

Let's look at the symbolism in this list. The first thing to observe here is the order in which the visitors are listed. Such an order is never incidental in China. The dignitaries will always be listed in order of importance, as perceived by the narrator. In this case the Party organization of Ji'ning Municipality appears to be more important that the Municipality itself. Phrased differently: in this visit, the unity seems to be less important than its Party organization. The Deputy Mayor is the Mayor's direct representative, while the Vice-Mayor is one of several (a large Chinese city always has a number of Vice-Mayors). The Municipality's Vice-Secretary should not be confused with its Vice-Party Secretary. The Director of the Economic Committee ranks last. Conclusion: this is above all a Party delegation.

Another aspect that immediately attracts attention is the fact that almost all organizations are represented by the seconds in command: vice-this, deputy that, etc. Lukang is an important enterprise, but a generic type of activity like a general inspection does not require the Mayor or the Party secretary to appear. Such leaders can be represented by the seconds in command. The Municipal Economic Committee, however, is represented by its Director. Lukang is an enterprise, an economic unit. This visit therefore calls for the number one leader to appear.

Youth League

The Communist Youth League is the incubator organization of the Communist Party. Young people complying with the requirements (family background, political and moral attitude, etc.) are stimulated to become members of the Youth League. Their development will then be closely monitored and as soon as a Youth League member is deemed fit to be promoted to membership of the Communist Party, the person is stimulated once more to make this step, which is seen as instrumental for smooth climbing of the social ladder in China.

Although the Youth League and the Communist Party are officially profiled as totally independent, in practice many Youth League activities are guided by the CPC. I therefore choose to regard the Youth League as a special segment of the CPC organization in the context of this study.

Like the CPC, each unit has its own Youth League organization. The corpus of narratives contains a report on a conference held by Lukang's Youth League. This conference was attended by representatives of the Youth League of Ji'ning Municipality. During the conference, the attendants were addressed by Lukang's CEO, in his capacity as the company's Party-Secretary.

Municipal Youth League representatives were also present at a collective wedding ceremony that was organized to offer an alternative for excessively expensive wedding ceremonies (see below). Newlyweds are usually young people and regardless of whether they are Youth League members or not, the Youth League is required to be adequately represented at such a ceremony with an obvious propagandist character.

Apparently the interactions between Lukang and the Youth League organizations mainly take place at the municipal level.

Lukang's internal bulletin

Lukang publishes a news bulletin that has recently also been added to the company's web site. Texts of this bulletin constitute an important segment of my corpus of Lukang-related narratives.

A meeting was organized by Lukang to celebrate the first anniversary of this publication. The ceremony was attended by the following persons:

- Lukang second-level Party Committee;
- The News Section of the Propaganda Dept. of the Municipal Party Committee;
- *Ji'ning Daily*.

The second-level Party Committee refers to the Party leaders of divisions of the Lukang Group. This term is always used in the corpus as opposed to the Group Party Committee. It is interesting to see that the compilation and publication of news is not a Group-level matter within Lukang, but is delegated to the divisional level. Apparently the production of news is perceived as a function of the working divisions, where the economic activities take place. On the other hand, this may also be regarded as a less important activity of Lukang and therefore not worth the limited time of the Group's leadership.

The second organization provides valuable insight into the general function of the Party apparatus on news production in China. News is a matter of the Propaganda Department, which has a special section for it. News and propaganda have always been highly overlapping notions in the CPC context. In the Marxist view of the world, there is no such thing as 'news' that happens out there. News has a class character and is always the product of a certain class, published with a specific political motive. The production of news has therefore to be scrutinized by the Party, through the propaganda departments of the Party groups in each unit.

The appearance of the *Ji'ning Daily* is therefore not surprising. The title of this newspaper already indicates that it is the publication of the Ji'ning Municipal Party Committee. A newspaper whose title is derived from its geographic name + the word 'daily' (*ribao*) is always produced under the auspices of the Party committee of that location (usually a province or a municipality). Although the *Ji'ning Daily* is a separate legal entity in economic terms, its contents are the responsibility of the News Section appearing in second rank in the above list. This is exactly the reason why the News Section ranks second, while the *Ji'ning Daily* ranks third; the News Section is more important.

This item shows that publications by an influential economic unit like Lukang are closely monitored by the Party Committee of the local government. Lukang's bulletin should tell the outside world of the company's great achievements. Lukang's success will add to the success of Ji'ning Municipality's economic policies.

In terms of identity, Lukang is part of the identity of Ji'ning and its success adds to the perception of Ji'ning as a successful economic region. This is a good example of a bidirectional identity construction process. Lukang and Ji'ning Municipality are two separate units. One of the social-economic contexts they share is Ji'ning, i.e. the administrative region as opposed to Ji'ning Municipality as a social-economic unit. Ji'ning Municipality is strongly included in the Ji'ning space and if Ji'ning disappeared for whatever reason, Ji'ning Municipality would disappear with it. Lukang is located in Ji'ning and is therefore also included in that regional space. However, Lukang is less strongly included in the Ji'ning space, as it also has reasonably strong inclusions in the Shandong space and the Pharmaceutical Industry space. As one of the major enterprises in Ji'ning, it is important for Ji'ning Municipality to work actively on its relations with Lukang and in the profiling of Lukang as a successful Ji'ning enterprise. Lukang, on the other hand, needs the support of Ji'ning Municipality in a wide range of matters. Lukang therefore can be seen as trading its success for the support from Ji'ning Municipality.

Shandong Outstanding Management Enterprise award

Lukang received an award as a Shandong Outstanding Management Enterprise in 2002. At an official ceremony to celebrate that honour, the following Party representatives were present.

- Vice-Secretary of Lukang's Party committee;
- Lukang Political Study Association;
- Vice-Chief of the Propaganda Dept. of the Municipal Party Committee.

The very first thing that should strike the reader is that representatives of any provincial organization were lacking, in spite of the fact that the title seemed to indicate that it concerned a provincial award. Apparently the title contained the word 'Shandong', but the award was not granted by provincial authorities.

Lukang was first of all represented by its Vice-Secretary. This indicates that it was not a major issue for Lukang to receive this award. The Political Study Association is a group of political activists who study policy statements of the government and the CPC and how they can be understood in such a way that they can be made applicable to their own organization. All larger units have such a group. It is not directly part of the Party organization, but its activities are closely monitored by it.

Ji'ning Municipality was represented through its Propaganda Department. Apparently, granting such an award is again something that simultaneously adds to the honour of Ji'ning Municipality. In terms of identity construction this event therefore shows close similarities to the event introduced in the previous section.

Collective wedding

Chinese wedding ceremonies tend to be lavish. It is not uncommon that newlyweds are deeply in debt after their marriage. To oppose the excessive spending on wedding ceremonies, units, often through their Party organizations, frequently organize collective weddings. A number of employees register to marry on the same date and a unit leader, again often the leader of the Party organization, will oversee the ceremony and publicly declare the couples married. One such ceremony is described in my corpus. The officials present included:

- several Lukang leaders;
- the Vice-Secretary of the Lukang Party Committee;
- representatives from the Propaganda Dept. of the Ji'ning Municipal Party Committee;
- representatives from the Municipal Youth League;
- representatives from the Municipal Labour Union;
- representatives from the Municipal Women's League.

Earlier in this chapter, I mentioned the organizational similarities of the Youth League, the Labour Union and the Women's League with the CPC. The fact that all these organizations were represented during the collective wedding corroborates this view. As most brides and grooms will be relatively young people, the Youth League cannot be absent. At least one of the couples in this particular ceremony was an employee of the company Lukang, hence the involvement of the Labour Union. The Women's League, finally, was needed to emphasize that husband and wife should treat one another as equals (which is not always the case in Chinese practice).

On the Lukang side 'several leaders' are presented before mentioning the Vice-Secretary of the local Party committee.

From an identity point of view, this ceremony seems to be more valuable to Ji'ning Municipality than to Lukang. The family is frequently described as a 'cell of society' in Chinese Communist parlance. Social stability is the single most important source of concern for any Chinese municipality and this type of collective wedding is regarded as instrumental in creating a stable society, as the newlyweds do not have to borrow money from friends, relatives, loan sharks, etc., to finance expensive weddings. Local large enterprises are therefore stimulated to facilitate collective weddings. More simply stated: Lukang is an instrument to create social stability. We can observe a trade-off once more: Lukang trades social stability for (unnamed) services from the part of Ji'ning Municipality.

Fraud

The last, but probably most illuminating, example of how the Party organization affects Lukang on the municipal level has already been introduced in the historical section of this chapter: the Lingzhi fraud case. Mr Wu, the former CEO of Lingzhi, accused the management of Lukang of tampering with the Group's financial figures to facilitate a second issue of shares. Soon after his return home to Ji'ning, Mr Wu was arrested and interrogated. The most salient detail was that he was not formally booked in prison, but first locked up in a hotel room. Moreover, he was not so much interrogated by the Prosecutor, but by the representatives of Lukang's Party organization. He spent almost a week in that hotel room, kept incommunicado from the outside world.

This situation is referred to in Chinese 'double restriction' (*shuanggui*), i.e. the Party organization is allowed to detain a member for interrogation in a restricted location for a restricted period of time. This power is only granted to Party organizations of large units. Lukang certainly suits that condition.

Mr Wu's treatment is an almost perfect illustration of complexity caused by multiple inclusions. The direct motive to contact the National Securities Supervisory Commission to blow the whistle was his conflict with Lukang's top management regarding the way Lingzhi was stripped after being taken over by Lukang; he wanted to get even. In terms of cognitive space, this conflict was constructed in the Lukang space. However, the particular way Mr Wu was treated afterwards in Ji'ning took place in the CPC space. Mr Wu's conflict with the Lukang management directly involved Lukang's CEO, Mr Zhang Jianhui. Although the reports on Mr Wu's interrogation do not reveal names of Lukang officials present, we can presume that the operation was at least sanctioned by Mr Zhang, as this is probably the most severe form of punishment a Party organization in a unit can carry out. Presuming that these observations are correct, this means that the procurator who arrested Mr Wu was also acting in the Party space. Lukang's Party commission and the local procurator entered into a configuration to neutralize the source of the problem that interfered with Lukang's smooth second share issue. Not all procurators involved need to be Party members to qualify as members of such a configuration. The initial contact will have taken place between the Party secretaries of Lukang and the Ji'ning Procurator, who will then have mapped out the proper way to proceed.

How then can we explain this severe reaction from the Ji'ning Party space to what seems to be an internal conflict of Lukang? I believe that the answer should be found in the identity of enterprise, in particular large enterprises like Lukang, as local units, i.e. providers of subsistence to a large number of people. Earlier in this chapter I already pointed out that at the Ji'ning level Lukang's foremost identity is that of major employer. Through the social role of provider of subsistence, Lukang contributes to the maintenance of social order; belonging to Lukang is not only a source of income, but of almost any resource a person needs to lead a quality life. Besides such material aspects as salary and housing, being a Lukang person also is a source of pride, earning the person respect from those who belong to lesser units. Endangering the position of Lukang therefore amounts to jeopardizing the livelihood of a large number of people. As social order is the main concern of a Chinese municipal government, that same government will be aroused by the news that Lukang's second share issue procedure was stopped. This news immediately caused the appearance of speculative articles in the financial media, which further endangered the position of the company, as rumours about problems lowered the price of Lukang stock. Financial problems may result in lay-offs, which would increase the number of unemployed people in the Ji'ning region. Unemployment is a breeding ground for social unrest, hence Lukang's problems must have been a cause of concern on the part of Ji'ning Municipality. The short period between Mr Wu's return to Ji'ning and his arrest indicates that the parties involved did not need much time to agree on measures to be taken to neutralize the source of the problem. Ji'ning Municipality must have been involved in this 'double restricted' treatment of Mr Wu, even though it was hiding behind the procurator's office.

When the officials of the National Securities Inspection Commission arrived in Ji'ning to investigate the accusations further, they first contacted their local daughter organization. This is regular procedure, as they belong to the same cognitive space. However, they received little assistance there. Apparently the inclusion of the local Securities Supervisory Commission in the Ji'ning space was stronger than the one in the Securities Supervision space.

Finally, the family of Mr Wu had to endure threatening telephone calls and had their windows smashed by stones. None of the press reports of this commotion mentioned a police enquiry or any other signs of official concern. This harassment must have been caused by local people, while the local public security organization either ignored the case, or Mr Wu's family did not report the harassment because they did not expect any action anyway.

Summarizing, the detention of Mr Wu and the commotion around the event demonstrate the extreme power of Lukang in its identity as a local Party organization. The task of the CPC organization is to maintain the conditions in which that same organization can continue to retain power over all aspects of Chinese society. The Party organizations of individual units are the lowest level in the CPC hierarchy, but also the most essential ones in terms of context construction. The people belonging to a certain unit are almost completely dependent on their unit for their day-to-day existence. The Central Committee may be the most powerful CPC organ on the national level, but without the continuous self-sustaining efforts of the lowest level Party organizations, those of the individual units, the Central Committee would be a construction built on quicksand. The Party organization of a large unit like Lukang, or formulated in terms of identity, Lukang in its identity as Party organization, can therefore exercise powerful influence at the level of the Party organization above its own level, which is the Party organization of Ji'ning Municipality.

It is here that Lukang in its CPC identity and Lukang in its Ji'ning identity meet. To understand fully the mechanism in which these multiple identities are constructed and interact I will analyse the Lukang–Wu conflict more formally than the previous sections of this chapter, in a separate section. The following section will then simultaneously function as a formalization of the main theme of this chapter: the identity construction of Chinese enterprises and their mothers-in-law.

Enterprises and their mothers-in-law – an organizational perspective

Earlier I have attempted to present a detailed description of how mothers-in-law affect the operation of a large state-owned enterprise like Lukang by collecting and categorizing concrete occurrences of interaction between that company and two types of mother-in-law. In this final section of the chapter on mothers-in-law I want to attempt to formalize the identity construction process of Chinese enterprises vis-à-vis their various mothers-in-law and the interaction of how aspects of one identity can be put to use in matters related to another identity, using the model of Social Integration theory described in Chapter 2. I will use the Wu–Lukang conflict as an example.

A strikingly common aspect in the behaviour of mother-in-law type of organizations towards their daughters-in-law is that the content of their interaction is often largely restricted to the nature of the business of the mother-in-law. For the Pharmaceutical Industry, Lukang is a unit producing a number of pharmaceuticals, for the CPC it is a large unit, which means it controls the political attitude of a large number of people. We may presume that the same holds for mothers-in-law that have not been studied in this chapter. For example, for Public Security Lukang may be an important vehicle to control a large number of citizens and it will communicate with Lukang through the company's Security Department.

A consequence of the inclusion of a number of employees of an enterprise like Lukang in different spaces is that their loyalty to Lukang in its Lukang identity (I will revert to this identity later in this section) can be weaker than that to a mother-in-law space, while in other cases the reverse holds. The actual relation between the inclusions is determined by the relative strength of each inclusion, which in turn can vary from case to case. For example, when the security officers of Lukang are contacted by the Public Security Bureau of Ji'ning with the request to monitor the behaviour of one of Lukang's janitors, who is a suspect of a criminal case, the officers will probably readily comply with this request and will even consent to keeping that activity confidential within Lukang, pending the investigation. However, if a similar request involved one of the senior managers of Lukang, the same security officers would have to think twice before they went along with the request. When a janitor is involved, the officers' inclusion in the Public Security space supersedes that in the Lukang space. When the suspect is one of their senior managers, this fact will construct a stronger inclusion in the Lukang space, as the officers have to anticipate what will happen if the senior manager finds out, or even worse, when the senior manager finds out and his guilt cannot be established.

The first step in the formalization of the Wu–Lukang conflict is to describe the two main identities of Lukang that are involved in this conflict: Lukang as an enterprise in Ji'ning and Lukang as a CPC unit.

Lukang = Ji'ning

When we analyse how Lukang is defined in the corpus in relation to Ji'ning, one of the most conspicuous designations is that Lukang is one of the largest employers in Ji'ning. The fact that Lukang is a pharmaceutical enterprise is less relevant in the Ji'ning space. Chinese municipal governments are more interested in units as employers, i.e. providers of the material and spiritual foundation for living, than as manufacturers of products or providers of services. This is related to the fact that municipal governments are held directly responsible for public order and material and spiritual wellness are regarded as essential conditions to avoid social unrest.

As an employer, Lukang is a major one in its home region. This means that Lukang is also a major cornerstone in the maintenance of public order in Ji'ning. As long as Lukang is doing well, Ji'ning is doing well too. This may not necessarily mean that Ji'ning will cease to exist if Lukang went bankrupt, but Lukang's bankruptcy would pose a serious social (and financial) problem to Ji'ning Municipality.

Lukang = CPC

When looking at the section above analysing interactions between Lukang and Party (or Party-related) organizations as described in my corpus of texts on Lukang, it is clear that the intensity of the interactions increases as the administrative level of the interaction becomes lower. For the national Party organization, Lukang is of no importance.

On the provincial level, Lukang, being a major enterprise in Shandong province, is mainly a vehicle to propagate national and provincial policies and make them more applicable in the context of that particular unit.

It is on the municipal level that most interaction seems to take place. Lukang is one of the largest units, and hence one of the largest employers, in Ji'ning. It provides a basis for living for a large number of people. In that capacity, Lukang significantly contributes to the local social stability, which is the main concern of the municipal government. Party and Party-related organizations like the Youth League, Labour Union and Women's League will maintain close relations with each other within Lukang.

As a grass-roots Party organization, Lukang's Party group is responsible for the behaviour of Lukang's Party members as worthy CPC members. As CPC members, the Party members among Lukang's employees have to obey a different set of rules of conduct than non-members. The Disciplinary Commission is responsible for this supervision of Party members' conduct.

Lukang = Lukang

Every enterprise constructs a cognitive space of its own. This holds even stronger in China, where the enterprise is the unit of its employees. As the unit influences almost every aspect of its employees' life, belonging to the same unit creates a strong bond between Chinese. This is further reinforced by the fact that employees of larger units, which have the means to provide housing to their employees, tend to live together in the same residential area.

Lukang is a source of pride for its employees. Belonging to such a large unit like Lukang gives its employees a higher status than those of smaller ones. It is a job that comes with desirable perks, even for those lowest in the hierarchy. Lukang is a company with nationwide fame as one of China's top pharmaceutical enterprises. On the provincial level, Lukang is active in organizing go contests, especially for young people. This gives Lukang a more intellectual identity than other major Chinese companies, which tend to sponsor sports teams.

Lukang in its Lukang identity is strongly linked to the person of its CEO, Mr Zhang Jianhui. Mr Zhang's name appears frequently in the texts in the corpus, regardless of the subject matter of the text. He led the company from a state-owned and -operated 'factory' to a major Chinese corporation, listed at the Shanghai Stock Exchange. Mr Zhang's activities as reported in the corpus show that he is always personally in charge of major actions. For example, he led the Lukang team to Beijing to prepare for the second issue of shares, an activity that many Chinese CEOs would rather delegate to others.

After describing the major cognitive spaces, the second step in analysing organization processes like the Wu–Lukang conflict is identifying the major actors and their inclusions in those spaces and configurations.

Mr Zhang Jianhui

I have already mentioned Mr Zhang's strong inclusion in the Lukang space. This inclusion is so strong that he seems to have become part of Lukang's corporate identity (Lukang = Lukang). However, as the Party Secretary of such a large unit as Lukang, Mr Zhang's inclusion in the CPC space is also considerable.

Mr Wu

Mr Wu is included in the Lingzhi space. Lingzhi is a separate company within the Lukang Group and hence it constructs a space of its own. Mr Wu has been included in the Lukang space since Lingzhi became part of Lukang. His behaviour indicates that his inclusion in Lingzhi is stronger than that in Lukang. Some observers may perhaps propose that his opposition to Lukang's takeover of Lingzhi means that Mr Wu refuses to be included in the Lukang space. I believe such an observation is incorrect. Whether Mr Wu approved of it or not, after Lingzhi's entry into the Lukang Group, he started interacting with Lukang people within the Lukang space. From an organizing perspective he was therefore included in the Lukang space.

As an inhabitant of Ji'ning, Mr Wu is also included in the Ji'ning space.

Having described the major cognitive spaces, the contexts of the organizing processes and the inclusions of the main actors in those spaces, we can now attempt to re-interpret these processes in a more integrative way.

Mr Wu and Mr Zhang developed a conflict within the Lukang space. As CEO of Lingzhi, Mr Wu had to report his activities to the management of the Lukang Group. From the day that Lingzhi was added to Lukang, Lukang started to disassemble Lingzhi, apparently according to a premeditated plan. Here once more, some observers may presume that Mr Wu was not interacting with the Lukang management, as he opposed the measures that would lead to Lingzhi's de facto disappearance. However, I would like to differentiate between negative interacting and not interacting. Two or more actors who have no social relation whatsoever and do not couple their behaviour in any way are not interacting. However, actors who are deliberately not co-operating with other actors because they disagree are still interacting. In terms of Weick's theory of double interact, it is an instance of independence, but there is still interaction.

In my model of cognitive space each instance of social interaction takes place in a specific space. This means that, when we observe that Mr Wu and the management of Lukang, in particular Mr Zhang, are interacting, we have to link that interaction to an appropriate context shared by the actors involved. Lukang then seems to be the obvious choice. Other spaces are available. All actors involved are, for instance, also inhabitants of Ji'ning, but the nature of the interaction, the position of Lingzhi within the Lukang Group, seems to be more closely connected with 'Lukang' than with 'Ji'ning'.

Mr Wu apparently was unable to find a way to solve the conflict to his advantage within the Lukang space itself. He then started seeking useful cognitive matter in other inclusions. One of his other inclusions was in a configuration with his colleague, a securities specialist specifically hired to prepare Lingzhi's listing on the Shanghai Stock Exchange. This configuration was constructed within the Lingzhi space, which means that it also became part of the Lukang space after the management of Lingzhi was transferred to Lukang. However, exactly because it is a configuration, a cognitive space with a small group of actors who are frequently interacting on a very specific matter, the inclusion of Mr Wu in this configuration is stronger than that in Lukang. His colleague was well included in the securities space, a rather broad national space of actors dealing with the securities trade in China. Through this inclusion Mr Wu found his way to the National Securities Supervisory Commission.

After the initial success in delaying Lukang's second share issue, Mr Wu returned to his home town, Ji'ning. His associate did the same to his own home town, Wuhan. This seems to indicate that they were well aware of their personal danger. However, Mr Wu's home town happened to be the same as that of his fellow actors in the conflict with Lukang. Moreover, he also had to consider yet another inclusion: that in his family space. In China, close relatives of criminals, traitors, etc., are also regarded as such by society. Mr Wu would no doubt have felt safer in joining his colleague to hide in Wuhan, but he had the obligation to return home to protect his family as much as possible.

Because of Mr Wu's accusations in Beijing, his conflict within the Lukang space had intensified considerably. The conflict was even perceived as threatening the smooth continuation of Lukang as an enterprise. This affected the identity of Lukang as a major unit (= employer) in Ji'ning. Lukang's demise would threaten the livelihood of thousands of Ji'ning citizens, which would then become a problem for Ji'ning Municipality. More formally stated in terms of corporate identity, the conflict within Lukang = Lukang was transferred to Lukang = Ji'ning. Meanwhile, the decision by the National Securities Supervisory Commission to put Lukang's second share issue on hold was reported in the national press. This not only affected Lukang = Lukang, but also Lukang = Ji'ning, as it decreased Lukang as a source of pride for Ji'ning. The conflict had now escalated to such a degree that severe measures were in order.

Mr Zhang, as the CEO of Lukang, had to search through his inclusions to find a workable solution. He was also the Party Secretary of Lukang. Moreover, Mr Wu was a Party member as well. This means that Mr Wu and Mr Zhang also shared inclusions in the CPC space. As the Party Secretary of a major unit, Mr Zhang opted for a rarely used privilege: the double fixed measure. This measure was controversial even in Party circles, but apparently the situation was so grave that he preferred to take the risk of being criticized for using such a heavy measure over the risk of losing his position in Lukang. Through his CPC inclusion, which, as I demonstrated earlier in this chapter, was strongest on the Ji'ning level, Mr Zhang could easily invoke assistance from leaders of various municipal organizations, most of whom would be CPC members. It was in the CPC space that he configured with the Ji'ning Procurator to organize the arrest of Mr Wu, a Party member himself, and his detainment in a local hotel. From there on, he let Lukang Party officials interrogate Mr Wu. It was also in that space that the Ji'ning branch of the Securities Supervisory Commission decided to side with Lukang rather than protecting the main witness of the National Securities Supervisory Commission in their case against Lukang.

In plain English we would say that Mr Zhang 'had Ji'ning in his pocket'. However, with the Social Integration model we have a strong tool to explain how he had Ji'ning in his pocket in terms of social-cognitive contexts and the various inclusions of the actors involved, in particular Mr Zhang himself, in those contexts. We can describe how actors interact within a certain context, but simultaneously can access other contexts through their inclusions to search for cognitive matter that can be beneficial to that interaction. Moreover, with this model we can explain how interactions in one context can affect other contexts. Figure 3.1 provides a graphic explanation of the Lingzhi incident in terms of Lukang's various identities.

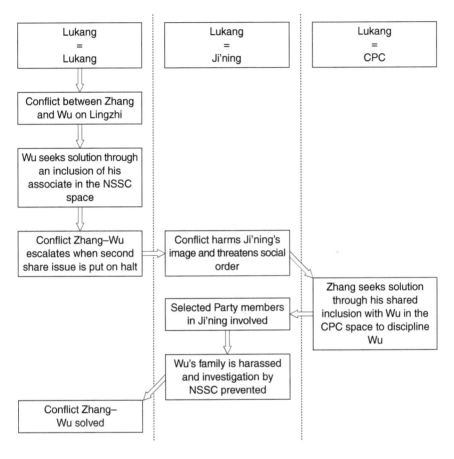

Figure 3.1 Graphic representation of the Lukang incident in various contexts.

4 Henan vs Zhengzhou
Conflict of identity between administrative levels

The construction of geographic spaces in China

One of the contexts in which Chinese actors construct (a version) of their self is their region of origin (Peverelli 2000: 69–77). The Chinese are very sentimental concerning their roots. Numerous poems, songs, novels, feature films, etc., have been produced with the home region/town of the author as their main theme. The Chinese used to be infrequent travellers. The Daoist ideal was that 'one could hear the neighbour's dog barking, but did not know what the neighbour looked like'. While this is an extreme rendering of Chinese geographic sentiments, it is indicative of the close relationship the Chinese have with their place of birth. Such a close, sentimental, relation with the home region provides an excellent environment for the preservation of the local dialect, cuisine, customs, etc.; or, in our terminology, for construction and continuous reconstruction of geographic cognitive spaces.

Another constructive force of geographic spaces is the market. In a rural economy like (traditional) China, the market or market town was the economic and social centre of a region. Such a market community often not only shared a market place, but also such scarce resources as a well (Zhang Yimou's famous feature film *The Old Well* is a splendid illustration of the social impact of a well in water-deficient North-West China). These material local interests supplemented the immaterial, sentimental, interests referred to in the previous paragraph. Such material interests still play a role in modern times. For example, Shanxi is a rather resource-deficient province; one of their few resources being coal. However, the national government regards coal as a potential hard currency generator and has heavily invested in railway connections between that region and a number of ports (China's first electric trains were not carrying passengers, but were transporting coal). Only a small amount of the hard currency thus earned flowed back to Shanxi. Many people from Shanxi can be heard complaining about this situation. Such complaints are even voiced by loyal Communist Party members, who readily let local sentiments ('we = Shanxi') prevail over political sentiments ('we = Communist Party').

Geographic spaces have had an enormous impact on the development of social stratification in the Marxist point of view. Marxists, including their Chinese proponents, tend to discern the class structure of a given society at a given point in history on a national level. They will typically describe the life of 'farmers during the early Qing period', referring to Chinese farmers in all regions of China. Such an approach can easily lead to reduction and therefore loss of information. Farmers toiling the soil of Shandong during that period would be in quite a different position from those living on the barren loess plains of North-West China. Investigation may show that the cognitive elements of the Shandong Farmer space were quite different from those of the Gansu Farmer space. However, an even more important flaw of a Marxist class-based description of Chinese society of any historical period is that it tends to neglect the alliances between local farmers and elites in defending the local interests against infringement from other regions. At times, tenants (the oppressed) and landlords (the oppressors) of the same region teamed up together against people from a neighbouring region, or the central authorities. Our theoretical framework can deal with these organizational activities in such a way that all differentiation remains intact. Sticking to our example, we could investigate cues that would justify discerning something like a Farmer space in early Qing China, but we would also distinguish a Shandong space, Gansu space, etc. Farmers of Shandong would be both Shandong and Farmers. In some activities, 'we = Shandong' would be more in the foreground than 'we = farmers' and in other activities, the opposite would be the case. However, Shandong farmers would always be regarded as multiply included in the Shandong space and the Farmer space. The realities constructed in each space would be different and could even be conflicting in some aspects.

Even now, when the Chinese travel much more inside China and around the world, most Chinese prefer to maintain close ties with their home region. Even after emigrating, Chinese from the same region tend to maintain close contacts and often settle in the same neighbourhoods and organize 'home town associations' (*tongxianghui*). The actual 'region' with which a Chinese person identifies at a certain moment can vary considerably. It can start with the neighbourhood, go up to the city district (in the major cities), the municipality, the region, the province, up to the national state: China. Each level is constructed with its own symbols, way of doing things, etc., and therefore each level can (and therefore will) constitute a cognitive space of its own. We will only present a few examples.

Neighbourhood

Here, we use the English word neighbourhood as a translation of the Chinese term *jiedao*, which literally means 'street'. The neighbourhood is geographically constructed by an official delimitation and a Neighbourhood Committee (*jiedao weiyuanhui*) consisting of volunteers, usually elderly people, who take care of the household registration, mediating if there are quarrels between neighbours or spouses, etc. This system has a historical background in the old *baojia* system. In imperial China, not only the cities were surrounded by a wall, but also parts of a city. The inhabitants of these areas were supposed to take care of each other's safety, hence the term *baojia*, literally: 'guarding armour'. Each day after sunset the city gates would be closed and simultaneously the gates of each *baojia* unit. This was seen as the best way to keep unwanted elements outside. This is an interesting illustration of how certain construction rules can persist through adapting to changes in the context. There is no wall around a neighbourhood, so bad elements can no longer be kept out by closing the gates at night. However, a small army of elderly people spending the better part of the day sitting outside at street corners chatting with each other are able to spot every person entering and leaving their neighbourhood. Each stranger is noted and if irregularities occur (such as burglary) they will be able to tell the police what suspicious individuals (= non-residents of their own neighbourhood) have entered the neighbourhood around the probable time of the crime, which home they visited, how long they stayed there, etc.

Municipal district

The urban areas of larger cities are divided into districts (*qu*). Urban Beijing, for example, is divided into: West City, East City, Chaoyang, Haidian, Chongwen, Xuanwu, Shijingshan and Mentougou Districts. The number of inhabitants of such a district can be quite high and are therefore governed through a professional District Government. Such a government will already have sector organs for the economic sectors as described earlier in this chapter. For example, the West District Government of Beijing Municipality has an Internal Trade Bureau, taking care of the distribution of commodities within the district. Several aspects of the daily life of the inhabitants are affected by the District. We already mentioned the distribution of commodities. Not so long ago, staple foods were distributed in China through a system of coupons. This distribution system was co-ordinated at the level of district in the larger cities. This distribution system now exists in a reconstructed way, similar to the reconstruction of the *baojia* system mentioned above. In one of the cases described later, we will show how the municipal district is constructed as a cognitive space affecting the activities of a European retailer in China.

Municipality

The municipality (*shi*) is defined as an urban centre with a certain economic strength. It is equivalent to the rural geographic space of county (*xian*). When a county has developed economically to a certain level, it can apply for and will receive municipality status. Besides an urban centre, municipalities usually also comprise a rural area, divided into counties. Some of these counties can also develop into municipalities, called 'local municipalities' (*dijishi*). Municipalities play an important role in the lives of their inhabitants. They are large enough to have a certain history, folklore, etc., and originating from City X already has a certain emotional content. Inhabitants of the larger cities have their own language, customs, peculiar habits, ways of doing things, etc. Citizen identity cards, passports, driving licences, and such, are provided by the municipal authorities. The municipality usually is a strong cognitive space. As already mentioned above, the urban area of cities used to be walled in imperial China. Although many of these walls have been demolished in recent decades, they have left their traces on the map and are often still shaping the geography of Chinese cities.

The walls of Beijing, for example, were demolished in the 1950s and 1960s. However, the ground of the former walls was used for the construction of a ring road and underneath this road, the underground brings people rapidly from one part of the town to another. As a result, the wall of Beijing still exists on the map of that city. Moreover, the names of gates have been retained (recognizable by the suffix -*men*, 'gate'), even after the gates have been demolished. Their former locations have been turned into major crossings and many underground stations have been named after the gate that used to top their location (e.g. Dongzhimen Station). In other words, not only the demolished wall, but also the gates still cognitively exist. Even one of the social roles of city gates as places where artisans used to gather waiting for work was retained. For example, many carpenters from outside Beijing sit down at the Dongzhimen 'Gate' with their toolboxes every morning. Beijingers in need of a new bookcase or other carpentry will go there to discuss prices with a few of the carpenters. If an agreement can be reached with one of them, the carpenter will go home with his new principal. The presence of the underground station no doubt plays an important role in bringing the carpenters and their customers together, stimulating the reconstruction of this social function.

Province

In a huge country like China, provinces are comparable in size to individual states in a continent like Europe. The same applies to the power of their governments. Provinces are important administrative units and their governments often seem to act as governments of sovereign states.

China is a vast country divided by a number of mountain ridges and rivers. In the course of history, these mountain ridges and rivers have become natural barriers surrounding plains with fertile soil. Most Chinese provinces are shaped with such a plain as its centre. The role of geography in the constructing of several provinces is reflected in their names: Shandong (East of the Mountains), Shanxi (West of the Mountains), Hebei (North of the (Yellow) River), Henan (South of the (Yellow) River), etc. This is an interesting example of how geographical structure can affect cognitive processes through the formation of a network of functionally linked cities, towns and villages. People living in such a plain will frequently interact with other people from the same plain, but contacts with people from other plains will be much more difficult due to the mountain ridges, especially in times when such ridges could only be crossed on foot or horseback. Skinner (1977) has defined nine such macro-economic regions for late imperial China and contends that these regions still matter in modern Chinese economy. Indeed, Chinese economists regularly talk in terms of the Northeast, Northwest, Southwest, etc.

One of the provincial symbols that frequently reconstructs the notion of province is its short name. Every province has a single character name often used for convenience in official documents. This character appears on the licence plates of motor vehicles registered in that province, which is possibly the most frequently viewed occurrence of that name. The short name is also frequently used in names of enterprises to denote their geographic origin and to show to the outside world that the founder(s) is proud of that origin. For example, the short name of Shandong province is Lu. Lu is the name of the ancient state of Lu, the birthplace of Confucius. The latter gives the name of Lu a strong emotional load. It expresses that this is not just any province, but the birthplace of a philosopher who is perceived as one of the major thinkers of the entire East Asian region. The character Lu appears on licence plates of Shandong-registered cars. It is also part of the name of China's largest fruit juice manufacturer: Zhonglu (literally: 'China Shandong') Group and one of the country's largest producers of antibiotics: Lukang (literally: 'Shandong Health') Group, which featured in the previous chapter. A large chemical company in the south of Shandong is called Lunan ('South Shandong') Chemical Corporation. The largest hotel in Shandong's capital Ji'nan is called Qilu (Qi was another ancient state in the present Shandong region) Hotel.

Dialect does play a role in the construction of geographic spaces, but dialect isoglosses do not always coincide with provincial borders. Fujian province, for example, is divided into two, mutually unintelligible, dialect areas. People in its capital, Fuzhou, and those of the major port city of Xiamen have to communicate in Mandarin. Interesting in this respect is that the dialect of most Chinese in Indonesia (as well as some other South-East Asian countries) is that of Xiamen, because their ancestors emigrated from that region. Although it is based on the dialect of Xiamen, this version of Chinese produces a language-based space often referred to as Hokjan, which is the Xiamen pronunciation of Fujian. This space covers large numbers of ethnic Chinese in Indonesia, Malaysia, Singapore, the Philippines, China's Hainan, Guangdong and Fujian provinces and

Taiwan. This metaphorization of Xiamen for the entire province is no doubt due to the economic importance of Xiamen as a large international port city. This aspect was further emphasized when the central government decided to make the entire municipality of Xiamen one of the Special Economic Zones.

Provinces were made into the main administrative regions of China after the establishment of the People's Republic, but their political and economic powers were strictly controlled by the central government in Beijing. With the start of the economic reforms in the early 1980s, more and more decision-making power was moved from the central to the provincial governments (Hendrischke and Feng 1999: 4ff.). As a result, provinces, in particular the ones in the coastal region, became a major source of revenue for the central government.

The increased policy-making powers become an important constructor of provincial space. Provinces no longer regarded other provinces as sister-provinces and the richer regions no longer felt obliged to share their wealth with the poorer inland provinces. Differences between provinces became powerful constructors of provincial identity. One area in which this shift in provincial identity became more and more evident was the interprovincial political and economic rivalry. Economic reporting in the media is very often oriented around the provinces. If we take China's major bulletin for the food industry, the China Food Newspaper (*Zhong-guo Shipin Bao*), as an example, the main story on its front page usually deals with provincial matters. We can, for example find an article introducing the fruit juice industry of Shandong. Such an article may describe the problems in that industry and urge the companies to improve their performance 'in order to keep up with the other fruit juice producing regions'. This discourse of interprovincial competition is also used by the fruit juice manufacturers themselves. The two main apple producing regions of China are Shaanxi and Shandong. Because Shaanxi is the poorer of the two, labour cost is lower there. Moreover, most apple juice producers in Shaanxi are so-called Town and Village Enterprises owned by the lowest level authorities, or private enterprises. Those in Shandong are mainly state-owned enterprises or ventures with foreign investment. The cost of labour is therefore considerably higher in Shandong. This situation, combined with a surplus of apple juice on the world market, has caused a price war between the apple juice manufacturers of both regions in 1998, in which the Shaanxi companies can undercut the prices of those in Shandong. Judging by the accusations from the Shandong companies towards those in Shaanxi, the use of the war metaphor is not an exaggeration.

The more intense interprovincial rivalry has also increased the opacity of provincial politics, as provinces are not willing to share their strategies for creating provincial wealth with their competitors. Provincial politics have always been less transparent than those on the central level. The (inter)national media tend to concentrate their attention on what is happening in Beijing, which is already considered rather opaque. Provincial politicians do not have to worry that much about those media and the media on their own level are to a large extent controlled by the various local authorities (see Lukang's relation with the press as introduced in the previous chapter).

One area of provincial politics in which obscurity is especially evident is the attraction of investment, both domestic and from abroad (Hendrischke and Feng 1999: 8). Although the central government still has a say in the allotment of foreign investment and aid programmes, each province tries its utmost to lure a fair share of foreign investment to itself through their permanent representative offices in Beijing. All provinces, as well as a number of large cities, have such offices in the national capital. The representatives spend their working days lobbying for their home region's interests. Provincial governments are wary of sharing their strategies in these matters with outsiders. The rules and regulations officially promulgated by the governments are usually written in very general language, while details are hidden in 'internal documents' that are kept strictly confidential. In this way, crucial details can be filled in, or adapted, for particular opportunities, whenever such opportunities occur.

A similar situation can be observed where investments by large national corporations are concerned. A process of conglomeration through mergers and acquisitions is going on in many Chinese industrial sectors. Successful companies are vying to obtain a foothold in key economic regions by establishing greenfield subsidiaries, but more often by acquiring a local company that is in dire straits. Such companies are often state-owned or collective enterprises, which means that the potential buyers have to negotiate with the respective governments, provincial or lower.

The case around which this chapter on administrative layers as sources of corporate identity is written involves both foreign and domestic investment and the corpus of narratives for this case study includes ample information regarding the machinations by various local parties in dealing with those investors.

Provincial capitals – a forgotten topic

In the previous section I introduced a number of the most important administrative levels in China. Two of those levels were the municipality and the province. However, there is a special type of municipality that is closely tied to its home province: the provincial capital. I have so far found no existing literature about this particular topic. This should probably not surprise us, as the fact that this strikes me as a problem is a consequence of my theoretical model.

The physical environment of the provincial government organizations (the buildings) needs a geographic space. The provincial capital is the logical candidate for such a space. The construction of provincial capitals shows similarities with that of the provinces. They are often located at advantageous locations such as places where a major river can be easily crossed, multimodal transportation nodes, plains of fertile soil, etc. Some of them have developed from important central markets in a macro-economic region as discussed earlier.

A provincial capital will share all typical traits of a municipality, but the presence of the provincial government organizations creates a strong inclusion in the provincial space as well. If we state that Nanjing is the capital of Jiangsu province, we are simultaneously saying that Nanjing is the seat of the provincial government, or in my notational convention: Nanjing = Jiangsu. However, apart from the provincial government, a provincial capital is also the seat of the (physical environment) of the municipal government: Nanjing = Nanjing.

This has consequences in a broad range of areas. In the economic realm, we can expect to see enterprises in the same line of business located in the same city, but operated at the provincial and the municipal level. This difference in inclusion will affect the competition between those enterprises and we will never be able to understand that competitive relation properly without a keen insight into the rivalry between their respective provincial and municipal parent organizations.

The central theme of the case study of this chapter includes two dairy companies located in Zhengzhou, the capital of Henan province, one belonging to a provincial organization, the other operated at the municipal level. A foreign party has been involved with the provincial company. This chapter intends to clarify two key issues:

1   the way the difference in affiliation complicates the competition between the two companies;
2   the fact that the foreign party has been active in Zhengzhou without being aware of this difference has negatively affected the economic success of their venture.

The case

The case study that constitutes the core of this chapter concerns the competitive relation between two dairy companies that dominate the Zhengzhou market. However, my personal involvement with this subject matter started as an assessment of a dairy project financed by the Dutch government. The Chinese side of this project was the mother organization of one of the dairy companies. It was in the course of my research that I noticed that the main problem so far impeding a proper understanding of the local situation by the Dutch side was their failure to appreciate the role of the other dairy company and its relation to their partner.

I believe that this case reveals a typical problem that afflicts a large number of Sino-foreign co-operations. I have therefore opted to organize this chapter in a similar way to the one I used when I conducted the assessment of this case. After a brief description of the situation up to the moment I started to be involved, I will follow my footsteps as a consultant once more, describing what I did, why I did it and what I concluded using the model of corporate identity as my guide.

Henan

Henan could be defined as the most centrally located province of China. It is situated in the centre of the North China Plain and is therefore often referred to as Zhongyuan, the Central Plain. Its name literally means 'South of the (Yellow) River', as opposed to its northern neighbour Hebei, or 'North of the (Yellow) River'. This is another example of how important the geological conditions are in Chinese geographic sense-making.

Henan's economy is distinctly agriculture based. The province is the largest cereal producing region of China, in particular wheat. China's largest manufacturer of instant noodles, Hualong, is located in Henan. It is also an important producer of meat. Again, the country's largest meat conglomerates, Chundu and Shuanghui (now trying to profile itself as: Shyneway), are based in Henan. A third agricultural sector of importance in Henan is fruit, in particular apples. Henan's Northwest is part of one of China's main apple belts, which also includes a large part of neighbouring Shaanxi.

Most of this agricultural industry is concentrated in the northern part of the province, a broad belt along the Yellow River. The Henan government, supported by the central authorities, have launched a project to improve the embankments of the Yellow River, thus forming a so-called green belt. This green belt will by used to develop modern agriculture, in particular dairy cattle raising and fruit growing.

Henan is not a traditional dairy region of China, but provincial government have been supporting the dairy industry as a key development sector in the local economy. Local authorities list a number of reasons for this support. Apart from the growing demand, the importance of dairy products to improve the Chinese diet, etc., a more region-specific motivation is the abundance of raw materials for feed: agricultural waste (wheat stalks, etc.). This waste used to be burned, causing tremendous pollution. Since the government has forbidden the burning of leaves, straw, stalks and other plant materials for environmental reasons, other ways to deal with these materials had to be sought. Feeding it to animals came out as a solution that simultaneously created value. We can metaphorize this as: dairy cattle raising = improving the environment.

Table 4.1 indicates the historic development of raw milk output of Henan. Although the local milk output has increased almost 2.5 times

Table 4.1 Historic development of Henan milk output

Year	Total milk (t)	Cow's milk (t)
1998	123000	78000
1999	159000	103000
2000	202000	161000
2001	300000	270000
2003	n.a.	310000

Sources: Various.

during that period, Henan's share in the national production is still less than 3 per cent. Compared with Heilongjiang's 18 per cent, Henan is relatively insignificant.

In the eyes of other Chinese, Henan people have the name of being habitual liars. It is hard to find a reason for this reputation. Henan has always been one of the poorer regions of China. Even today, its economic development is largely based on agriculture, which is regarded as less prestigious than, for example ICT, space technology or biotechnology, by many younger Chinese people. Chinese city people tend to look down on farmers and Henanese have a farming image. One of the big entrepreneurial debacles in the Chinese economy of the 1990s was the Yaxiya (Asia) Group, a retail conglomerate that started out as an agricultural enterprise. After quick financial success in its home town, Zhengzhou, Yaxiya started to establish subsidiaries in other major cities, including Beijing and Guangzhou. Soon, one after another had to file for bankruptcy or had to be sold. The one in Guangzhou was hardly able to start business. The story of Yaxiya was widely told, in official and less official circles. In the latter, the Yaxiya fiasco was posed as a corroboration that the Henanese were just a bunch of liars and cheats. However, if one studies the narratives around Yaxiya more carefully, it seems that the reputation of Henan people was used to make it virtually impossible for Yaxiya to conduct its business properly. Some of Yaxiya's subsidiaries found it extremely difficult to find suppliers in their local markets. However, I will not go into this story further. What has been told so far is sufficient to see how a provincial reputation can be enacted, at times leading to a self-fulfilling prophecy. It does affect foreigners as well. Whenever I tell people in Beijing that I am going to Henan, I am warned to be wary of doing business with the Henanese.

Zhengzhou

Zhengzhou is the capital city of Henan Province located in the central part of China, facing the Yellow River in the North, the Songshan mountain ridges in the West and with a connection to the Huanghuai plains in the

Southeast. The total surface reaches 7446 km². Zhengzhou Municipality consists of six counties (*xian*, see above) and the Zhengzhou urban region (comprising six districts; *qu*, see above). The total population amounts to about 6.5 million people (figure 1999) of which 2.4 million people live in the wider urban area of Zhengzhou. In the newly emerging residential areas within a radius of 20 km from central Zhengzhou city an additional 600 000 people are living. The population growth is about 2 per cent, allowing for migration.

Zhengzhou is located at a multimodal transportation node, including water (the Yellow River) and a number of railways. The Yellow River itself is too shallow for heavy transportation like the Yangtze, but its symbolic value cannot be overstated (the symbolic value of the Yellow River will be treated in more detail later in this chapter). Zhengzhou is a major city along the Eurasian Continental Bridge, a (still largely virtual) rail link between the Chinese port city of Lianyungang and Rotterdam in the Netherlands. This project has received more attention in China than in Europe, but it seems to work for the Chinese side. This railroad has already become the import/export channel for Kazakhstan, making this new Central Asian republic less dependent on its previous mother state Russia.

The old Beijing–Guangzhou railroad runs along Zhengzhou. A new railroad, the Beijing–Kowloon railway, was opened in 1996, providing a direct connection between Beijing and Kowloon in Hong Kong. This newer railroad actually crosses the Eurasian Continental Bridge at Shangqiu, rather than Zhengzhou, but Zhengzhou is close enough to participate in the economic advantages.

Finally, Zhengzhou is situated at the crossing of a major north–south express way, linking Beijing with the Shenzhen Special Economic Zone on the border with Hong Kong and an east–west express way. The national capital can be reached by car from Zhengzhou in about eight hours.

In 1998, the per capita income in urban areas reached about RMB 5700, while in rural areas it was only RMB 2500; the average for Henan Province amounted to RMB 4220 per year. In 1998, the net growth of per capita income in urban areas was 2 per cent. The per capita expenses on food items in urban Zhengzhou in 1998 amounted to RMB 1925, out of which about RMB 55 would relate to dairy products (IDC 2002: 13).

The assignment

The original research assignment was to assess the entire SIDDAIR project from an organizational perspective and make an inventory of possible ways to let the project create value for the Dutch industry after the handover of the project to the Chinese side.

My research strategy was to focus on the sense-making of the project by various parties involved. I started discussing the project with a number of people in the Netherlands, prior to my visit to Zhengzhou in March 2004. In preparation for that visit I also began building a corpus of texts on the project and the dairy industry in Zhengzhou and Henan.

A visit to Zhengzhou took place on 19–21 March 2004, during which I was able to discuss in various degrees of formality a large number of actors.

Another aspect of the assignment was to make an inventory of viable ways to build further on the infrastructure created by the SIDDAIR project. A number of parties had already indicated that the Chinese side was interested in producing cheese. The Dutch side had made a market research and business plan for a cheese plant in 2002. The intended location of that project would be Huahuaniu (Colourful Cow), a milk processing daughter of Yawei, the Chinese partner.

Already during my initial reading of the texts that gradually formed the corpus, before my discussions on the spot in Zhengzhou, I noticed that another dairy processor in Zhengzhou, Shanmeng, kept being mentioned as a serious market player, while it was never part of the narratives of the Dutch actors whom I talked to before the visit to Zhengzhou. Shanmeng was named in the above-mentioned business plan for a cheese plant, but only as a major competitor of Huahuaniu. I learned that none of the Dutch actors actively involved in the project had an opinion of what Shanmeng was other than 'another local dairy company'. None of them had ever thought of paying Shanmeng a visit. In my methodology, this discrepancy between the Chinese and Dutch narratives is a cue pointing at a major difference in the sense-making of both partners. I therefore made the difference between Huahuaniu and Shanmeng a major issue in my final report, focusing on the differences between Henan province and Zhengzhou municipality as social-cognitive contexts.

This case is extremely complex and my report described it from a number of other contexts as well. As I am using this case here to illustrate how a Chinese enterprise located in a provincial capital and operated by a provincial organization has to cope with its provincial and municipal identities, I will focus on the identity of Huahuaniu, Yawei's dairy company.

In the course of this case study, I will try to illuminate the following issues:

1 How does Huahuaniu make sense in the two different contexts?
2 Who are Huahuaniu's competitors in the two different contexts?
3 Who are Huahuaniu's allies in the two different contexts?
4 How does SIDDAIR make sense in the two different contexts and how could the Dutch party have used this insight to achieve the goals of the SIDDAIR project?

The major players

Henan and Zhengzhou as cognitive spaces have already been introduced in the previous section of this chapter. In this section, I will introduce three major players: SIDDAIR, Huahuaniu (Yawei) and Shanmeng. In the theoretical framework of this study these also constitute separate cognitive spaces. However, they belong to a special section on the imaginary scale on which cognitive spaces can be categorized, i.e. those cognitive spaces usually referred to as 'organizations' in everyday speech. Such spaces are often perceived as behaving in a similar fashion as human actors. The coining of the term 'legal person' has been based on this perception. This is also the reason that we have no problem with talking about a company like Huahuaniu as being a market player, as if it were an active subject. We would be much more reluctant to apply the same term to Henan or Zhengzhou.

However, there are occasions when we actually do. When describing a controversy between the government of Henan and the central authorities in Beijing, we may use a phrase like 'Henan is not content with Beijing's tax policy'. Henan then refers to the provincial government, which is perceived as 'acting' on behalf of the entire province, bestowing it a role of active subject.

To provide maximum insight in the way the actors directly involved with that player perceive their own organization, the account of each player is divided into an account of the self-perception, followed by my analysis of the identities. The sources of SIDDAIR's self-perception are:

- the self-introduction on SIDDAIR on its web site (SIDDAIR 2004);
- the introduction at SIDDAIR's facilities in March 2004.

The main source material for Yawei's story is a lengthy interview I had with representatives of Yawei. Because Shanmeng was identified as a major player in a later stage of the research, no visit to this company was scheduled during my visit of March 2004. Shanmeng also lacks a web site, at least at the time of writing this text. Introductory articles on Shanmeng can be found in a number of places. As it is common practice in China that companies provide their self-introductions to editors of newspapers, magazines, news sites, etc., which will publish them without post editing, we may presume that such introductory texts reflect the self perception of Shanmeng.

SIDDAIR – self-perception

In October 1997, the Minister of Agriculture, Nature Management and Fisheries of the Netherlands visited China on the invitation of the Chinese Minister of Agriculture. During his visit to Henan Province, the

Dutch minister signed a Letter of Intent with Mr Ma Zhongchen, Governor of Henan Province and the Chinese Vice-Minister of Agriculture, expressing the intention to set up an agricultural development and demonstration project in Henan, within the framework of developing and promoting bilateral trade and co-operation between Henan Province and the Netherlands. In this agreement, the preference from the Dutch side for a dairy project was stipulated. The project was approved during a final appraisal mission which took place in June 1998. In March 1999, Zhengzhou Yawei Industry General Corporation and International Dairy Consultants BV (IDC), the Netherlands, were assigned by the Chinese and Dutch sides respectively to implement the 'Sino-Dutch Dairy Training and Demonstration Project' (SIDDAIR). Through joint efforts a final Letter of Agreement was signed on 12 April 1999, officially launching the project.

SIDDAIR – mission statement

The joint management of SIDDAIR perceived as its prime task the establishment of a Centre for Innovations in Dairy Production that will introduce, demonstrate and disseminate sound farm management practices, sustainable production methods and Dutch applied technology and knowledge to the Chinese dairy farming community, in order to develop dairy farming systems which would be able to compete effectively in a market-oriented environment.

SIDDAIR – project concept

SIDDAIR aimed to contribute to sustainable development of the dairy sector in Henan and the rest of China, playing a vital role in promoting dairy farming as a profitable economic activity by demonstrating the opportunities for improving financial returns through raising productivity, improving production efficiency and producing consistently high quality milk.

SIDDAIR intended to bridge the differences between Chinese and Dutch management approaches in the field of dairy production. SIDDAIR would demonstrate various managerial and technical options, ranging from low input to the more advanced production systems. Visitors should be able to recognize the opportunities as offered by the various systems and translate them in terms of how to incorporate the exhibited technology and management methods and approaches into their own farm enterprise.

The applied concept entailed a demonstration of a logical sequence of farm development under Chinese circumstances. Introducing and demonstrating Dutch applied technology and knowledge in the field of dairy production, well adapted to Chinese circumstances, three different models of technically sound, environmentally non-degrading and economically viable dairy farming systems were exhibited.

One system would demonstrate Dutch innovative technology and state-of-the-art management methods and techniques, including a free-stall housing system, milking parlour, milk cooling tank, and fodder crop production and management. The other two systems were based on existing traditional Chinese dairy farms run by private households. The latter was inspired by the intent to demonstrate that the performance of existing dairy farms could be easily upgraded with technology introduced by SIDDAIR.

To demonstrate the next step in the logical sequence of farm development, a tie-stall for 20 milk cows plus followers was developed with mechanized milking and milk cooling, and on-farm fodder crop production.

The project intended to facilitate the process of gradually changing farmers' attitudes towards modern management practices by showing them in practice. With the aim of introducing appropriate farm management approaches to allow efficient and profitable farm operations in a competitive environment, emphasis was laid on (re)productive performance, production efficiency and product quality. The technical package (extension message) aimed at providing dairy farmers with practical advice that should contribute to a more efficient use of available resources (i.e. improved input to output ratios). Geared towards optimal performance and efficiency, the farm activities would be centred around fodder crop production (grassland or alternative fodder crops), accurate feeding strategies, reproduction management, calf rearing, and milk harvesting and handling.

Although open for demonstration purposes, the various dairy farm units were considered as separate farm enterprises, i.e. profit centres which would be able to recover their own recurrent costs and generate sufficient capital to assure the continuity of the farm operations.

SIDDAIR – project facilities

SIDDAIR is located in the river bank area of the Yellow River, near Babao village, Huayuan towns, at about 21 km north-north-east of Zhengzhou. The total project area covers about 113 hectares, including 88.3 hectares of arable land. The land has been allocated to the project on the basis of a long-term lease (50 years). The soil type varies between sandy loam and loamy sand of good quality. In order to control soil hydrology effectively, a comprehensive drainage and irrigation system has been developed.

The project buildings comprise:

1   three dairy farm units, with a capacity of 90, 20 and ten milk cows plus followers, respectively, including storage facilities for fodder;

2   a shed for the machine park, including a work shop for maintenance and repair;
3   office buildings, including meeting and conference rooms; a permanent information and exhibition centre.

SIDDAIR – project activities

Training of Chinese staff and farm employees

The permanent labour force of the project is trained on-the-job by the resident Dutch farm manager in order to carry out their duties according to the required professional standards. Key staff may have the opportunity to participate in tailor-made training courses in the Netherlands.

Farming systems research and development

To support the development of appropriate technology and production methods, farming systems research and development was conducted. The main objective was to optimize and fine-tune Chinese dairy farming systems and related extension packages on the basis of the outcome of applied and adaptive on-farm and on-station research. Applied research referred to the creation and development of new technologies. Adaptive research assisted to adjust the introduced technology, production and management methods to the requirements of the local environment.

Farm demonstration, field days, subject matter workshops

In order to assure maximum impact on the development of dairy farming in Henan Province, it was envisaged to organize on a regular basis one-day subject matter courses, demonstration and field visits for dairy farmers, professionals, technicians and officials working in the field of dairy production or related services. In addition, open days for the public would be organized once or twice a year.

Dairy farm management courses

On a regular basis, comprehensive dairy farm management courses would be organized for Chinese dairy farmers, consultants, researchers, extension officers and other relevant technicians/officials. These courses would comprise the following subjects:

- dairy farm management;
- farm economics and business administration;
- grassland and fodder crop production;
- animal nutrition;

- animal reproduction and health;
- milk harvesting and handling.

The course manuals would be presented and published in the Chinese language.

The project was completely transferred to the Chinese party on 24 March 2004.

SIDDAIR – other narratives

The above text is a collation of the information on SIDDAIR's web site and the stories told during my visit to SIDDAIR. The following paragraphs contain stories about SIDDAIR from various other parties.

Dutch professionals

The 'official' story conspicuously does not explain the reason for selecting Henan–Zhengzhou as the location of the Dutch project. Another narrative, private communication of one of the Dutch actors involved, points out that this location was more or less dictated by the Chinese side as the only location it was willing to consider for the project. It was either Zhengzhou, or China was not interested in the project. Within the context of this story it is believed that the Henan government has been lobbying for the project in Beijing.

Henan Agricultural University (HAU)

There is a plaquette stuck near the main entrance of SIDDAIR naming SIDDAIR as one of HAU's official training sites. HAU students sometimes stay there for a short period to receive practical experience. Other organizations sharing that designation mentioned in this case study are: the Henan Provincial Dairy Cattle Reproduction and Breeding Centre and Huahuaniu.

HAU has a co-operative relation with the Dutch Wageningen Agricultural University. A joint dairy farming research project of these two universities has been running parallel to SIDDAIR. Although the participants in both projects do regularly interact, they are separate cognitive spaces, making sense of SIDDAIR in different ways. To avoid unnecessary complication of this case study, I have left the HAU–Wageningen project out of this chapter.

Yellow River Project

The various texts in the corpus of recent publications show large differences in their treatment of SIDDAIR. A three-page article on 'the Henan dairy industry of 2003' does not mention it at all. Another recent article on the development of the Yellow River banks does. This seems to indicate that SIDDAIR makes sense in the context of the Yellow River Project, rather than the Henan context. This Yellow River Project identity of SIDDAIR is further strengthened by the wall-sized map of the project on the wall of SIDDAIR's exhibition room and the scanned article on the project on SIDDAIR's web site. Moreover, Mr Sijtsma received the Yellow River Friendship Award in September 2003. This is an award for experts who have made outstanding contributions to Henan province, but the symbolic power of the name of this award is enormous.

SIDDAIR = SIDDAIR

An organization like SIDDAIR is not only part of a number of cognitive spaces, it is one itself as well. The actors that made up the social element of the SIDDAIR space, the employees, could be divided into two groups according to their attachment to the enterprise. A small number of local managers, usually Yawei employees, lived in Zhengzhou and worked at SIDDAIR during work days. The Dutch manager, with his Chinese wife, and the local staff hired by SIDDAIR lived on the premises. The Dutch manager's account of his work at SIDDAIR made it clear that SIDDAIR had become a major part of his life and during my visit to Zhengzhou, he regretted that the project would soon be handed over to the Chinese side. The Chinese side had agreed to keep him as a manager for the time being following the handover.

SIDDAIR – identities

In the framework adopted in this study, the number of possible identity constructs of an organization is infinite. However, usually only a limited number play a significant role in a certain case study. This section makes an inventory of the most important social-cognitive contexts and the way SIDDAIR makes sense in each context. I will not do much more than presenting the inventory and revert to the consequences later in this chapter.

Original configuration
Social: Dutch Ministry of Agriculture (minister), Chinese Ministry of Agriculture (vice-minister), Henan Province (governor)
Cognitive: SIDDAIR = Dutch agricultural development and demonstration project

Enlarged original configuration
Social: as previous one + Yawei and IDC

Cognitive: SIDDAIR = Dutch dairy agricultural development and demonstration project

HAU
Social: SIDDAIR, HAU, Henan Provincial Dairy Cattle Reproduction, Breeding Centre and Huahuaniu
Cognitive: practical training facility for HAU students

Yellow River Project
Social: Henan Province, SIDDAIR . . .
Cognitive: SIDDAIR = part of the project to create a Yellow River Basin Green Belt

Huahuaniu
Social: SIDDAIR, Huahuaniu
Cognitive: SIDDAIR = milk supplier to Huahuaniu

Yawei
Social: Yawei, SIDDAIR
Cognitive: SIDDAIR is part of the Yawei group with the functions of breeding dairy cattle, providing milk to Huahuaniu

SIDDAIR
Social: Dutch manager, specially hired staff of SIDDAIR
Cognitive: SIDDAIR = foundation of existence

Yawei–Huahuaniu – history

It is not easy to find a written self-introduction produced by Huahuaniu. The guided tour through the plant I made only included a superficial introduction by a tour guide, who was unable to answer the simplest technical or commercial question. A number of web sites provide general introductions that are so similar in phrasing that they seem to be provided by Huahuaniu (HAU 2004; ZZNET 2004; HNXMY 2004). I will use these narratives as self-introductions.

The Henan Zhengzhou Cattle Farm was established in 1956. The highest administrative level mentioned in this name, Henan, reveals that it was operated at the provincial level. It was reorganized into the Zhengzhou Yawei Industrial Co. in 1993, which brought its first batch of Huahuaniu ice cream on the market in June 1994. This was exactly the time that international brands like Wall's (Unilever) and Nestlé started entering the local market. Although Huahuaniu ice cream was well received, it had a hard time conquering market share. To strengthen Huahuaniu's position, Yawei combined its dairy products and ice cream production in 1997. Furthermore, Huahuaniu Dairy Co. was established as an independently operating daughter company of Yawei in 1999. Yawei owned 60 per cent of the equity, while the remaining 40 per cent was in the hands of the employees.

Around the turn of the century, competition in the Zhengzhou dairy market was enormous. Along with a number of local companies, all major national players were active in the region. It was felt that Huahuaniu could only continue its existence as a local dairy manufacturer by linking up with a major national company. After an agreement with the active newcomer New Hope, from Sichuan, was called off at the very last minute, Yawei reached an agreement with the Sanlu Group of Hebei to reform Huahuaniu into the Sanlu Huahuaniu Dairy Co., Ltd in October 2003; 50 per cent of the equity was owned by Yawei and the other 50 per cent by Sanlu.

Yawei as context of Huahuaniu

Huahuaniu is frequently introduced as part of the Yawei organization. Before looking into the identity construction of Huahuaniu, we need to understand the identities of the parent company Yawei as well. For Yawei too, it is almost impossible to obtain a written self-introduction. It seems to be an aspect of the cognitive element (corporate culture) of Yawei as a cognitive space to put little value on standardized written materials introducing the company. However, a three-hour interview with the CEO of Yawei, Mr Ouyang, and one of his aides, Mr Wang, on 16 March 2004, provided a comprehensive picture of how the Yawei leadership perceives the company. As my role as interviewer played a significant role in the course of the discussion, I will not attempt to filter out the various remarks by the Yawei leaders and rearrange them into a neat story, but instead reproduce the course of the discussion, to preserve the flow of sense-making.

Mr Ouyang opened the discussion by stating that Yawei was an independent corporation, detached from the Henan Bureau of Animal Husbandry. Yawei is often identified with the Henan Bureau of Animal Husbandry. One text on Yawei's web site puts the designation 'Henan Province Zhengzhou Breeding Farm' (the original name of Yawei) in brackets behind Yawei's name, stating that it directly resides under the provincial Bureau of Animal Husbandry. In the Chinese hierarchy, the use of 'province' behind Henan and not using 'municipality' behind Zhengzhou is a way of indicating that Yawei is an enterprise physically located in Zhengzhou, but owned and operated at the provincial level. The provincial government is obviously also located in Zhengzhou, but it makes a significant difference, for example in the political clout of the management of Yawei.

Mr Ouyang's remark during the discussions on the afternoon of 16 March that political and commercial activities were now strictly separated in China confirms that both are highly intertwined. Such a very emphatic statement usually points to the opposite, in this case: that the link between the administrative and commercial contexts is still close.

The brochure of the Henan Provincial Dairy Cattle Reproduction and Breeding Centre states that it is 'subordinate' to the Henan Bureau of Animal Husbandry. Mr Ouyang introduced it as one of the subsidiaries of Yawei. This once more stresses the strong link between the Bureau (administrative organization) and Yawei (commercial enterprise).

Yawei is an abbreviation of Yazhou Weixing, 'Asian Satellite'. The name was originally the brand name of another of Yawei's subsidiaries, a plant for veterinary medicines. The discovery of this company's first patent medicine coincided with the launching of Asia's first satellite. Yawei Nr 1 was therefore chosen as that product's brand name. When the Breeding Farm was transformed into a corporation, the brand name Yawei was selected as the company name, because of its accumulated fame. It is very common in present-day China to make a noted brand name into the corporate name of its manufacturer. Mr Ouyang mentioned that they are even considering renaming Yawei as the Huahuaniu Group (this plan was actually carried out a few months after the research took place). Huahuaniu itself started out as a brand name, which was later used to name the Huahuaniu Dairy Co.

Mr Ouyang further introduced the eight subsidiaries of Yawei, which I have listed in Table 4.2 for easy reference. The provincial identity of Yawei is attested by the fact that a majority of these subsidiaries have 'Henan' in their official name. This table contains two pairs of very similar organizations:

- 3 and 7: embryo transplanting;
- 4 and 5: cattle breeding/raw milk production.

Table 4.2 Subsidiaries of Yawei

	Subsidiary	Core business
1	Sanlu Huahuaniu Dairy Co., Ltd	Milk processing
2	Henan Yawei Veterinary Medicine Co., Ltd	Veterinary medicines
3	Henan Chuangye IND Bioengineering Co. – Sino-Canadian co-operation	Embryo transplantation
4	SIDDAIR	Cattle breeding + raw milk production
5	Henan Provincial Dairy Cattle Reproduction and Breeding Centre	Cattle breeding + raw milk production
6	Henan Imported Cattle Quarantine Farm	Quarantine of imported cattle
7	Henan Dairy Cattle Embryo Transplantation Centre	Embryo transplantation
8	Asset Management Co.	Management of Yawei's assets

The common trait of these pairs is that one involves foreign invest-ment, while the other is wholly Chinese (though not necessarily 100 per cent Yawei). When we look at the time of establishment of the organi-zations, we can observe that the 100 per cent Chinese one is established in the same year as the foreign partnership or later. It seems as if Yawei has created parallel organizations to practise and see if what has been learned from the foreigners can but put into practice without their assis-tance as well. This phenomenon has been very common since the incep-tion of foreign co-operative ventures in China and is a constant source of complaints that Chinese counterparts have secret agendas. However, the Chinese Foreign Joint Venture Law stipulates that the duration of the venture is specified in the agreement. As a result, such ventures are easily perceived as temporary. The 100 per cent Chinese counterpart venture could then also fulfil a backup role, to guarantee the con-tinuation of the business after the co-operation is finished without exten-sion or if it is terminated prematurely.

This already points at an identity of SIDDAIR within the Yawei space: an inlet for foreign cattle breeding knowledge. However, I will revert to the identities of SIDDAIR later.

Henan played an important role in the self-introduction by the Yawei leaders. This part of the self-introduction was carefully structured and might have been used before on similar occasions, to put Henan on the map in the preferred perspective. This construct of Henan started by stating that it is a major agricultural province of China. This phrase, in almost exactly the same words, can also be found in other sources intro-ducing Henan (provincial web sites, industrial yearbooks, etc.). Three reasons were given why dairy used to be so weak in Henan in the past:

- insufficient government support;
- low local consumption;
- no interest in dairy on the part of the local government.

Currently the situation is said to be improving for all three aspects. The government is supporting the regional dairy industry as a major develop-ment sector for the Henan economy. For example, the government has subsidized the importation of dairy cattle. Consumption of dairy products is increasing. Milk is no longer regarded as something for babies or the old and the sick; people of all age groups drink milk. Dairy is now considered a good money maker.

While introducing the current positive attitude of the government, Mr Ouyang listed a number of major dairy companies in Henan. He used geo-graphic terminology (east, west, etc.) to indicate that these were well dis-tributed over the province. However, the south of Henan was not represented. The same discourse can be found in a news article (*People* 2002) about the Henan Animal Husbandry Bureau, which once more

Table 4.3   Key Henan dairy companies as perceived in the Henan space

Location	Company
East (Shangqiu)	Kedi
Central (Zhengzhou)	Shanmeng
West (Luoyang)	Ju'er

indicates the identity relation between Yawei and the Bureau. Table 4.3 illustrates the perceived geographic distribution of these 'key companies'.

Although not described so verbatim, Zhengzhou is presumed to occupy a central position in this concept. An interesting detail was that their own dairy company, Huahuaniu, was not mentioned. This could be explained as modesty, but could also indicate that Huahuaniu is perceived as having a different status. Yawei is not only *the* dairy producer in Henan, but also the Henan Animal Husbandry Bureau and therefore the governing organization of the other dairy companies mentioned. As such it is obviously located in the provincial capital, Zhengzhou, but it is not Zhengzhou's main dairy company. This role is performed by Shanmeng. Phrased differently, Huahuaniu is geographically located in Zhengzhou, but administratively in Henan.

This geographic distribution cognitively links up with the map of the Yellow River Project as painted on the wall at SIDDAIR. The Henan dairy processing industry is depicted as dependent on the source region for the raw milk: the Yellow River basin. The cities in which the above-mentioned dairy companies are located were all indicated on that map.

In order to stimulate the Yawei people to reflect more deeply and spontaneously on this subject outside their own regional perspective, I deliberately raised a challenging question: from a national point of view would it not make more sense to invest all money and effort in the typical traditional dairy regions like Inner Mongolia, Heilongjiang, etc., and distribute the products to other regions of China, now that the necessary infrastructure is rapidly improving? Why Henan? Mr Ouyang listed a number of aspects and Mr Wang spontaneously added some comments of his own. I will first reproduce the list:

Mr Ouyang:
• dairy consumption is increasing in Henan;
• the Yellow River Project, a project to develop the Yellow River basin for agriculture, in particular dairy cattle raising;
• Henan is a good stepping stone to other regions of China;
• the government of Henan supports the dairy industry;
• most major national dairy companies are active in Henan.

Mr Wang:

- the number of (potential) consumers is enormous, including a considerable number of unregistered people.
- although Inner Mongolia and Heilongjiang do have grasslands, these are mainly used for grazing sheep. Dairy cattle in those regions are also fed with stalks and other agricultural by-products. The latter are actually more abundant in Henan.

While all of these arguments do indeed make sense, most of them also hold for other Chinese regions. Dairy consumption is increasing everywhere in China and most eastern and central provinces are densely populated, including a number of unregistered people, as Mr Wang jested. Chinese investment, both by governments and private people, is heavily steered by vogues. As soon as word has it that a certain product or industry is a real money maker, all provinces and many smaller regions will immediately allot funds to invest in that industry. Dairy is currently such an industry, all over China, not only in Henan. All Chinese provinces and cities are heavily investing in infrastructure, again not only Henan, and Zhengzhou is certainly not the only, or even the largest, multimodal transportation node in the country. As a still mainly agricultural nation, agricultural waste that can be utilized as animal feed is available in all provinces, the only difference being the composition. Henan may have more wheat stalks, but Shandong has an equal amount of maize stalks available for the same purpose. The only argument that remains standing as specific for the Henan dairy industry is the Yellow River Project.

Other narratives – Zhengzhou Municipality

A large number of texts produced by various sources connected to the Zhengzhou government mentions Huahuaniu as a 'dragon head' company in the local dairy industry. 'Dragon head' is trendy terminology in present-day China to denote leading companies in their own industry. On most occasions Huahuaniu is mentioned in combination with Shanmeng. Apparently, the Zhengzhou government recognizes the strength of Huahuaniu and wants to let Shanmeng share some of it by always mentioning both in one breath.

Other narratives – Sanlu

Often, something can make sense by being missing. As Sanlu owns half of Huahuaniu, we would expect to find stories of how Huahuaniu makes sense in the Sanlu space. However, I have not been able to find such a narrative. Sanlu's web site contains a news section, but the acquisition of Huahuaniu is hardly reported. Sanlu had been heavily engaged in acquisitions during that period and apparently obtaining a 50 per cent stake in Huahuaniu was regarded as just a part of the overall strategy. Sanlu is located in Shijiazhuang in the southernmost part of Hebei, while Zhengzhou is situated in the northern part of Henan. From this geographical point of view, both regions form one continuous home region for the Sanlu Group. Viewed in this way, Huahuaniu is located in that home region, making this acquisition less 'special' than those in other provinces.

Huahuaniu identities

The number of cognitive spaces in which Huahuaniu makes sense and constructs an identity seems to be much smaller than that of SIDDAIR. Huahuaniu mainly makes sense within the Yawei space. However, we can discern two identities, constructed in two different identities of Yawei:

Yawei (as Henan Province Bureau of Animal Husbandry)
Huahuaniu = the leading manufacturer of dairy products in Henan

Yawei (= Yawei)
Huahuaniu = Yawei

As the dairy company operated by Yawei in its identity of Henan Province Bureau of Animal Husbandry, Huahuaniu is *the* number one dairy company of Henan. As a company, Yawei is less known among the general products. As a manufacturer of consumer goods, the Huahuaniu brand name is better known in the Zhengzhou region. This is no doubt the reason that the CEO of Yawei, Mr Ouyang, was playing with the idea to rename Yawei as Huahuaniu.

Zhengzhou Municipality
Huahuaniu = one of the two leading dairy companies, together with Shanmeng

Sanlu
Huahuaniu = a local subsidiary of Sanlu

Shanmeng – history(-ies)

Self-perception

If it is hard to find a text even resembling a self-introduction of Huahuaniu, this is virtually impossible for Shanmeng. I am once more relying on the practice that the Chinese media regularly print 'news' articles on companies that are prepared by the companies themselves, without much post-editing.

The Shanmeng Dairy Co., Ltd was officially established by Zhengzhou Municipality (Zhengzhou Agricultural Commission + Zhengzhou Dairy

Bureau) on 28 May 2001, by merging Tianyun Dairy Co. (formerly known as the Municipal Labour Union Dairy Factory), owned by the Labour Union and the Ouyuan Dairy Factory, operated by the municipal government. This project was partly funded with financial aid from the European Union (Gu 2003; ZYQNW 2003). The municipal government considered Shanmeng a 'key industrial project' (*Zhengzhou Evening News* 2001).

The story of Shanmeng after its establishment resembles that of Huahuaniu. The company is reported to have expanded, but also that it is too weak to survive on its own in the fierce competition that the Chinese dairy industry experienced during the early years of this century. Shanmeng started looking out for a partnership to become a player in the national dairy industry. A number of national leading companies were already reported to be showing interest. Shanmeng finally opted for a partnership with Bright from Shanghai. The breakdown of the ownership is as follows: Bright 60 per cent, Shanmeng 30 per cent, managers 10 per cent.

Regret

I have found only one story that explicitly criticizes Bright's closing in on Shanmeng (Wang 2002). The journalist reports that 'many people in Zhengzhou' regretted the takeover of Huahuaniu by Sanlu, which was regarded as a loss for Zhengzhou. They were weary of losing another major dairy company to Bright. According to this story, Shanmeng was already distributing Bright's UHT milk in Zhengzhou, before Bright acquired Shanmeng.

It is interesting to observe that such regret was not heard after the Sanlu–Huahuaniu deal. This may indicate that in this context Shanmeng was perceived as 'more Zhengzhou' than Huahuaniu. Losing Shanmeng to a party from another province would therefore be a bigger loss than in the case of Huahuaniu.

CEO

One narrative introducing Shanmeng's CEO, Mr Dong Bo, tells us that Shanmeng was already provisionally formed in late 2000 (Hu 2003). Mr Dong, who was then Vice-General Manager of an electronics group, was instated as Shanmeng's General Manager by the Zhengzhou government. At that time, the story continues, Shanmeng was extremely short of cash, while Zhengzhou Municipality had made it very clear that it was not willing to provide financing. Mr Dong started lobbying and obtained a loan from the municipal Labour Union of RMB 500 000. Only then did Shanmeng officially start operating on 28 May 2001.

Labour Union

The two stories introduced above seem to indicate that Shanmeng makes special sense within the local Labour Union space. In this transitory period of the Chinese economy, we can see organizations like the Labour Union, in particular local branches, invest in commercial enterprises, even though the trend is to separate administrative organizations and commercial enterprises operated by them. This case is especially intriguing, as it makes the Labour Union a de facto employer. There is no indication that this is regarded as a conflict of interests by any party. In less formal Chinese parlance, the municipal Labour Union is one of the mothers-in-law of Shanmeng.

Shanmeng + Huahuaniu?

While most narratives in my corpus describe Shanmeng and Huahuaniu as competitors, one story (Wang 2002) reports that the two companies had been negotiating a merger in July 2002. Although it is only one story, the author is describing the merger as inevitable. The reporter claims to have heard such a rumour during a local dairy conference and that spokespeople of both companies as well as the municipal government had confirmed it. Zhengzhou Municipality had further indicated that it was only playing the role of go-between. This story has never been followed up, but the author's comments offer an interesting insight into the differences between Huahuaniu and Shanmeng. The journalist specifically points out that Huahuaniu belongs to a provincial organization, while Shanmeng is a municipal investment and sees this as a major obstacle to forge a successful merger. He emphasizes this point with the sentence 'how on earth could they be linked up' using the local dialect. Using dialect words seems to place the problem in a very local and informal context. It is an issue specifically involving the people in Zhengzhou. Moreover, the fact that the journalist does not add any further comments, seems to indicate that this information itself should be sufficient for Chinese readers to understand the consequences. He then continues reporting that both companies were being courted by national players like Bright and Sanlu, offering lucrative alternatives for merging with a local party.

And what about Bright?

Similar to Sanlu's silence regarding the way it makes sense of Huahuaniu, Bright is not generous with stories about its Henan subsidiary Shanmeng, even though Bright holds a majority share of 60 per cent. Bright is one of China's top five dairy companies, with subsidiaries spread over the country. Shanmeng apparently does not stand out among Bright regional daughter companies. However, Shanmeng can derive political clout from its alliance with such a powerful national player.

Shanmeng identities

As with the other two players introduced above, I will here present an inventory of Shanmeng's major identities. Shanmeng first of all makes sense in the Zhengzhou Municipality space.

Zhengzhou Municipality
Shanmeng = key industrial project
Shanmeng = one of the two leading dairy companies in Zhengzhou, together with Huahuaniu

Zhengzhou Labour Union
Shanmeng = investment project

Mr Ouyang of Yawei included Shanmeng in his list of major regional dairy companies of Henan (see above):

Yawei
Shanmeng = one of the major regional dairy companies of Henan

And then there is Bright:

Bright
Shanmeng = Henan subsidiary of the national top dairy maker

Huahuaniu vs Shanmeng

I will use the last two sections to demonstrate how the different identity constructs of Huahuaniu and Shanmeng work in practice. In this section I will look at the competition between the two companies in their home region, Zhengzhou. Later in this chapter, I will demonstrate how the Dutch actors involved in the SIDDAIR project may have missed opportunities, as they failed to understand the local competitive environment.

Looking at the competition from shared social-cognitive contexts, we can compare the ways the two companies are made sense of in the same context. The inventories of contexts provided above show two share contexts:

Yawei (as Henan Province Bureau of Animal Husbandry)
Huahuaniu = the leading manufacturer of dairy products in Henan
Shanmeng = the major dairy company in Zhengzhou

Zhengzhou Municipality
Huahuaniu = one of the two leading dairy companies of Zhengzhou, together with Shanmeng

Shanmeng = one of the two leading dairy companies in Zhengzhou, together with Huahuaniu

Although the narratives in both contexts recognize that Huahuaniu and Shanmeng are competitors in the sense that both are manufacturers in the same industrial sector, trying to maximize their share of the same market, the leading theme of these identity constructs seems to convey the perception that there is enough room for both, they are supplementary in nature, rather than competitive. The main difference between these two spaces is that Yawei evidently places Huahuaniu at a higher administrative level, while Zhengzhou Municipality implies that they are equals in the Zhengzhou region.

Observation of the behaviour of Huahuaniu and Shanmeng as told to us via the various stories in the media shows that both regularly take similar strategic decisions. However, Shanmeng usually makes its decision after Huahuaniu. This seems to indicate that Shanmeng is perceiving Huahuaniu as a kind of role model, imitating each of its major strategic steps. Three such strategic decisions can be discerned.

Consolidation of the dairy business

Yawei officially established the Huahuaniu Dairy Co., Ltd in 1999. Zhengzhou Municipality started forming Shanmeng in late 2000. Although it has never been expressed so verbatim, it would make sense that the formation of Huahuaniu by bundling the dairy and ice cream manufacturing activities of Yawei was perceived by the Zhengzhou authorities as a threat to its own dairy interests. They then followed suit by bundling two dairy plants operated by different municipal organizations into Shanmeng.

Foreign funding

Henan Province (with Yawei as its vehicle) signed the SIDDAIR agreement in March 1999. Zhengzhou officially incorporated Shanmeng Dairy Co., Ltd in mid-2001, adding that the company was partly funded from an EU programme to aid the development of the Chinese dairy industry. From the SIDDAIR narrative we already know that the agreement was conceived during a visit of the Dutch Minister of Agriculture in 1997. We may assume that the activities preceding the signing of the SIDDAIR agreement were known by the Zhengzhou authorities. It is not unlikely that the formation of Shanmeng in 2000 was part of their own preparatory activities to be elected as part of the EU programme, initiated to counter the Province's Dutch project.

Local partner

Huahuaniu and Shanmeng both sold part of their equity to a national leading dairy company in late 2003, within two months of each other. The various stories about Huahuaniu and Shanmeng speak of New Hope, Sanlu and Bright courting both companies simultaneously. Sanlu came out of this with Huahuaniu as its bride, while Shanmeng opted for Bright, with which it reportedly already had a commercial relation. At the time this chapter was written, it is not clear in what ways these partnerships will affect the competitive relation between Huahuaniu and Shanmeng.

I have arranged the main differences in competitive aspects and identities of Huahuaniu and Shanmeng in Table 4.4 to illustrate this matrix of companies and their differences in various contexts. The consequences of this competitive relation between Huahuaniu and Shanmeng can be discussed from a number of angles. As the main theme of this sub-section is to reveal how Shanmeng imitates the major strategic decisions of Huahuaniu, I will focus my discussion on that particular aspect.

After the handover of the SIDDAIR project to the Chinese side in March 2004, some actors on the Dutch side are still contemplating ways to follow it up with a new project (this will be discussed more fully in the following section of this chapter). Because of the SIDDAIR project, which was retained without a change of name after the handover, good working relations have been established with Yawei–Huahuaniu. A number of people would therefore like to see a new dairy processing project with Huahuaniu as the Chinese partner. This makes sense, not only because of the Dutch-oriented attitude at Yawei, but also because dairy processing would be the logical next step after SIDDAIR, which was about raw milk production.

However, suppose that parties started negotiations towards such a project, what reaction could we expect from the market? It is not unlikely that Shanmeng would perceive such news as a new threat to its position from the side of Huahuaniu. In view of the competitive relation between Huahuaniu and Shanmeng as analysed above, we could then expect Shanmeng to start looking for a similar move. Most international dairy companies have at least representative offices in China and many of them are already producing locally. Moreover, Bright, Shanmeng's national partner, has close relations with Danone.

Table 4.4   Differences between Huahuaniu and Shanmeng in various contexts

Context	Huahuaniu	Shanmeng
Geopolitical	Henan	Zhengzhou
National partner	Sanlu (Hebei)	Bright (Shanghai)
Foreign funding	Netherlands	EU

Finally, I would like to point out that this spiralling way of competing has been overall beneficial to the Zhengzhou region. If Huahuaniu and Shanmeng had been merged, it may have formed such a large company that the owners would not have deemed it necessary to link up with national partners. On the other hand, the resulting company may not have had the size and financial strength to have made it join the ranks of the national leading dairy companies. Although Huahuaniu's major policy decisions are now partly made in Shijiazhuang (Sanlu's home city) and Shanmeng's in Shanghai (Bright's empire), which is regarded by some people in Zhengzhou as a loss of power in the local dairy industry, it also links that industry up with the national industry. In terms of organizing: the inclusions of Huahuaniu in Sanlu and Shanmeng in Bright simultaneously construct inclusions of the Henan in Hebei and Shanghai. While Shanmeng has benefited from following the ideas of Yawei–Huahuaniu, the latter has also been saved from complacency by Shanmeng.

Dutch sense-making of identities

In the final section of this chapter, I will observe the way the Dutch involved in the SIDDAIR project made sense of the identities of Huahuaniu and Shanmeng. I will first look at the relevant remarks made during conversations, followed by an analysis of the remarks on Shanmeng in a written assessment of the local dairy market from late 2001.

Conversations

During conversations, the Dutch actors, with no exception, all perceived Yawei–Huahuaniu as *the* dairy processor in the Zhengzhou region; all others being marginal. None of them had ever visited Shanmeng or any other plant in Zhengzhou. One motive for not doing so was probably the Western perception that, as Yawei was the partner organization in SIDDAIR, it would have been inappropriate to contact one of Yawei's competitors. However, contacts between competitors in the same region is quite common in China. The two organizations' common inclusions will create ample opportunities for interaction. Moreover, in this particular case some of the leaders of Yawei–Huahuaniu and Shanmeng had been educated in the same school. This also made them schoolmates, which is as good an occasion for keeping in touch in China as elsewhere in the world. One of the stories introduced above reports on contacts between Huahuaniu and Shanmeng regarding a possible merger in July 2002.

The evident unawareness of the Dutch in Zhengzhou regarding Shanmeng also indicates that their interaction with their partner organization left much to be desired. They either never brought up that subject during interaction with their partners, and/or Yawei people did not bring it up voluntarily.

For SIDDAIR, Huahuaniu was the only buyer of its milk. The Dutch manager privately remarked that he might start talking to other prospects, to see if he could negotiate a better price, but his tone of voice did not sound very convincing.

All discussion held between various Dutch actors regarding a possible dairy project to follow up the SIDDAIR project centred around Huahua-niu as the designated location for the new project. It is very likely that this was still based on the perceived partner relation with Yawei, even though this relation officially ceased with the handover of the project to the Chinese side in March 2004. The SIDDAIR project had legally ended, but cognitively still continued. This behaviour is quite common, but can easily lead to reifying the relation. Actors are then less open to alternatives.

This conclusion is corroborated by a remark made by the Dutch manager of SIDDAIR during the interview with the Yawei leadership. When I asked Mr Ouyang in Chinese how much of SIDDAIR was owned by Yawei, the Dutch manager privately remarked in Dutch 'probably 100 per cent'. Mr Ouyang refrained from mentioning a percentage, but said that SIDDAIR was operated by Yawei. While the CEO of Yawei was reluctant to give an explicit reply to this question, which he apparently regarded as sensitive, the Dutch manager eagerly exposed his perception of the Yawei identity of SIDDAIR.

Written assessment

An assessment was made of the possibilities of adding a dairy processing module to the SIDDAIR project in late 2001. The tenor of the assessment is that such a module would be located at Huahuaniu. I have therefore made a collation of all remarks on Shanmeng in the report, supplemented with private communication from the market researchers, to focus on how the researchers made sense of the most important 'marginal' player.

The newly established Shanmeng dairy factory was perceived as being in the process of capturing a market share of the local (= Zhengzhou) market in addition to (or at the expense of) Yawei. Their current overall market share was estimated at around 13.2 per cent. I have arranged some key figures concerning Yawei and Shanmeng in Table 4.5 for ease of comparison.

The market for fresh dairy products in urban Zhengzhou was being dominated by Yawei. Yawei was the single largest supplier of pasteurized milk (62 per cent market share) and yoghurt (55 per cent market share). Runner-up was the 'newly established' Shanmeng Dairy, representing 27 per cent and 17 per cent of the market volume of pasteurized milk and yoghurt, respectively. Product range, prices and quality of the two main suppliers are similar. However, further in the report it was remarked that Shanmeng had been able to capture that share of the market in a 'fairly short period of time'.

Table 4.5   Key figures of Yawei (Huahuaniu) and Shanmeng in tonnes/day as perceived by Dutch market researchers at the beginning of the Dutch project

	Pasteurized milk	Yoghurt	Flavoured milk	UHT milk
Yawei Co.	16	33	8	3
Market share	62%	55%	55%	100%
Shanmeng Dairy	7	10	1	0
Market share	27%	17%	7%	

Source: Compiled from IDC report and private communication.

Shanmeng Distribution Model

The network of Shanmeng Dairy was said to be under development and its design looked similar to that of Yawei. It entailed 26 wholesale/retail centres supplied by their own transport means (eight trucks of 2 t each). Sales were mainly oriented towards wholesalers and retailers, while grocery shops, supermarkets and institutional outlets (hotels, restaurants) would become more important in the future.

The most conspicuous aspect of these remarks is the repeated reference to the fact that Shanmeng was a new player. Phrases like 'newly established', 'in phase of development', etc., abound. Shanmeng is perceived as a completely new company, without any reference to the Chinese stories that Shanmeng had been formed by merging two existing dairy plants. The researchers had neither read those stories, nor heard them from their Chinese counterparts.

However, it is also clear that Shanmeng is making remarkable progress, for such a newly established company. Shanmeng has gained certain market share 'within a fairly short period of time'.

We should not expect market researchers to be familiar with organization theory and models of organizational identity. However, even then it is remarkable that the results of this study had aroused sufficient curiosity on the Dutch side to look more into the background of Shanmeng, this obviously growing threat to their local partner's market position.

This then leads me to the conclusion that the Dutch involved in the SIDDAIR project had such a strong Yawei identity, that it impeded them from looking beyond the Yawei horizon.

This conclusion corroborates the conclusion I made regarding the conversations with the Dutch actors. SIDDAIR was regarded as strongly included in the Yawei space. In line with the Western cultural inclination to perceive identity as singular, the Dutch then found it extremely hard to consider other inclusions (identities).

5 Mengniu the follower

A case of intertwined identity

This chapter not only follows the previous one in the physical sense, its theme also links up with that of the previous chapter. The case of Chapter 4 illustrated how Chinese companies in the same type of business, located in the same geographical region, but linked to different administrative levels were operated in such a way that they appeared as competitors in some contexts, but in others seemed to be confining themselves to their own 'space'. Although both companies were part of the sense-making of the other, this influence was extremely subtle and could only be revealed by a certain research effort. Foreigners co-operating with one of the companies had hardly noticed the relation between the two.

The case matter of this chapter may strike the reader as more of the same: two companies operating in the same region, but in spite of their fierce competition, one appears to be making up an essential part of the identity construction of the other. However, the differences between the two enterprises are considerably more complicated than was the case in the previous chapter. Moreover, the incident in this chapter is the way these two companies re-enacted their competition in another region in China. To facilitate the comparison between this case and the previous one, I have once more selected two dairy companies.

The company that constitutes the focus of this chapter is Mengniu (literally: Mongolian Cow) situated in Huhhot, the capital of the Inner Mongolia Autonomous Region. Inner Mongolia, the Chinese section of the Mongolian territory, is one of China's few regions where the production and consumption of milk is part of an age-old local tradition. I will first present a section on the region in general and its dairy industry in particular and then introduce the story of Mengniu's founder and CEO.

The region – a bit Chinese and a bit Mongolian

Inner Mongolia, or officially: Inner Mongolia Autonomous Region, is an administrative region of northern China at the same level as a province, but with a larger degree of political autonomy. The region is bordered on the north by Russia and the Republic of Mongolia; on the east by the provinces of Heilongjiang, Jilin and Liaoning; and on the south and south-west by Hebei, Shanxi, Shaanxi and Gansu and by Ningxia Autonomous Region. Inner Mongolia is one of China's largest administrative regions, with a total area of about 1.2 million km².

The region that is now Inner Mongolia first came under Chinese control during the Han dynasty (206 BC to AD 220). Han Chinese farmers com-peted and fought with the Xiongnu (a nationality usually identified with the Huns), the nomads who occupied the steppes and deserts of north-western China and what is now the Republic of Mongolia. The conflicting lifestyles of the earth-bound Han farmers and the nomad peoples of the north has played a major role in the history of northern China and was the occasion for starting the construction of the Great Wall. The Han pushed back the Xiongnu and settled in southern Inner Mongolia. In the Tang dynasty (618–907) much of the territory came under Chinese control. Mongols took the region back in the tenth century, and it subsequently became part of the Mongol Yuan dynasty (1279–1368) under Kublai Khan. Mongol power retreated once more during the Ming dynasty (1368–1644), and Chinese control over the Mongol population and occu-pation gradually extended out onto the Mongolian steppes and areas where settled farming was possible. Outer Mongolia gained independence as the Republic of Mongolia in 1912 and Inner Mongolia became an administrative territory of China. In 1947 the Chinese Communists gained control of Inner Mongolia and established an administrative organization, two years before the establishment of the People's Republic of China.

The greater part of Inner Mongolia is a plateau with elevations of about 1000 metres. The Yellow River flows north from Ningxia and forms a loop that encloses the Ordos Desert. Grasslands predominate on the plateau, where they sustain large numbers of grazing animals such as cows, sheep, goats, camels and horses. Milk from all those animals has been part of the traditional diet of the Mongols. Apart from drinking the fresh product, milk is processed into a number of cheese and yoghurt-like products. Horse milk is even fermented into an alcoholic beverage.

The population of Inner Mongolia is approximately 25 million, up from only 6.1 million in 1953. The rapid population growth since the 1950s is a result of better nutrition, increased health care services, and a substantial migration into the region of Han Chinese. More than 80 per cent of the current population is Han. Mongols comprise the largest minority group in Inner Mongolia, and their presence is acknowledged by the government's designation of Inner Mongolia as an autonomous region. Other minority groups in the region include the Hui (Chinese Muslims), Manchus, Daur Mongols, Koreans, the Evenki and the Oroqen.

About one-third of Inner Mongolia's population lives in cities and towns. Baotou is the largest city and is a major industrial centre with a large iron and steel complex, as well as cement, chemical, fertilizer, machine tool and textile manufacturers. Huhhot, the capital, is the region's main administrative and cultural centre and an important transportation and industrial hub.

Traditionally, Inner Mongolia's economy is agricultural, with products associated with animal husbandry. Farming is productive along the Yellow River; important crops include oats, wheat, millet, sorghum, sunflowers and sugar beets. In recent years a manufacturing sector has developed as well. Much of it is related to processing natural resources of the region, including agricultural products, wool, iron ore, coal, alkali soda and salt.

Inner Mongolian infrastructure is still limited. The Chinese leg of the Trans-Siberian Railroad passes through northern Inner Mongolia on its route from Russia to Heilongjiang. The Trans-Mongolian Railway that links Beijing with the Republic of Mongolia and Russia runs through the middle of the region. Another rail line extends from Baotou to far western China. A number of express ways are in various stages of construction.

Niu Gensheng – the man, the myth and the company

The CV of Mr Niu Gensheng (born 1956), Mengniu's founder and CEO is one of the most mythical ones among present-day China's famous entrepreneurs. The contents of this section is been mainly derived from Alibaba (2004) and BJSSE (2003: 299–313).

Story has it that he lost his parents at the very early age of three months and was raised by a farmer called Niu, who paid the, then huge, adoption fee of RMB 50. His foster parents gave him the name: Niu Gensheng. Niu grew up at a cattle farm in Huhhot, the capital of Inner Mongolia, so he literally took cattle raising in with his mother's milk.

Niu was hired by what was then called the Yili Dairy Factory in Huhhot, as a bottle washer, in 1978. From that humble position, he gradually worked his way up from work shop supervisor, subsidiary director, vice-director of the mother factory to Vice-President in charge of production of, what was then transformed into, the Yili Group. Niu's career did not pass by unnoticed. He has been granted a number of regional awards, like the Huhhot Building the City through Science & Technology Award and the designation Huhhot Special Labour Model and he was included in the ten Top Young Entrepreneurs of Huhhot. In terms of administrative levels, all of Niu's awards are linked to Huhhot Municipality.

For reasons that have never been actually expressed, a conflict developed between Niu and the other board members, resulting in his removal from the board in November 1998. The Board issued a statement indicating that 'Comrade Niu Gensheng no longer fitted his position'. He was 'advised' to find a place to study outside his home region for at least two years. Judging by this 'advice', it could have been that his fellow board members no longer felt comfortable with a self-made man among their ranks. Niu grabbed this opportunity to enrol himself in the MBA course of the prestigious Guanghua Business School of Beijing University. He left Yili the following year.

Within only a year, 1999, Niu Gensheng, a group of more than 50 of his old subordinates at Yili and a number of private individuals raised RMB 1.3 billion to establish the Mengniu Dairy Co., Ltd. The company was officially registered in July 1999. When asked during an interview how Niu could so easily convince a considerable number of his former colleagues at Yili not only to quit their comfortable positions, but also entrust a considerable amount of their savings to him, Niu's own rationale was that he had the habit of sharing his income with his subordinates. His last salary as a Vice-President of Yili exceeded RMB 1 million, which he found more than he needed to make a good living. He often shared part of it with subordinates who he regarded to have contributed to his success. In Niu's eyes, he was cashing in on the goodwill thus accumulated during the establishment of Mengniu.

This goodwill extended over the small circle of Niu's former subordinates. His former colleagues also mobilized their relatives, friends and business associates to invest in the new project. The first assets of Mengniu consisted of a one-room office rented for RMB 200 per month. Many of the 'investors' brought their contribution personally to this office, in cash. This aroused the suspicion of the local authorities, who started to suspect that Niu was engaged in the 'illegal accumulation of capital'. Although, after considerable effort (read: networking), the problem was resolved, once more relying heavily on Niu's sound social network, Mengniu remained under close scrutiny of the financial authorities for some time.

Three months after its establishment, Mengniu moved from its one-room office to the Shengle Economic Park in Linge'er County of Huhhot. Here Mengniu had to tackle another bureaucratic hurdle. The only patch of land still available in the Park consisted of an area with trees. Cutting down trees required a permit of the Forestry Bureau and Niu knew that such a permit would be hard to obtain. He cut the trees down anyway, without a permit, but under the protection of the County Magistrate of Linge'er, who deemed the economic development more essential than a few trees. Niu Gensheng repaid nature later by planting fruit trees all over the premises of Mengniu, which also provide added value through the sales of their fruits.

At this point in Mengniu's development, the company was still in a situation Niu himself recalls as 'four deficiencies': no milk source, no factory, no brand (he had registered a brand name, but it was unknown among Chinese consumers) and no market. Niu's strategy to emerge from such an unfortunate situation is the third aspect of his mythological success, again in Niu's own words: 'emulated combination' (*xuni lianhe*). He contacted dairy plants all over China with a surplus capacity and contracted those to produce for Mengniu. Mengniu provided specifications, a brand name and technological assistance. Mengniu first created a market and only then built its own production facilities.

Mengniu turned out to be of the fastest growing companies in China's history. The company generated a turnover of RMB 43 million in the first year of its existence, which was approximately 4 per cent of Yili's turnover of the same period. The turnover for 2002 had already increased to RMB 2 billion, exactly half of Yili's turnover of that year.

A milestone in the short history of Mengniu was its acceptance of foreign participation in late 2002. Niu Gensheng himself had repeatedly stated in the national press that he was not in a hurry to follow Yili's example in seeking registration on the stock exchange and expose Mengniu to the whims of speculators. It therefore was even a surprise to insiders when it was reported that Morgan Stanley, CDH Fund and China Capital Partners had signed an agreement with Mengniu to invest US$ 26 million in the Chinese dairy company. As a result of that deal, the three foreign investors held a total share of 32 per cent in Mengniu. According to a spokesperson of Mengniu, the Chinese side have attracted foreign participation to compete better with the other dairy giants like Sanyuan and Bright, which are heavily supported by their respective local governments. Morgan Stanley had already invested in a number of Chinese enterprises including Ping An Insurance Company, Nanfu Battery Company and Heng'an International Group. CDH Fund had invested in 12 Chinese enterprises, also including Nanfu Battery and Sina.com, an important Chinese business Internet portal. China Capital Partners, a UK fund for investment in China, had invested US$ 55 million in China since it was established in June 2000 (FIF 2002).

Following opening its door to foreign influence, Mengniu's next step was to seek listing on the Hong Kong Stock Exchange in June 2004. The company expected to raise as much as HK$ 1.37 billion. Mengniu was reported to be betting that China's economic growth and increasing affluence will underpin demand for dairy products. Mengniu and its existing shareholders, including Morgan Stanley's private equity unit, planned to sell 350 million shares (*China Daily* 2004).

Niu himself made the headlines in the first month of 2005, when he announced that he, and all of his family members, had placed their Mengniu stock (close to 10 per cent) in a fund called: 'Old Niu Fund' (the Chinese word *lao* (old) can be prefixed to surnames to express a sense of familiarity to an elderly person). The main aim of the fund is to reward people who have contributed in an exceptional way to the development of Mengniu. Actually, the idea for such a fund had been mentioned by Niu a number of times since late 2003, but was made official in January 2005. The timing of this publication, right after the news of the arrest of the leadership of Yili (see below) aroused a fierce debate in the media whether this was yet another example of Niu's beneficial leadership or a scheme of Niu to show that he was 'clean' (CEW 2005).

Yili – the company and its founder

The Yili Dairy Group started out as the Huhhot Red Flag Dairy Factory. This enterprise was renamed the Muslim Dairy Food Factory in 1984. Following the general trend of the economic reforms of state-owned enterprises, the factory was reorganized as a limited company under the present Yili name in 1992. Yili obtained its listing in 1996.

From its initiation to, at least, the end of 2004, Yili's history is one long success story. In the initial period of the economic reforms, the dairy companies of the two large urban conglomerates, Beijing and Shanghai, benefited most from the new challenges and opportunities. The traditional socialist Beijing Dairy Corporation and Shanghai Dairy Corporation reorganized themselves as respectively Sanyuan and Bright (Guangming), which started expanding by setting up branches, but especially by acquiring state-owned dairy companies that fared less well in the new competitive environment, in various regions of China. However, after the establishment of Yili, the company rapidly obtained a top position on a par with Sanyuan and Bright.

Yili has no doubt benefited from its proximity to the grasslands of the Mongolian highland. However, the rapid and sustained success of Yili is usually for a major part attributed to Mr Zheng Junhuai, who has been Yili's CEO up to his arrest for fraud in late 2004.

Mr Zheng was born in Huhhot in 1950. He has a bachelor degree in business administration. In late 1970, when he was still an officer in the Huhhot Bureau of Agriculture and Forestry (Sina 2004), Mr Zheng was transferred to a state-run cattle farm where he performed the functions of Party Secretary and Vice-Director. He became the Manager of the Guest House of the Huhhot Dairy Corporation in 1980. Finally, Mr Zheng was transferred to the Huhhot Red Flag Dairy Food Factory in January 1983, as the Director. It was under his leadership that the factory developed into the present Yili Dairy Group.

Yili never really made the headlines with internal strife, conflicts with government organizations, etc. The company was only reported in the media for its concatenation of successes.

It was therefore all the more spectacular when Mr Zheng and a few close associates in the Yili board announced a management buyout. The rationale for this move was that it would give them more freedom to move in the new competitive environment. Although Mengniu was never mentioned as the main cause for this strategic decision, it was generally believed, both in the public media and in the rumour circuits, that Mengniu's ties with Morgan Stanley were the primary incentive for this step. The proposal was approved (a management buyout had to be approved by the local authorities) in spite of the scepticism. However, one early morning of December 2004, Mr Zheng and six of his associates were arrested under the accusation of having embezzled public funds. Those

funds were the capital they had used for their management buyout operation a few months earlier. The veracity of these accusations are not an
issue in this study, so I will not discuss them further here. The case is still
under investigation while this chapter is being written.

Mengniu–Yili: who follows whom?

Re-enacting Yili

The above concise historical introductions of Mengniu and Yili already
show that it is practically impossible to say anything about one without
mentioning the other.

From an organizing perspective, the important role of Yili in Mengniu's
sense-making can be explained by the fact that so many top level managers of Mengniu, including Niu Gensheng himself, were former
employees of Yili, where they had also occupied managerial positions.
Especially in the initial period of Mengniu's existence, this group of people
were still enacting a Yili style of management, while constructing a new
company. They were all using their personal inclusions to build a support
base for Mengniu, but those inclusions, the configurations of actors
involved, the cognitive matter (perceptions, ways of doing things, etc.)
would not have changed fundamentally. In situations like this, actors will
first continue to enact their social-cognitive contexts more or less as usual.
Then only gradually will the changed situation (in this case the newly
formed configuration around Niu Gensheng for the construction of
Mengniu) cause a change in other configurations in which Niu and his new
associates were included.

A slightly different, but not necessarily conflicting, organizational
explanation of Mengniu's rapid success is that already during his work at
Yili Niu had formed a tightly coupled configuration with a number of his
colleagues. After Niu had de facto been dismissed by Yili, this configuration continued, but outside Yili. This altered the nature of their inclusion
in the Yili space, but did not sever it completely. When people change
jobs, they usually remain socially and cognitively linked to the former job
for a certain period. This link will gradually become weaker, but the speed
of that weakening depends on the discrepancy between the old and the
new job. When people remain unemployed, the social-cognitive link to the
old job can serve as an anchor to the outside world. When the new job is
very different from the former one, the speed of de-linking can be very
quick. However, when an actor takes up a similar job in a similar line of
business at a new employer, the link, especially the cognitive link, often
weakens slowly and sometimes never becomes completely extinct. Actors
can redefine their inclusion in the old employer's space.

My research in how Chinese make sense of their work context reveals
that this is especially the case in the Chinese cultural environment. In the

main case of Peverelli (2000: 127–156) I observed how a sales person of a metals trading company in Hunan province, who had formerly worked as a driver for the managers of a local metals processor, was used as the main intermediary between the trading company (his current employer) and his former employer. The companies were involved in a commercial conflict and the other sales people, including the Head of the Sales Department, of the trading company were unable to contact the metals company directly. However, when foreign guests of the trader wished to visit the metals processor, this person was able to make the appointment and accompany the foreigners during their visit, on the basis of his inclusion in the metal processor's space.

Back to Mengniu vs Yili, we can imagine that Mengniu's managers would have had at least a gut feeling of how Yili would react to their every move, but that it is equally likely that they would have continued to communicate with colleagues remaining in the employment of Yili. Using biological terminology, we could be tempted to refer to (young) Mengniu as a 'clone' of Yili.

(Don't) follow the leader

In the year that Mengniu was established the Huhhot region produced approximately 440 t of raw milk p.a. of which Yili alone purchased 400 t. However, in spite of Mengniu's desperate 'thirst for milk', Niu issued what he called 'the Three Don'ts' (BJSSE 2003: 301):

1   Mengniu will not erect milk parlours in regions where Yili is already operating one;
2   Mengniu will not purchase milk that does not come from milk parlours;
3   Mengniu will not purchase milk that does not comply with Yili's specifications.

Chinese dairy companies have a number of routes for purchasing raw milk. Farmers can bring their produce directly to the plant. There the purchasing department will analyse a sample. If the milk is found in accordance with the company's purchasing specifications, the purchasing manager will then determine the price according to the current market price and a number of essential specifications like fat and protein content. Often farmers bring their cows to so-called milk parlours, centrally located milking stations where the cows can be milked under more hygienic conditions. Milk parlours also have better storage facilities. Dairy processors can collect the milk from the parlours by means of cooling trucks. While some of the milk parlours are operated by private entrepreneurs, most of them are placed and owned by the dairy companies. This is the best way to ensure a steady supply of raw milk of required quality.

In the competitive environment of the present-day Chinese dairy industry, which is suffering from a structural lack of (good quality) raw milk, competing dairy companies often build milk parlours of their own in regions already 'served' by competitors. While this is beneficial to the farmers, who can, within certain limits, sell their milk to the highest bidder, it often leads to unfair competition when large companies, like Yili, build milk parlours in locations outside their own home region, outbidding the local dairy processors.

In this respect Mengniu followed a strategy similar to the 'emulated combination' mentioned above. While Yili owned and operated its milk parlours, Mengniu contracted independent operators to build and operate parlours (Webber and Wang 2003: 9). This constructed a major difference in operating costs between Yili and Mengniu.

What Niu Gensheng was saying was that Mengniu would not directly confront Yili in its source regions of raw milk. On the quality side, however, Mengniu would copy Yili's policy of only purchasing milk through milk parlours and adopting Yili's quality specifications.

Niu also has another favourite motto for not directly competing with Yili. He is often quoted as stating that he positioned Mengniu from the start as a market builder, instead of focusing on taking away the market share of others. Mengniu expands the market, which creates space for growth for both companies. Literally, the motto says: 'we promote the Chinese people to drink more milk, but it does not all have to be Mengniu's milk' (XBRY 2005).

Niu is regularly interviewed by the media. During such interviews he has a habit of, seemingly casually, alluding to the relaxed nature of the competition between Mengniu and Yili. One of such remarks states that: by the end of the tenth Five-Year Plan, Mengniu and Yili combined may be good for one-third of the national dairy market, representing a value of RMB 30 billion. Of this, Yili could be good for RMB 20 billion and Mengniu for RMB 10 billion, or each half, or a little bit more for Mengniu.

This aspect of Mengniu's relation to Yili goes a step further than the one discussed in the previous paragraph. Here Niu is not only stating that he keeps out of the way of Yili, but he is actually positioning Mengniu as contributing to the development of Yili (XBRY 2005).

This positioning vis-à-vis Yili is also continued in Mengniu's advertising campaigns. Slogans used in the company's early advertising include: 'striving to become Inner Mongolia's second brand', 'The vast grasslands have given birth to: Yili, Xingfa and Mengniu Dairy' and 'Promoting the national industry, learning from Yili'. The term 'national industry' (*minzu gongye*) used in the second phrase is a standard term referring to the indigenous Chinese industry as opposed to (threats from) the global industry. From the first foreign investment in China subsequent Chinese governments have expressed fear that foreign investment may harm the development of an indigenous industry. The Chinese term *minzu gongye* coined in this context therefore evokes a strong national sentiment; it is not simply Mengniu, or even Mengniu + Yili, it refers to the entire Chinese industry. After putting the reader in the proper mood, this slogan then moves on to Yili, thus attributing a considerable part of the national pride to Yili. Xingfa is another major Inner Mongolian company and one of China's top meat processors. The order in which the three companies are mentioned in the third slogan is significant. When Chinese enumerate people (e.g. state officials attending a ceremony) or organizations, they will virtually always do so in a particular order of importance. The criteria for this ordering are linked to what is regarded as crucial at that particular configuration of time and place. Mengniu's third slogan is therefore a double pat on the back for Yili: Mengniu mentions itself after Yili, but also positions Yili before Xingfa.

The Chinese, individuals and organizations, have a habit of using humility for self-promotion. Mengniu has developed this cultural inclination to an art. Western readers may tend to interpret many of Mr Niu's slogans as on, or even over, the verge of arrogance. Some may regard them as satirical. However, I understand this Chinese habit of referring to one's humble position vis-à-vis others as compliant with the Chinese cultural inclination. In earlier work (Peverelli 2000: 52–62 and 123–125) I attempted to redefine 'culture' as the way in which actors deal with organizational complexity, i.e. multiple inclusion. In this model, the Chinese seem to be positioned at the end of an imaginary scale with relatively rapid movements between different cognitive spaces. Mengniu is competing with all major national dairy brands. However, the relation between Mengniu and, for example, Bright of Shanghai is different from its relation with Yili, in that Mengniu shares its home region with Yili. Niu verbalized it like this in an interview (Xinhuanet 2004): 'Yili is the big brother and Mengniu the little brother, without Yili there would be no Mengniu, there is a bit of you in me and a bit of me in you'. Moreover, sharing a home region is an emotional issue for the Chinese.

Mengniu's (early) advertising strategy thus copes with the fact that the key actors of Mengniu and those of Yili share a number of inclusions not shared with those of a company like Bright:

- as ex-employees of Yili, Mengniu's top managers are still included in the Yili space;
- the people of Mengniu and Yili all share the same home regions: Inner Mongolia and Huhhot.

Dairy capital

The importance of the home region is further emphasized by another identity construction strategy of Niu Gensheng: promoting Huhhot as China's Dairy Capital. In his eagerness to express his societal commitment, Niu conceived the idea of promoting Huhhot as the 'Dairy Capital of China'. Mengniu hung banners with this slogan all over Huhhot in June 2001. This proved to be a clever move, as the campaign soon aroused the interest of the municipal government, which took over the slogan as its own (XBRY 2005).

Because both Mengniu and Yili were located in the Huhhot region, Yili in a suburb and Mengniu in an adjacent town, the honour of being part of China's Dairy Capital was shared by both.

The China Dairy Capital identity of Huhhot did not only refer to milk, but to high quality milk, pure and free of any contamination. Inner Mongolia has long been one of China's poorest regions. Its economy was almost entirely based on agriculture, with industry concentrated in a small number of cities. Baotou is still Inner Mongolia's main industrial town, although Huhhot is the capital. The special status of a Chinese regional capital, like Zhengzhou in the previous chapter, also played a role in this campaign. Huhhot, the seat of the Inner Mongolian government, had long been regarded by many Chinese from other regions as a large village, compared with Baotou. Naming Huhhot China's Dairy Capital gave the city exactly the foundation for prestige it was so desperately in need of.

An unintended bonus of the lack of industry was the low level of environmental pollution. China boasts some of the world's highest polluted urban regions. The head offices of other national top dairy companies, in particular Sanyuan (Beijing), Bright (Shanghai) and Sanlu (Shijiazhuang) (see the previous chapter), are located in highly polluted regions. China's oldest dairy companies are situated in Heilongjiang, in the vicinity of Harbin and Qiqihar, where the dairy plants have heavy industry as neighbours. It was yet another smart move of Niu to spot a positive aspect of a situation generally perceived as negative (underdeveloped local industry) and use it to the full (this background of a number of 'ecological agriculture' regions in China has been shared with me during private communication with a Chinese government official).

After the municipal government had picked up the concept of Dairy Capital, Yili followed suit and its CEO, Mr Zheng Junhuai, expressed his commitments to the Inner Mongolian cause as ardently as Mr Niu. In interviews, Mr Zheng stated that Yili strived to forge the glorious and clean Dairy Capital image in close co-operation with sister companies (Chinese speak of brother companies) like Mengniu (Xinhuanet 2004a).

An interesting aspect of Messrs Niu and Zheng's statements of commitment to a common cause is that, although their statements are very similar in content, they never actually react to one another's declarations. While Mr Zheng confirms that Yili is devoted to helping construct China's Dairy Capital, he seems to stop at saying that he does so 'in accordance with Mr Niu Gengsheng's statement of a certain time and place'. When reading Mr Zheng's statement cited above out of context, his language itself does not contain any indication that these ideas are not his own. However, if we believe that time matters and that Mengniu (Mr Niu) was the first to launch the concept of Dairy Capital, and further if Yili (Mr Zheng) agreed wholeheartedly, we would expect that Mr Zheng would refer to statements by Mr Niu and express his, complete or part, agreement. Instead, we can observe the representatives of two rival companies verbosely stating their common cause, but apparently doing so independently from one another.

It should be added here, however, that Yili had no choice but to ascribe openly to the concept of Dairy Capital, once the Huhhot government had started supporting Niu's initiative. Messrs Niu and Zheng were both included in the Huhhot and Inner Mongolia spaces. Mr Niu was able to make the concept part of the cognitive element of the Huhhot space, after which Mr Zheng, in particular in his function as the CEO of another dairy company, had to follow suit. Seen from the perspective of general organization theory, this is an important way in which actors who, in terms of classical management theory, possess little authority, can exercise considerable influence. Once you have an initial idea, you need to find ways to attract the interest of a sufficient number of other actors. This requires an instinct for how those other actors make sense of the world in one or more social-cognitive contexts. When such initiatives fail, they usually fail in that the initiator does not select a way to attract attention that suits the sense-making of a crucial context. A good idea is as good as the social-cognitive context that deems it good.

Visionaries are therefore not so much people who are good at putting forward lots of new ideas, but rather people with the ability to create a critical mass for their ideas, or in terms of organizing: people who are able to let their ideas make sense in a number of social-cognitive contexts. Mr Niu Gensheng is such a person. He started Mengniu by launching the idea among his friends and former colleagues, who brought their savings in cash to his one-room office. Mengniu was already generating a turnover while its own production facility was still under construction. The promotion of the Dairy Capital proceeded so rapidly, that Mr Zheng had to hurry to the press, to avoid the impression that he was getting sloppy.

Mengniu and Yili outside Inner Mongolia

The previous sections introduced the background of Mengniu, its main competitor Yili and the way they constructed their competition in their home region. After the introduction of the ways Mengniu makes sense of itself in terms of Yili, I now want to turn to the competition between Mengniu and Yili outside Inner Mongolia to observe how their competition in new markets relates to their competition at home. I have selected Shanyin county of Shanxi province as an example.

Gucheng in Shanyin

The northernmost part of Shanxi is another of China's traditional dairy belts, separated from the Huhhot region by only a mountain ridge. The major city in the region is Datong. Datong itself is best known as a coal mining area, but the counties Huairen, Shanyin and Yingxian, which belong to the Municipality of Shuozhou, are agrarian regions with dairy cattle raising as the key industry. The region used to be geographically quite remote, as it is locked in on the north and east sides by mountain ranges. However, after the completion of the Datong–Beijing expressway in 2000, trucks can bring products from the region to Beijing in a four- to five-hour drive. Before, the same journey could take an entire day.

The region is the base of one of China's top ten dairy companies: the Gucheng Dairy Group. The Group was formed by combining a number of smaller dairy plants in Shanyin county at the end of 1998. These plants included a joint venture between one of the local companies and a Dutch partner. I described the case in Peverelli (2000: 3 and 106–111) and Peverelli (2001). In both publications I concentrated on the relation between the Chinese and the Dutch partners. In this chapter, I will switch my focus to the way Mengniu and Yili (re-)enacted their competition in Shanyin and how the position of a local player like Gucheng was affected by it.

Gucheng used to be the leading dairy processor in its home region. The name Gucheng started as the brand name of the founder of the core company, a local private entrepreneur. He had developed his company starting from scratch as a small dairy plant to a relatively modern company, when he contacted his future Dutch partner with the aid of a Hong Kong trading company. This led to a joint venture contract between the Chinese and Dutch companies, in which the Hong Kong trader also became a party. Compared with the bulk of Sino-foreign joint ventures, this project proceeded quite well, technically as well as financially. The Chinese CEO played a significant role in this success. His successes as an entrepreneur had won him considerable support of the Shanyin authorities and he was even selected as the local representative in the People's Congress, a kind of parliament that convenes twice a year in Beijing to discuss major decisions by the central government.

When the joint venture had been operating for just over a year, the government of Shanyin County decided that the dairy industry in its region was too dispersed over too many small plants. The latter sentence is literally taken from the official announcement of the county government. This is a gross simplification of the organizing processes involved in the formation of Gucheng, but I will not present these details here, as they are less relevant for the subject matter of this chapter. Interested readers can consult Peverelli (2006). The Gucheng Dairy Group started operating as a group company from January 1998.

During a visit to Gucheng in 2001, the CEO of Gucheng stated that he intended to bring order to the local dairy industry by acquiring all dairy companies in the region. However, this plan was never realized. A number of plants were indeed incorporated into Gucheng, but a number of others remained operating independently. Moreover, new companies were established as well. When studying what types of companies were acquired by Gucheng, I noticed that one of the aspects involved was the hierarchy to which a certain company belonged. As introduced in Chapter 2, the Chinese economy is divided into a number of hierarchies, led by a ministry or ministry-like organization in Beijing, with branches in all provinces, autonomous regions and major cities. To what hierarchy a certain enterprise belongs is usually clearly determined by the nature of its products. A paint manufacturer in Anhui province is likely to be operating in the hierarchy of Chemical Industry, headed by the Ministry of Chemical Industry in Beijing, which is represented by the Anhui Department of Chemical Industry. If the paint company is located in a major city, such as Hefei, Anhui's capital, another administrative level will be involved: the Hefei Bureau of Chemical Industry.

These hierarchies are cognitive spaces of their own. The Ministry of Chemical Industry is engaged with the supervision of the production of chemical products, drawing up quality specifications for chemicals, etc. However, its activities go far beyond 'chemicals'. For example, each hierarchy operates its own hotels (Peverelli 2000: 66). When an official of the Ministry of Chemicals has to undertake a business trip to visit a local chemistry organization, he is likely to be put up in a guest house operated by the latter. This type of sector-based hotel facilitates the construction of the sector space. Such hotels and guest houses are important meeting places where actors from the sector meet and interact. They will exchange the latest rumours, discuss directives issued by 'their' ministry, etc. They are crucial places of sense-making. Other such occasions are national and regional conferences, trade fairs, etc.

For some industries, however, the enterprises are dispersed over a number of hierarchies, with the food industry as the most notorious one. Food is basically a matter of Light Industry, but many dairy enterprises are operated by Agriculture. The hierarchy of Commerce is in charge of the distribution of goods (wholesale and retail), not with production. Still, a number of food companies, in particular cereal and dairy processors, belong to the hierarchy of Commerce. The processing of raw milk into dairy products is closely linked to the production of that raw milk. While (raw) milk is produced by farmers and therefore an Agricultural product, its production is surrounded by such a strict system of quality control that the distinction between agricultural and industrial production becomes extremely vague. This could be an explanation why milk producers gradually changed into dairy companies. Close links between dairy farmers and the dairy industry are also common in other parts of the world as well.

Dairy is an important element in the nutritional policy of the Chinese government. The fair distribution of milk powder was emphasized from the early days of the People's Republic. This applied to cereal products as well. A good way to ensure the distribution of products is not to rely entirely on the supply of those products by others. Hence, organizations of Commerce started to be involved in dairy processing as well. Finally, there is a special section of the Agriculture space: State Farms. To develop less favourable regions for agriculture, the Chinese government established large, industry-like, farms in the early 1950s. Some of these farms, in particular in Xinjiang, were set up by army people that stayed on after the opponents of the People's Republic had been defeated. Although State Farms are officially operated by the Ministry of Agriculture, they are organized as a separate hierarchy.

Gucheng fell under the hierarchy of Agriculture, under the Ministry of Agriculture. This ministry had a Department of Agriculture in the provincial government of Shanxi, located in its capital Taiyuan, down to the Bureau of Agriculture of Shanyin County. One of the older dairy processors in the region that seemed to be out of reach of Gucheng was operated in the hierarchy of Commerce, headed by the Ministry of Commerce, with a similar hierarchy of departments and bureaus. It would not have been legally impossible for Gucheng to acquire a company of Commerce, but it would have been highly unlikely according to the established unwritten rules of Chinese practice. Another local company belonged to the hierarchy of State Farms. The battle between hierarchies is often quite fierce. As dairy was already considered a very promising industry at the time that the Gucheng Group was established, the local Commerce organization (Commerce space) would not easily agree to give up its own dairy plant.

In spite of the fact that a number of competitors remained, Gucheng was the undisputed leader of the local dairy industry for a number of years. Gucheng was given the status of 'Dragon Head' (*longtou*) company by the Shanyin government. Being a Dragon Head enterprise means that the company is protected by the local authorities from competitors by giving it priority in the allocation of resources, etc. I will return later to the consequences for Gucheng of being a local Dragon Head.

Early in 2002 the relation between the Dutch and Hong Kong investors chilled, which almost led to a withdrawal of the foreign investment from Gucheng. Although it did not go that far eventually, the foreign identity of Gucheng, one of the pillars of its local authority, had been damaged. On top of that the old CEO was diagnosed with cancer. He retreated from the day-to-day operation of Gucheng, which he handed over to his sons.

It was in the middle of that year that the news broke through that Mengniu was to open a daughter company in neighbouring Huairen County. Mengniu's company, called Yanmen Dairy Co., Ltd, a joint venture with a local company, started producing UHT milk and ice cream before the end of that year. Mengniu's activities seem to have stimulated the local authorities to invest in the local milk production. In January 2003 the Huairen government announced the establishment of a special dairy cattle raising zone. The zone included facilities like milking parlours that could be shared by the local individual farmers (*People's Daily* 2003a).

Mengniu further encroached on Gucheng when it entered into a strategic alliance with Rongrong Dairy in May 2003. Rongrong was also located in Shanyin. It belonged to the hierarchy of State Farms and was the main regional competitor of Gucheng that Gucheng was never able or willing to acquire.

In March 2003 it was announced that Yili and a recently established dairy company in Shanyin, Kangxi Dairy Co., Ltd, had signed a joint venture agreement to set up the Shuozhou Yili Group. The Shuozhou authorities had provided a number of beneficial conditions, like a tax holiday, to make the investment attractive to Yili. Now it was both Yili and Mengniu knocking on Gucheng's front gate. When asked for comments by the local media, Gucheng spokespersons jokingly replied that they were not afraid to 'dance with the wolves'. This is an interesting piece of sense-making, as on one hand it states that Gucheng is not disturbed by the news, but on the other hand acknowledges that Yili is a wolf, a creature attributed a similar image in China as in Europe. Gucheng, however, did protest (private communication) against the 'special incentives' handed out to Yili. While Gucheng had not only never applied for financial support from the government, but even contributed in the form of tax, the outsider Yili was now being attracted with financial bait.

A complicating aspect of Yili's appearance in Shanyin was already indicated by the official name of the joint venture: Shouzhou Yili. Shanyin County is a region under Shuozhou Municipality. This means that sense-making that led to attracting Yili was taking place in Shuozhou. Gucheng has always been the favourite of the Shanyin authorities. Shanyin's official web site mentions Gucheng as the main dairy company (Shanyin Gov. 2005). It is therefore no wonder that another local company, like Kangxi, would try to find allies in an administrative level higher: Shuozhou. The official Shuozhou web site has a page on local dairy products. This page introduces three companies, not including Gucheng (Shuozhou Gov. 2005). This means that the competition between Gucheng and Kangxi is not only a matter of one hierarchy against the other, but also one between different administrative levels. The competition between Gucheng and Kangxi is not the main theme of this chapter. However, we can observe that Yili is using the local competitive situation to gain a foothold in Shanyin.

The most recent development of this ongoing construction of the dairy industry in North Shanxi is a combined decision by Gucheng and the local subsidiaries of Mengniu and Yili to lower the purchasing price of raw milk. This move met with fierce criticism from the dairy farmers, who regarded it as a threat to their subsistence (*Shanxi Evening News* 2005). As this chapter is written, local authorities are still studying whether this decision is illegal. However, from an organizing perspective this event shows that Gucheng has opted for an 'if you can't beat them …' strategy; Mengniu and Yili were too large to beat or to ignore. Seen from the point of view of Mengniu and Yili, Gucheng, as the local Dragon Head, was a party they would have to interact with on a day-to-day basis. This inter-action will automatically lead to the construction of a configuration. This agreement on a common purchasing price for raw milk is a sign that such a configuration has already take shape. A new local dairy industry has been constructed in which Gucheng, Mengniu and Yili are the market leaders.

The recent history of the Shanyin dairy industry can be summarized as follows: the Shanyin government attempted to decrease the number of dairy processors in its region by forming the Gucheng Group. Although never stated so verbatim, the ultimate aim seems to have been to allow Gucheng to incorporate as many local plants as possible. This did not succeed, as the competition between various hierarchies in the Chinese economy proved to be too powerful an obstacle for Shanyin to overrule. Remaining competitors of Gucheng were approached by a number of major national companies, including Mengniu and Yili, which resulted in alliances. In the new competitive environment, Gucheng started interact-ing with the local subsidiaries of Mengniu and Yili, resulting in a configu-ration of 'the top dairy companies of Shanxi'. The construction of this configuration has become noticeable in a tripartite agreement to lower the purchasing price of raw milk in April 2005.

Mengniu and Yili in Shanyin

We now have sufficient information to try to see how Mengniu and Yili are competing in Shanyin.

Mengniu arrived first in 2002, entering into a joint venture with a local company. In its home region, Mengniu was a so-called People-Operated Enterprise (*minying qiye*) (also see Chapter 4) and so was its partner in Huairen County. In this respect similarity in company type may have played an important role in forging the relation. While People-Operated Companies as a category cannot be simply compared with sector hier-archies like Agriculture or Chemical Industry, from an organizing point of view, there is a similarity. In the chapter on Lukang (Chapter 3) I have already pointed out that, in spite of the parlance of liberalization, cutting red tape and freeing enterprises from their mothers-in-law in Chinese poli-tics, companies still need mother-in-law-like organizations. Once People-Operated Companies were allowed, local governments started setting up People-Operated Enterprise Bureaus in charge of that section of the local economy. As mothers-in-law, these Bureaus operated on a more or less similar level as the Bureaus of Agriculture, Commerce, etc., at the same administrative level. As a consequence local People-Operated spaces were constructed. A major difference with the classical sector spaces is that there is not yet a hierarchy all the way up to Beijing. However, if this trend is carried on, we can expect the establishment of a kind of State Administration of People-Operated Enterprises in the near future.

Having arrived at this interpretation of Mengniu's entry into the region, we can observe that Yili entered along a similar line. As a state-owned enterprise operated at the municipal level, Yili sought connections with a government organization with similar connections (Webber and Wang (2003: 10) also report that Yili's contacts with local governments for securing its supply of raw milk is a feature distinguishing it from Mengniu). Although I have not been able to unravel the exact relations of Kangxi in Shuozhou, the name of the resulting joint venture, Shuozhou Yili, indicates that Kangxi was operated at that level. No written law or regulation forbade Yili from approaching the government of Shanyin, but Shuozhou was a more 'natural' administrative level for Yili. I have arranged this analysis in Table 5.1, comparing the administrative levels involved in Shanxi and in Inner Mongolia.

In its home region, Mengniu was located in Linge'er county, outside the Huhhot urban area. In north Shanxi, it started its activities in Huairen county, while Yili, located within the urban region of Huhhot, sought contacts at the Shuozhou level.

Mengniu's second step in this region, its alliance with Rongrong, followed the same pattern. Mengniu directly approached the company. In terms of hierarchy, Rongrong operated in the State Farms space, as such it was not a People-Operated Enterprise, but the alliance was still forged on the local level.

Using sector identity as a resource for a company's regional expansion strategy can be observed elsewhere in the Chinese dairy industry. Another national top company, Wandashan, is a State Farms enterprise in Heilongjiang. It set up its first subsidiary in South China in Guangxi in 2003, in co-operation with the local State Farms Bureau (Redland 2003). Apparently companies from the same sector share so much cognitive matter that it facilitates forging co-operative relations between companies from different regions, but similar sectors.

Table 5.1 The analogy between the competitive environments of Mengniu and Yili in Inner Mongolia and Shanxi

Region	Inner Mongolia	Shanxi
Municipality	Huhhot	Shuozhou
County	Linge'er	Shanyin/Huairen

How the locals were affected

Another way of looking at the competition of Mengniu and Yili in other regions is from the perspective of the local players. The participation of new actors always influences existing organizing processes. The newcomers will input new cognitive matter from their various inclusions. Especially interesting is to study how the arrival of the new actors affects the existing configurations. At the beginning of this section I have briefly described the situation of the dairy industry in Shanyin county at the time of the appearance on the scene of Mengniu and Yili. Here I will revert to two of the players, Gucheng, the local favourite that intended to acquire all local plants and Rongrong, one of the smaller plants that stayed out of reach of Gucheng.

Gucheng

Gucheng has been the favourite of the Shanyin government almost from the day it was established. In the course of the 1990s it became fashionable among local governments to designate one or a small number of enterprises in a key sector in their own region as key enterprises. These were referred as 'Dragon Head enterprises' (*longtou qiye*) using a very traditional Chinese mode of sense-making. Gucheng is regarded as the Dragon Head of the Shanyin dairy industry (this section draws heavily from Xinhuanet 2004b and personal communication from the CEO of Gucheng).

The status of Dragon Dead comes with a package of privileges. Dragon Heads have better access to government subsidies. In times of bad sales, the government may help its Dragon Heads to find new sales channels. They have priority rights on scarce resources, etc. However, this privileged status can also turn into a pitfall, when a Dragon Head enterprise fails to use its privileges to build a basis for a sustainable existence outside the context of government favours.

Yili is a good example of a Dragon Head enterprise (of Huhhot) that has used that position to grow into the number one player in its own industry in China (DAC 2003). Obviously, Yili's location in China's major dairy production region has also contributed to its success, but the fact that Yili was able to grow faster than its local competitors of a similar age should be largely attributed to the protection of the Huhhot government.

This is exactly the point on which Gucheng has failed, or at least has lost opportunities. Gucheng was also located in a major dairy belt and was in fifth position on the list of national dairy companies in 2002. However, this was mainly based on its enormous output of dairy powder, by that time already considered a traditional product, gradually being replaced by pasteurized or UHT milk. A sales person of a dairy company in Beijing (private communication, 2002) described Gucheng as follows: 'mainly a manufacturer of milk powder that is sold in the south to be rehydrated'. This meant that Gucheng was first of all a manufacturer of industrial bulk products and as a result was less known by consumers outside its own province. Yili on the other hand concentrated on consumer products, which made its name known all over China.

When Mengniu and Yili started looking for ways to enter the local dairy industry, both opted for alliances with existing partners rather than constructing green-field plants. However, neither of them knocked on Gucheng's door.

Yili was the first with its joint venture in Shanyin, but initiated this activity through an administrative level above Shanyin. It seems as if it was difficult for an outside Dragon Head to link up with a local one. Shuozhou Yili Dairy (the former Shanyin Kangxi Dairy) is now presented as one of the three dairy companies of Shuozhou (Shuozhou Gov. 2005). Although the sources (written or oral) never mention a conflict between Shuozhou and Shanyin regarding the local dairy industry, the fact that Gucheng is not mentioned as a 'Shuozhou dairy company', while it has the status of dairy Dragon Head enterprise of Shanyin, is a strong indication of a large difference in sense-making of the dairy industry between the authorities of these two administrative levels. Shuozhou used Yili to gain clout in this matter and Yili simultaneously deftly utilized this cognitive conflict to link up with the party that lacked a Dragon Head of its own, Shuozhou. Although Shuozhou Yili is never referred as a Dragon Head enterprise, Yili's status as Dragon Head of Huhhot is carried on to its subsidiary in Shanyin.

Mengniu positions itself as 'a good second after Yili'. In line with that motto, Mengniu could not afford to stay behind after Yili had established itself in Shanyin, threatening not only Gucheng but also Mengniu's earlier plant in Huairen county. Gucheng was a local Dragon Head enterprise and therefore virtually out of reach for Mengniu. Kangxi was taken by Yili, so Mengniu sought a partnership with the largest remaining dairy company in Shanyin: Rongrong.

After Mengniu had become its neighbour as well, Gucheng was in a difficult position. A constant stream of raw milk, already a scarce resource, was more and more difficult to attain. The Shanyin government remained faithful in that it continued to regard Gucheng as the only dairy Dragon Head in the county. It even issued a decree to divide the local milk parlours fairly over the three competitors: 49 for Gucheng, 36 for Yili and 20 for Mengniu. However, this was still not enough for Gucheng (or the others).

Gucheng itself also tightly stuck to its position. Gucheng's CEO stated (private communication) that 'Mengniu's arrival in the region would not alter Gucheng's status as Dragon Head'. In an interview (Xinhuanet 2004b) Rongrong's CEO talked about Gucheng's situation as follows: its position as the favourite of the government had made Gucheng sloppy.

Moreover as an enterprise set up by farmers, Gucheng had more or less attained the highest status it could hope to achieve. Gucheng's old CEO was being replaced by his children which, according to Rongrong's CEO, proved that Gucheng was really nothing more than a traditional Chinese family enterprise.

Opportunity seemed to knock on Gucheng's door when Bright approached the company to explore ways for co-operation. Bright also ranked among China's top dairy producers, but belonged to the category of socialist-style big city dairy corporations that had been transformed into quasi-independent commercial enterprises. Bright started out as the Shanghai Dairy Corporation in the 1950s. Its main task was to ensure that the population of Shanghai, in particular the senior officials and the foreigners, had an uninterrupted supply of basic dairy products. Although weak in terms of raw material, raw milk, Bright has a strong political and economic base in Shanghai. The company had benefited from the almost mythical economic growth of the Yangtze Delta region. By the time Bright visited Gucheng, it had already acquired dairy plants and established milk stations in all major Chinese dairy belts. Moreover, Bright had started to attract foreign investment: Danone owned 5 per cent of its equity (this was recently increased to 7 per cent).

However, the Bright delegation left Shanyin without having reached any agreement at all. According to Gucheng, Bright demanded too much control over the operation in Shanyin. Rongrong's CEO (Xinhuanet 2004b) attributed the wariness of Gucheng of giving up control to its status of Dragon Head enterprise. It allegedly had made a spoilt child of Gucheng that was not used to the big bad world out there.

At the time I am finishing this sub-section, Gucheng still seems to be going strong and remains the dairy Dragon Head of Shanyin county. We can conclude that within the cognitive space of Shanyin, Gucheng can retain its position as long as Shanyin continues to make sense of Gucheng as its dairy Dragon Head enterprise. However, the arrival of Mengniu and Yili, who carried on their relation established earlier in their own home region, Huhhot, brought new social-cognitive contexts to Shanyin in which Gucheng plays a much more humble position. The most crucial aspect determining Gucheng's position seems to be the development of the differences in sense-making of the local dairy industry between the administrative levels of Shuozhou Municipality and Shanyin County. Yili is actively participating in these differences to provide Shuozhou with a Dragon Head enterprise. Mengniu is enacting its good-second-after-Yili identity.

Meanwhile, Gucheng and the local daughters of Mengniu and Yili have also constructed a configuration as the local big three dairy companies. As long as Mengniu and Yili perceive Gucheng as necessary in their local power play, this will be another leg supporting the continuation of Gucheng.

Rongrong

Rongrong Dairy Co., Ltd was established in 1983 as the Shanyin Animal Husbandry Dairy Factory. It derived its name from its main investor, the State Animal Husbandry Group Corp. This corporation was operated under the Ministry of Agriculture, but, like State Farms, formed a sub-hierarchy of its own. All provinces and many smaller administrative regions had companies whose names were formed by adding 'Animal Husbandry Co.' (*mugongshang*) to its geographic name. Other investors were Shanxi province and two smaller regional governments, including Shanyin county (most of the history here is drawn from Rongrong 2005).

There are no sources directly reflecting on the relation between Gucheng and Rongrong within the Shanyin space. However, we can observe that it was Gucheng and not Rongrong that received the designation of dairy Dragon Head enterprise, even though Rongrong was a few years the senior of Gucheng. The personal networks of the respective CEOs must have been a major factor. Gucheng's CEO was elected as People's Representative for the benefit his entrepreneurial activities have brought to his home region. Gucheng was established and developed by Shanyin people in Shanyin. Rongrong represented outside investment to cash in on Shanyin's identity as dairy belt.

Rongrong does not frequently make the news. It has been operating since its establishment without interruption, but its development seemed to be hampered by the favourable treatment of Gucheng. Rongrong was one of the companies that Gucheng never acquired and of which Gucheng's CEO remarked that that was 'another matter' (see above).

Yili's entry to the Shanyin scene through a connection at the Shuozhou level was even more a threat to Rongrong than it was to Gucheng. Now Rongrong had to cope with two Dragon Heads.

Although no sources are available describing the interaction between Mengniu and Rongrong leading to their alliance, it is easy to imagine that Mengniu did not have to try too hard to convince Rongrong of the benefits of such a co-operation. The alliance definitely placed Rongrong in the spotlight. The alliance was well covered in the local and national food industry publications. The entire nation had learned of Rongrong and that its co-operation with Mengniu was shaking one of China's top ten dairy companies, Gucheng. If we compare Rongrong with David and Gucheng with Goliath before the alliance, then we can conclude that the roles had now (seemingly) been turned around. The words of Rongrong's CEO in the press interview, mentioned above, corroborates this view.

In terms of cognitive space, the situation actually seems to be more complex. The sense-making of the dairy industry in Shanyin seems to take place in at least three separate geographic spaces. In the Shanyin space, Gucheng retains its position as Dragon Head. The distribution of milk parlours over Gucheng, Yili Kangxi and Rongrong Mengniu is quite symbolic in this respect: 49:36:20. In the Shuozhou space, Kangxi and Rongrong are positioned as equals, together with a third party, Chuncheng (which does not seem to play a role in the sense-making processes described in this chapter, apart from its being part of this list). Gucheng is not mentioned, which indicates that it does not make sense in the Shuozhou dairy context. Although the reporting on the activities of Mengniu and Yili in Shanyin are worded in terms of the influence their competition has on the operation of the existing local players, the general purport of the reports, articles, discussions, etc., usually point at the national level. Once Mengniu and Yili left their home region to re-enact their competition elsewhere, they became national players on the national dairy scene. In this respect, Mengniu and Yili not only helped to put a small local company on the map of China, but also facilitated the breakthrough of Shanyin as a region that mattered in the Chinese dairy industry.

Mengnu/Yili in Shanyin – conclusions

In the first sections of this chapter I have described how Mengniu has been constructed as a kind of clone of Yili. Part of Yili's DNA in the shape of a group of high level employees, led by Yili's former Vice-President Niu Gensheng. The sense-making of Mengniu was tightly linked to and phrased in terms of Yili. Mengniu was positioned as a follower, a worthy second after Yili. It was not an objective of Mengniu to push Yili out of the market. On the contrary, Mengniu's activities would enlarge the market to such an extent that it would provide Yili with room for growth as well.

From the perspective of ownership type, Yili was a state-owned enterprise. Moreover, the dairy industry was regarded as a pillar of the local industry and the municipal government of Huhhot treated Yili as a key dairy enterprise. Mengniu was a typical People-Operated enterprise, owned by a number of individuals, later joined by some institutional investors. Yili was located in the suburbs of Huhhot, while Mengniu created its head office in Linge'er county outside that city. Mengniu's geographic location followed its perceived relation to Yili, where Yili was the larger, more central, of the two, with Mengniu operating in Yili's vicinity.

Mengniu was the first of the two to set up shop in Shuozhou. This step already re-enacted the identity constructed in its home region. Mengniu settled down in Huairen, an outer county of Shuozhou, far away from the urban centre of Shuozhou.

Yili followed soon, but, apparently likewise re-enacting its central position, initiated its activities in the region via Shuozhou. Yili forged an alliance with Kangxi, a dairy company located in Shanyin, known as the main milk region of north Shanxi.

With Yili settled down in Shanyin, we saw Mengniu following suit only a few months later. Mengniu linked up with another company in Shanyin:

Rongrong. Once more, there is no talk of assistance, etc., from any administrative level.

The local government of Shanyin county has been supporting Gucheng as the key dairy company in the region, honouring it with the designation Dragon Head enterprise. Gucheng ranked among the national top ten dairy companies. As such, we can understand the preference of the Shanyin government. However, while Yili is also often referred to as the Dragon Head enterprise of the Huhhot (even Inner Mongolian) dairy industry, Yili did not succeed in entering into an alliance with Gucheng. It seems that being a Dragon Head stimulates the feeling of staying independent. When you find a company like Yili knocking on your door to seek co-operation, you can expect a serious package of demands. The incentives given to Yili/Kangxi corroborate this. Gucheng was apparently found unwilling to comply for fear of being taken over. This in turn is corroborated by the fact that another of the top ten dairy companies, Bright, had to leave Shanyin without a deal with Gucheng as well.

After this summary I would like to attempt to describe Mengniu and Yili activities in Shanyin in terms of organizing processes from two angles:

1   the local organizing before the advent of the Mongolians and the changes they brought about;
2   the use of identity as strategy by Mengniu and Yili.

Understanding the organizing activities in the dairy industry in north Shanxi can only start by discerning a number of cognitive spaces. Moreover, these spaces were divided over at least two dimensions: administrative level and economic sector. The Municipality of Shuozhou recognized the dairy industry as one of the regional key industries. Within the Shuozhou dairy industry three companies were designated as main enterprises: Chuncheng a People-Operated enterprise, Kangxi (state owned) and Rongrong (Agriculture (Animal Husbandry)). A common trait of these three companies is that they are all located in Shanyin.

However, in the Shanyin dairy space, another company was recognized as the central player: Gucheng. A number of local companies had been combined into a conglomerate on instigation of the Shanyin government, with Gucheng as the core enterprise. The central strategy evoked by Gucheng's CEO and confirmed by Shanyin officials (private communication) was Gucheng would gradually incorporate all local dairy plants.

This reveals a major cognitive conflict between the Shuozhou dairy space and the Shanyin dairy space, in which Shuozhou seems to favour the maintenance of a certain level of variety, while Shanyin strives for unification. This type of conflicting sense-making, heterogenizing versus homogenizing, has been described by van Dijk (1989: 79–80) and A. van Dongen (1997: 156–169). One perception is that too little variety is detrimental to creativity, while the opposite one is that too much variety is distracting and that scarce resources (in this case raw milk) can be used most efficiently when placed into the hands of one player. Social Integration theory is wary of designating one perception as better or more correct than another. However, there is an ethical constraint that warns against blocking social interaction. If the Shanyin government had attempted to force all dairy plants within its region to join the Gucheng Group, it would have violated the ethical restraint. However, while promoting such a development, the Shanyin authorities left it to the parties involved to negotiate whether or not to become part of Gucheng. This does not violate the ethical restraint.

The recent action by Gucheng, Mengniu and Yili to lower the purchasing price of raw milk jointly is yet another indication that the conflict between heterogenizing and homogenizing is an important aspect of the local sense-making. After the arrival of Mengniu and Yili in Shanyin had intensified the heterogenizing trend, the local subsidiaries of the two, in interaction with the local leader Gucheng, formed a configuration resulting in a homogenizing decision to fix the price of raw milk, the single most important scare resource.

Outside north Shanxi, Gucheng was recognized as one of China's top ten dairy companies. This sense-making took place in a more formal fashion, by comparing key figures like turnover, production volume, profit per employee, etc. A link between the Shanyin space and the national space was Shanyin's CEO who was the local delegate in the People's Congress. This position was given to him by the Shanyin government as a reward for his contribution to local development, but once in position, the CEO could use his access to delegates from all over China to gain political clout in his home region. Shanyin made the CEO an important man by selecting him as their delegate and consequently he became an important man because of his new social networks, which reinforced the conviction that he was the right choice for Shanyin's delegate.

This was the situation Mengniu and Yili found at the time of their entry into the local market. As a 'marginal' player in the literal sense of the word, Mengniu instinctively linked up with a local marginal partner and geographically in the margin of the Shuozhou municipal region. Mengniu's local subsidiary may have lived long and happily ever after, if Yili had not ventured into the region as well. Yili's point of entry, Shuozhou municipality was equally 'natural' in the sense that Yili simply continued to enact its position as a state-owned enterprise, the number one in its home region, situated in the central urban area of that home region. Yili's local partner was one of the three key enterprises recognized in the Shuozhou dairy space. Although it cannot be said to be located in the suburbs of Shuozhou, its location in Shanyin was closer to the Shuozhou urban region than Mengniu's plant in Huairen County.

This situation could again have continued for a long time. However, Mengniu apparently from its self-perception role as active second player, found it necessary to follow Yili a little closer and sought another ally in the region, Rongrong. Rongrong was also one of the three key dairy companies in the Shuozhou dairy space and also located in Shanyin. From a sector point of view, Rongrong belonged to a sector that was perceived as more rural that Kangxi, which had a more industrial image.

The intriguing question now is: did Mengniu and Yili make deft use of the local competitive situation, by seeking partnerships with companies that needed such partnerships to cope with the political clout of Gucheng? Or, did Kangxi and Rongrong skillfully exploit the competitive relation between Mengniu and Yili? The answer from the organizing perspective is: both. Organizational actors, like individual actors, do not act in a social vacuum, but interact with other actors. Mengniu's first partner selection was affected by its relation with Yili. In other words: although at that moment Yili was not yet physically active in the region, it already played a role cognitively. If Mengniu had started out in north Shanxi in Shuozhou, it would have violated its identity as a good follower. Instead, Mengniu started in Huairen, even further away from Shuozhou than Shanyin, which was recognized as the centre of milk production in that region. At that particular moment, Huairen had just decided to develop its own dairy industry, knowing that it had to compete with 'sister' counties like Shanyin. In a way, Huairen County was taking on a role as market expander, like Mengniu in the Huhhot region. Starting interactions with a number of parties in north Shanxi, Mengniu was likely to have the most efficient interaction with Huairen. With 'efficient' I mean to say that the interaction between Mengniu and the Huairen County government would more quickly lead to the construction of a sensible environment (Weick 1995: 30–38) than with any other party in that area. Mengniu was still re-enacting its role identity as 'market expander rather than predator of other companies' resources', which matched Huairen's ongoing identity construction with its neighbouring counties as new dairy region in north Shanxi.

I will pick up the most salient aspect as an example. A consequence of Huairen's decision to position itself as a dairy county was that it would start a competitive relation with other dairy counties like Shanyin, as well as with Shuozou Municipality, which had an identity of the centre of dairy production in north Shanxi. Mengniu had constructed an identity of non-state dairy player that competed with the state-owned sector by creating its own market space, rather than engaging in direct competition by fighting over the same resources. When Mengniu entered into north Shanxi, Huairen County was the party that could benefit most from Mengniu's experience.

Finally, the cognitive conflict between the sense-making processes in the Shuozhou and Shanyin dairy spaces has been intensified by Mengniu and Yili's activities in the region, but does not seem to have changed fundamentally, at least not by the time this chapter was written (early 2005). Gucheng is still the Dragon Head of the dairy industry in the Shanyin space. This is not contested by Kangxi/Yili, Rongrong/Mengniu or any other party. That status is constructed, and continues to make sense, in the Shanyin space.

6 Yanjing
The Emperor's messenger

Group companies

At the core of this chapter is a so-called group company or *jituan gongsi*, in Chinese. This relatively new type of enterprise in China was briefly introduced in Chapter 2. From the point of view of its legal status, the group is not a legal person. It is a conglomerate of companies with one enterprise, usually a larger, more successful, one as the core enterprise (*hexin qiye*). A number of other companies of horizontally or vertically related industries, often from different parts of China, can form a group around such a core enterprise. The other companies remain officially independent legal persons, but voluntarily give the core company the authority to interfere in their management. The core company will receive a management fee from the other group members.

The emergence of group companies in China is an extremely complex matter. Keister (2000: 50–51), while also recognizing that it was caused by a variety of circumstances, seems to regard the establishment of group companies above all as a means to retain a certain level of centralized management of enterprises after the break up of the command economy. She is almost describing enterprise groups as a separate administrative layer (op. cit., p. 61), operating under the sector ministries. I believe that this explanation is too simple, in the sense that it only describes the establishment of group companies as a means to put some order into the chaos that was the multitude of similar companies and fails to go into the reasons for this multitude. Incorporating the background of the vast number of similar companies in China will increase our insight into the nature of Chinese group companies.

Another criticism of Keister's treatment of Chinese group companies is that, although she herself stresses the administrative function of those groups, she fails to see the role that at least a number of these groups seem to have in the way the central government attempts to stay in control of what is happening in China outside the direct influence of Beijing. I believe that this other 'administrative' function emerged after the concept of group companies was launched.

Before explaining my latter remark, I would like to return to the mechanisms in the Chinese economy that have led to the multitude of (seemingly) similar enterprises in China. I have described this situation briefly in Chapter 2, when introducing the group company as a new type of enterprise emerging in the period of economic reforms. I will pick up that description here with considerably more details and illustrated with practical examples.

The first mechanism is Chinese federalism. The Chinese, in particular the successive Chinese governments, are keen on stressing the integrity of the nation's territory. Separatism, even when only expressed by words, is a bigger crime in China than robbing a bank. However, it has proved hard to impossible to rule such a vast territory as one integral state. After the official unification of China by the Qin dynasty, in the second century BC, China has known long periods of unification, interspersed with a number of periods in which the territory was divided into separate states.

Like nations in other parts of the world, Chinese governments had to divide the country into a number of smaller, more easily managed, administrative regions. The types and number of such regions have been subject to frequent changes, but in the current system, China is divided into 31 main geographic regions, consisting of provinces, autonomous regions (like Inner Mongolia, the home region of Mengniu, the core case of the previous chapter) and four independent municipal areas (Beijing, Tianjin, Shanghai and Chongqing). However, these main geographic regions act as if they were semi-independent states in a way comparable with that of the USA. Just as people from California tend to present themselves first as Californians and only then as Americans, Chinese from Liaoning province will tend to introduce themselves first as people from Liaoning, or perhaps from the Northeast, a multi-province region that also has a strong regional identity. The Chinese are proud of their regional identities, even of the stereotypical shortcomings (see Wu 2003 for a comprehensive Chinese compilation of such regional stereotypes and Wong and Stone 1998 for a similar collation of foreign perceptions of local cultural differences). One of the most frequently stated traits of people from the Northeast is their gullibility in business. While this may be perceived as a rather negative trait by Europeans, northeasterners can often be heard saying that they are 'too *laoshi* (honest, trusting)' and therefore an easy prey for tricksters. When interpreting this kind of statement of self-description, one should realize that the 'tricksters' referred to are the ones from other regions than the speaker's.

One consequence of this strong self-perception of the Chinese administrative regions is that each of them would prefer to produce virtually everything within their own region. For some products this is physically impossible, because the climate is unsuitable, no raw materials are available, etc. However this inclination for regional independence is so strong that some provinces are willing to support importing raw materials from far away regions to establish at least one manufacturer of a certain product in the home region. Guangdong does not really have the climate for sheep raising and one would therefore not expect a well-developed wool processing industry in that province. Indeed there is not, but woollen clothing is produced in Guangdong. The raw material has to be 'imported' from Inner Mongolia. Although no provincial government would dare to mention it, let alone do so, many Chinese provinces could venture to declare themselves independent states.

This strong us-and-them tendency in Chinese regional identities plays a significant role in the case history of this chapter. The example enterprise in this chapter is China's top brewing group, Yanjing. Yangjing's corporate head office is based in Beijing. However, the name 'Beijing' has at least two different meanings as a symbol: the geographic place and the location of the central government. Whenever Yanjing entered a new region, it had to cope with the perception that an entity from Beijing = central government was encroaching on the local autonomy.

The second mechanism is that of copying what others (are perceived to) do well. Imitating is an inherent part of Far Eastern culture in general and of Chinese in particular. This applies to individuals, organizations and regions. When a company is reported to be successful by producing and marketing a certain product, it is only a matter of time before more companies in its vicinity will start manufacturing the same product. Sometimes even special enterprises are established for this purpose, only producing that specific product. This explains why so many Chinese companies have the name of a specific product as part of their corporate name. For example, glucose is a sweetener produced from starch. In most parts of the world a company that produces glucose will also manufacture a number of other syrups produced from starch using similar processes. While such companies also exist in China, a considerable number of 'glucose factories' are still in operation all over the country. At some point in time, a party, in most cases a local government, had learned that it was possible to make money with glucose and therefore set up a dedicated plant for that single product. These plants are usually rather small, with basic equipment and employees who are only familiar with that particular process. They are often more like workshops than real factories. Their production processes are usually inefficient and wasteful. However, as a considerable part of these 'factories' are Town and Village Enterprises, they are regarded as a means to create employment for the surplus labour in the Chinese countryside (Wong *et al.* 1995 is still the best source for understanding these aspects of Town and Village Enterprises). This causes a conflict between identities. On one hand these factories, as work units, are the source of livelihood for the families of the employees. Without these units, they would be part of the rural surplus labour and thus a burden to society. This burden is both economic (who is responsible for feeding and clothing them) and political (long-term unemployment can be a cause of political unrest). On the other hand, these inefficient factories are an economic burden as well, as they waste raw materials, energy, etc. (Clissold 2004: 286).

This propensity for copying is emerging in this study as a major aspect of competition Chinese style. In Chapter 4 we observed that Shanmeng was imitating each major strategic decision by Huahuaniu. In Chapter 5 the competition between Mengniu and Yili was more complex, as they seemed to be continuously copying one another. Chapter 7, the final case chapter in this study will present yet another example, in which two subsidiaries of the same business group (a European and a Chinese one) are co-operating, but while the Europeans are developing the project on the basis of their own proven business formula, their Chinese colleagues, following their cultural propensity, are imitating the main local competitor. This leads to a most peculiar type of co-operation.

The third mechanism is a preference for small scale in Chinese culture. Traditional Chinese culture advocates harmony. One of the main causes of strife among people is inequality. If some people are much richer than others, it will create envy. Chinese politics through the ages has been affected by this. The rich were expected to share their riches with their community, either through taxes or through charity, like funding a local school. In more modern times, this practice is continued towards larger enterprises. Such a company is often regarded as a money machine and is regularly 'requested' to give financial support to various projects in their local community. Consequently, it was better to hide or disperse some of your riches, to avoid being called upon for money too often.

One way to cover up some of the apparent wealth within a company is to establish another company as a means of expansion, instead of rebuilding the existing facilities (Tang and Ward 2003: 135). A large company in a city can, for example, set up a smaller subsidiary in a suburban town, or smaller town in its home province, producing the same, or a similar, product. Although they are established and registered as separate legal persons, from an organizing point of view, the two plants can be regarded as one company. Seen from the angle of the topic of this chapter, we could also conclude that such companies, sometimes with active help of their mother-in-law, are gradually developing into a group company.

The fourth mechanism is more practical: tax. Chinese enterprises can be divided into different groups according to ownership and the tax regime for each type of ownership is different. State-owned enterprises pay 55 per cent income tax, while collective enterprises only pay 20 per cent. The other types pay about 30–35 per cent. This is almost an invitation for state-owned enterprises to set up new small companies somewhere else, disguised as collective enterprises run by the local government. In some locations we can see a state-owned enterprise and a foreign-funded enterprise engaged in exactly the same type of business (industrial indices are a good source for this type of information). In that case the latter has probably been set up in co-operation with the state-owned enterprise. It would then be advantageous to allocate the major part of the income to the joint venture, as that income will be taxed at a considerably lower rate. It will be interesting to see how recent changes in the Chinese taxation system will affect this practice.

The fifth mechanism is the division of the Chinese economy into industrial sectors. From the establishment of the People's Republic of China, the production of goods and services has been divided into a number of sectors like: Light Industry, Education, Agricultural, Metallurgy, Aviation, etc. These sectors are headed by central ministries or organizations on the same level as a ministry, located in Beijing. However, the link between one particular product and a certain hierarchical sector was never strictly implemented in practice. As the core company of this chapter is a brewery, the food and beverage industry is a good example. Food is primarily a matter of Light Industry, but some food manufacturers operate in the hierarchies of Agriculture and Internal Trade. Large farms (= Agriculture) can set up factories for the processing of primary agricultural produce, which then automatically are part of the Agriculture hierarchy. A dairy farm raises dairy cattle to produce raw milk. This milk can be supplied to a dairy factory as a single source of income. However, the farm can decide to establish a processing plant of its own. It can then typically produce milk powder, yoghurt, ice cream, etc. This is a multitude of products with a higher added value. As such a dairy plant will belong to the farm, its economic activity will be controlled by the local organization of Agriculture.

Another hierarchy with considerable activity in the food industry is Internal Trade, currently merged into the Ministry of Trade. A typical food sector with strong links to Internal Trade is cereal processing. The distribution of cereal products, unprocessed like wheat or processed like flour, used to be regulated using a coupon system in the first three decades of the People's Republic. Grinding wheat into flour is only a physical treatment of the raw wheat. The distribution of flour was therefore part of the same coupon system as raw cereals such as rice. As the distribution of the raw wheat and the processed product flour were both activities belonging to Internal Trade, cereal processing, also including products like noodles, steamed bread, etc., also became the business of this sector. Even after the abolition of the coupon system in the early years of the economic reforms, a large number of cereal processing companies (including animal feed) remained linked to the Internal Trade organization of their local government. In the previous chapter I have introduced Shanyin county in Shanxi province, in which the local dairy enterprises were divided into three sectors: Light Industry, Internal Trade and Agriculture. The forced establishment of a dairy group was an efficient means to bring those companies together into one conglomerate, while retaining a certain level of independence. The case in Chapter 4 also showed that the county government was unable to unite all hierarchies. The strife between local Chinese governments and the local representatives of the sector hierarchies is an ongoing battle between homogenizing and heterogenizing tendencies.

We can now combine these five mechanisms that create a multitude of similar enterprises in China and look how the formation of group companies could offer solutions to deal with the negative aspects, while retaining the positive side of each mechanism.

Federalism

The political strife between Chinese regions creates a need for each individual region to become as economically independent as possible. This poses a threat to the central government that is constantly battling to retain the territorial integrity of the State.

The development of group companies with subsidiaries in different administrative regions of the country can offer channels to take away small amounts of economic power from the control of the regional authorities. Once a dairy company in Hangzhou, the capital of Zhejiang, becomes a subsidiary of a dairy group whose core company is based in Chongqing, the original mother-in-law of that company loses its grip on the day-to-day operation of the enterprise. That mother-in-law will therefore in principle not be inclined to agree to handing over its power, unless for very good reasons.

Copying

The quickest way to wealth is to copy the way others gained wealth before you. This belief is present, more or less prominently, in all cultures, but is a salient feature of Chinese culture. Copying well, however, is usually not as easy as it may seem. Moreover, it leads to inefficient use of scarce resources. On the other hand, in China it also helps relieve rural unemployment.

Local, less efficient, enterprises can be incorporated into a group company. The group can then transfer production and management knowledge and make the plant operate more efficiently, while retaining the valuable employment. This is a typical reason why a local mother-in-law could be persuaded to give up its control of the plant. If the inefficient enterprise were to go bankrupt, the mother-in-law would face the burden of having to take care of the unemployed workers. This threat may outweigh the loss of some political and economic power.

Small is beautiful

This mechanism itself is actually constructive of group companies. A larger company can establish subsidiaries elsewhere in its home region, thus forming a group company. Sometimes, the mother-in-law of the company is actively involved. A state-owned chemical plant operating under the Bureau of Chemical Industry of its home province is in need of expansion. The Bureau can then decide to set up a subsidiary in another part of the province. This can be for a variety of reasons. The subsidiary can be located near a source of raw material. It can also be constructed in a place with a high ratio of unemployed people, to create job opportunities.

Tax

It can be advantageous for large state-owned enterprises to transfer parts of their profits to subsidiaries to which other tax regimes apply. Authorities can bring some of those subsidiaries back to a higher tax regime by incorporating them into group companies. The members of groups will retain their status of independent legal person, but their financial situation will be part of the consolidated accounts of the mother company and will thus be more transparent.

Sectorized economy

The Chinese economy is divided into a number of sectors. However, as a result of historic developments, the production of particular products and services in a region can be dispersed over a number of sector hierarchies. This can add political complications to economic competition. Establishing group companies to combine such companies offers an efficient way to neutralize such potential political struggles.

In most cases, the establishment of a particular group company involved more than one of the above aspects. This explanation of the multiple potential functions of group companies seems to have much more explanatory power than Keister's singular explanation. Keister's model is mainly administrative, while my model combines economic, political and cultural aspects.

Group companies also differ in respect of the voluntary nature of their establishment. Some groups have been established owing to a rational decision by the core company and an initial number of small members. However, usually the local government of the core company plays a certain role. This role can vary from suggesting, to a bureaucratic decision that cannot be refused.

The case of Chapter 3 on the Lukang Group has shown that the independence of group members is very relative indeed. Lingzhi was added to Lukang by a single stroke of the pen. Quite often group companies are formed by local governments to protect a major local brand. A good example, suiting the case company of this chapter, was the decision by the Beijing municipal government to support only a few local beer brands at the end of the 1990s. Smaller breweries were ordered to join one of the protected groups, at that time in particular the Five Star brewery (see below). For example, the Three Ring Brewery in Beijing's Huairou District was instructed to produce Five Star beer, against the will of Three Ring's management (private communication). Three Ring was operated by the Huairou government and had just successfully developed a new type of beer, the first dry (lite) beer produced in Beijing. However, protests were futile and the Three Ring plant had to switch to produce Five Star beer. Soon afterwards, it was virtually incorporated into the Five Star Group (Clissold 2004: 261). The case story of this chapter will demonstrate that this move failed, when the Beijing government apparently switched to another protégé among the region's breweries.

Another example of government-instigated group formation was seen in the previous chapter, when the government of Shanyin County ordered that a number of dairy enterprises in its region would be joined into a conglomerate. Refusal was not an option.

Core companies are often state-owned enterprises, while many of the other members are collective ones. Group members are often divided into close members, semi-loose members and loose members, according to the degree of involvement of the core company in their management (Keister 2000: 81 ff.). They often continue to produce their own products under their own brand name. In other cases, member enterprises produce the core company's product under the core company's brand name as well as their own product.

In the light of the main theme of this study, the construction of Chinese corporate identity, the emphasis of this chapter will be the group's corporate identity rather than its structure. I will demonstrate how the expansion of the structure (i.e. the addition of new members) affected the identity construction of the group.

The selected company is the Beijing-based Yanjing Brewing Group, currently China's number one brewery.

Yanjing: more Beijing than Beijing

Yanjing, literally meaning 'the capital of (the state of) Yan', is derived from Yan, the name of an ancient kingdom located just south of present-day Beijing. Before the unification of China in the Qin dynasty, China was divided into a number of small states with a king, duke or other feudal nobleman as its leader. As these states were in a constant state of war with one another, this period is generally referred to as the Warring States Period in Chinese history. These states were conquered by the state of Qin one after another, until the first period of unification of China started with the Qin dynasty in 221 BC. The state of Yan saw a very short revival around 350, during one of the periods of dispersion of power in Chinese history (Fairbank *et al.* 1973: 94). This indicates that the concept of 'Yan' continued to make sense almost six centuries after it ceased to exist as an independent state.

The influence of these states on the construction of local cultures has been so strong that many of their names are still used today as an indication of the origin of a company or government organization. In Chapter 3 we saw that the name of an ancient local state, Lu, is now often used to indicate that an enterprise is located in Shandong. The actual state of Lu was smaller than present-day Shandong, but this convention is now completely institutionalized. The occurrence of the character Lu in a company name, or on the number plate of a car, immediately betrays that the company (or car) originates from Shandong.

It was also the age of the great philosophers. People like Confucius, a native son of Lu, were advisors of the rulers of the various states. They often travelled from one state to another to offer their advice to the local ruler.

Yan is not used as frequently as other literary names like Lu. Number plates of Beijing cars carry the character Jing (literally: 'capital'). In modern usage, Yan is often combined with the name of another ancient state: Yan's southern neighbour state of Zhao. The compound Yanzhao seems to refer to Hebei province, in particular Hebei's capital Shijiazhuang. A local newspaper, for example, is called *Yanzhao City News* (*Yanzhao Dushibao*, www.yzdsb.com.cn). Zhao by itself would already have sufficed to refer to the Shijiazhuang region, which is part of what used to be called Zhao. Apparently, linking up with Yan, as a symbol of the national capital, adds symbolic power to Zhao. It adds a Beijing identity to Shijiazhuang.

The combination Yanjing seems to be used as an alternative for 'Beijing' in cases where a similar designation with 'Beijing' is already used for another organization. The Yanjing Hotel is located in the western part of Beijing. This hotel was originally named Fuxing Hotel, derived from nearby Fuxing Gate. However, story has it that this name often caused foreign guests to giggle, because they pronounced the 'x' in the English way, making the name sound like 'fucking'. At that time, the hotel was considered a show case of the municipal government, demonstrating that the Chinese were able to construct and run a modern hotel. However, the name Beijing Hotel was already used for the famous hotel along Chang'an Avenue, reserved for special state guests. Actually, in terms of identity, the Fuxing Hotel was meant to be the municipal counterpart of the State's Beijing Hotel. The government then coined the name Yanjing Hotel.

The case history (see below for the details) will show that the suggestion to change the brand name of the new brewery into Yanjing Beer was made under similar circumstances. Beijing Beer was already used as a brand name by the Beijing Brewery, which was located in Beijing and carried the word 'Beijing' in its name, but was tightly connected to the

State, rather than Beijing Municipality. Yanjing Beer then offered an ideal alternative for 'Beijing Beer'.

A highly interesting consequence of this play with the words Beijing and Yanjing is that Yanjing was actually more closely connected with Beijing municipality than the name Beijing. This is corroborated by a number of other institutions with the name Beijing that are more connected with the nation as a whole than the city. Beijing Opera is China's national opera. A number of years ago the 'Beijing Opera Troupe of Shanghai' made a tour through a number of European countries. Beijing University is one of China's top universities. It was originally located in the centre of the city. In the northwestern suburb of Beijing, there was Yanjing University, a local university founded by foreigners. In 1952 Beijing University was moved to the location of Yanjing University and the latter ceased to exist. So now there is Beijing University located in the space of Yanjing University.

A concise history of Yanjing

Yanjing is a company very conscious of its history. The corporate web site includes a number of pages in which the development of the company is tracked on a year-to-year basis. Yanjing's in house 'historians' have divided the young company's history into three periods. There is a separate web page for each period. On top of that, there is a special site for 'major events'. In this section I will follow Yanjing's own periodization, as it is reflective of the corporate self-perception. As is the case with all case histories in this study, I have supplemented this with information from a large corpus of narratives on Yanjing.

Period 1, 1980 to 1988: 100 000 hectolitres/year (hl/year)

For each period, the average increase of the beer output is indicated as the first parameter of a period. Yanjing evidently strongly anchors its self-perception in its core business: brewing.

Yanjing's story starts by stating that it was originally established to relieve the beer shortage in Beijing. At the eve of the economic reforms, beer was still regarded as a luxury good in China. The Chinese drank the traditional distilled liquor, called white spirit (*baijiu*) in Chinese, with their meals. Wine was hardly produced and most Chinese wine was very sweet, which made it less suitable to accompany meals. Beer was produced and served in hotels and restaurants, but in insufficient quantities to serve the total populace.

A typical sight in Beijing (and elsewhere in China) was people lining up to buy a few bottles, or even just a pitcher, of beer to treat special dinner guests. Yanjing's historians take this picture of people lining up for beer as the environment in which Yanjing was conceived.

Sometimes, what is left unsaid is just as significant as what is mentioned. The statement that Yanjing was established as a relief to the beer shortage in Beijing gives the company a strong Beijing identity. Yanjing is located in Shunyi County of Beijing and was initially registered as the Shunyi Brewery. However, the county identity is mentioned second in this account. The Beijing identity was stronger than the Shunyi identity.

Yanjing is positioned as the result of the combined effort of a number of parties. The historic account lists several of them:

- Shunyi County Government: co-investor;
- Shunyi County CPC: co-investor;
- Shunyi County Industry Bureau: co-investor; (multiple inclusion: the Chief of the latter two organizations was the same person);
- Beijing Municipal Government: approval;
- State Planning Committee: approval;
- Ministry of Light Industry: Vice-Minister He Zhihua suggested the change of the brand name from Shunyi Beer to Yanjing Beer in August 1981; probably the basis for the decision to change the company name from Beijing Shunyi Brewery to Beijing Yanjing Brewery on 13 March 1984;
- State Council: praise by Vice-Premier Wan Li in RMRB after visit to Yanjing on 19 May 1982; visit by other Vice-Premier Chen Muhua on 12 April 1986.

This is an impressive list of organizations and individual actors. A vice-minister is the one who suggests the change in brand name from Shunyi Beer to Beijing Beer. The physical plant was located in Shunyi, but the perceived enterprise had a Beijing identity. This ministerial support and the further attention bestowed on Yanjing by two vice-premiers even constructs a national identity, not only Beijing = Beijing (the city), but also Beijing = central government.

Once more, we need to pay attention to what is left unsaid as well. Mentioning a shortage of beer in the Beijing region should make us wonder how the existing breweries in the region were handling this problem. Beijing was the home region of two large national breweries: Beijing Brewery and Five Star Brewery. By stating that a new brewery had to be established to cope with the shortage of beer is also a statement that the existing breweries were deemed unable to alleviate the shortage. From a Western economic point of view, it would have made better business sense to expand the existing breweries, which were state-owned enterprises. We cannot ignore this aspect and need to have a closer look at the identity constructs of Five Star and Beijing Brewery relevant to the newcomer Yanjing.

Five Star, Beijing and Yanjing can be regarded as representatives of three major periods in recent Chinese history. All three seem to have been established around the initial years of a new period:

- *Five Star*: established at end of imperial China; a symbol of national pride;
- *Beijing*: established in the beginning of the 1950s; a symbol of the new China;
- *Yanjing*: established in the early 1980s; a symbol of the economic reforms.

It looks as if the coming of a new era needs to be celebrated by the establishment of a new brewery. A mere expansion of an existing brewery would not have sufficient symbolic power.

Moreover, if we compare the success story of Yanjing that will unfold in the course of this chapter with the ordeals that were waiting for Five Star and Beijing Breweries that would erase their names from the list of top Chinese breweries before the turn of the century, it is almost as if a supernatural power had taken away its blessing from the older two and given it to the newcomer. Five Star ended up being sold to an American investor. However, the investor was unable to manage the brewery and finally had to sell it to another old Chinese brewery: Qingdao (Clissold 2004: 251 ff.). Beijing Brewery was sold to an Indonesian investor of Chinese descent, who had acquired a number of Chinese companies in a selected number of markets, including the brewing industry. The Indonesian had used patriotic parlance to gain relatively easy access to these companies, as the local governments hoped that he would be able to revive these fledgling state-owned enterprises. Instead, however, the investor tried to make a quick buck by bringing his Chinese investment company to the stock exchange abroad, while doing nothing whatsoever to improve the performance of the member companies (Liu *et al.* 1997: 325–333). He then sold them one by one to other foreign investors. The breweries were acquired by Asahi and Beijing Brewery is now a Japanese brewery. At the end of the day, both Five Star and Beijing are still breweries and apparently reasonably well managed by their respective mother companies, but they are no longer independent companies and have been completely stripped of their old symbolic identities.

Back to the history of Yanjing, our new brewery was still only a concept, without even a physical location of its own. Instead of building a greenfield plant, the Shunyi government decided to build their brewery on the premises of an abandoned brick factory. Production started early 1981 and Yanjing developed gradually without too many turbulent events.

Yanjing's historiography specifically mentions that a number of state-level organizations doubted that the project would be a success. The rationale for this doubt was that a county government was deemed unable to establish and operate a state-owned brewing enterprise successfully. The people behind Yanjing were extremely proud that they could invalidate this perception.

Period 2, 1989 to 1993: 500 000 hl/year

By 1988 Yanjing had already attained a market share of 30 per cent of the Beijing market. This is the first time Yanjing's historians mention their two local rivals. In their own words, Yanjing now formed 'one of the three legs of the Beijing beer market with the Five Star and Beijing Breweries'. The graphic Chinese expression is that Yanjing, Beijing and Five Star were standing like a *Ding*, an ancient Chinese three-legged cooking vessel. The *Ding* was used in ancient religious sacrifices and was a symbol of imperial power. This is strongly symbolic language indicating that Yanjing was already in that early stage of its existence functioning as a pillar of the government, on an equal footing with Five Star and Beijing.

Some people in the Beijing government were sceptical about the expansion of the local brewing industry. They estimated the then Beijing market at a maximum of 200 000 hl p.a., which was less than the combined capacity of the region's three main breweries. Yanjing's management calculated it in a different way. They took into account that the per capita consumption of beer would increase considerably and therefore estimated the total local market at 500 000 hl, more than double the official estimate.

Moreover, Yanjing did not intend to restrict its sales activities to the Beijing region. The company had already laid out a rough expansion scheme:

Beijing > Tianjin > Hebei > China > the world

The port city of Tianjin, like Beijing, is a municipality with provincial status, or in Chinese terms: a directly governed city (*zhixiashi*). The regions of Beijing and Tianjin municipality are almost adjacent and the two can be regarded as twin cities. Apparently the Yanjing strategists believed that the experience accumulated in Beijing would be easily employed in Tianjin, a city so similar to their own. This strategy formulation shows similarities to the concept of Yanzhao mentioned earlier in this chapter. Beijing and Tianjin are both located in the region of Yan. Yanjing's strategy could then be paraphrased as:

Yan > Zhao > China > the world, or Yanzhao > China > the world

Hebei is the province surrounding the regions of Beijing and Tianjin. In fact, from an economic point of view, Beijing and Tianjin are cities located in Hebei, though directly controlled by the national government. Linguistically, geographically, culturally, etc., it is one region (Yanzhao).

It is interesting to observe the Hebei stage in the perceived development is immediately followed by 'China'. The Yanjing management did at that time not divide China into regions like Northwest, Central, East Coast, etc. Many Chinese companies with the intent to expand their business to the entire nation used such a division and planned to attack them one by one. Yanjing's development plan placed itself in an imagined central position and perceived its expansion as progressing like the ripples caused by a stone thrown into water. This self-perception, projected on a world map, resembles the self-perception of the Chinese nation. Any Chinese world map will place China in the central position (China – *Zhongguo* – the Middle Kingdom), with Europe and America at, respectively, the far left and the far right. This self-perception fits in with the symbolism expressed by the *Ding* vessel, used in ancient state rituals. Although not stated so verbatim, Yanjing's historiography places it in the centre of the world, it is not the Middle Kingdom, but the Middle Enterprise.

Yanjing rapidly climbed to the ranks of the top Chinese breweries in this period. Table 6.1 shows Yanjing's upward march to the number one Chinese brewery.

By 1995, Yanjing had a 70 per cent share in Beijing. Here, Yanjing's historians once more use the *Ding* metaphor, by stating that Yanjing at that moment formed one of the three legs of the national beer market with Qingdao and Zhujiang. Qingdao vied with Five Star to be China's oldest brewery. It was established by Germans in Shandong province in the beginning of the twentieth century. Until recently, Qingdao was the only Chinese brewery with some reputation outside China (better known with the old spelling Tsingtao). Zhujiang was established a few years after Yanjing in Guangzhou, the capital of Guangdong province. Zhujiang included investment from Stella Artois. Following my analysis of the use of the term *Ding* above, Yanjing now perceived itself as a pillar of the state, on an equal footing with Qingdao and Zhujiang.

Another feat of Yanjing achieved in this period was raising the percentage of its output so that it was allowed to sell directly to customers. In the old command economy, state-owned enterprises had to sell 90 per cent of their output through state-regulated sales channels, controlled by the Ministry of Commerce (or more in the terminology of those days: Ministry of Internal Trade; this ministry was merged with the Ministry of Foreign Trade and Economic Cooperation recently into one large Ministry of Commerce). Yanjing's management wanted more freedom in this respect

Table 6.1   Yanjing's way to the top

Year	Rank
1991	10
1992	5
1993	3
1994	2
1995	1

and started a campaign among its mothers-in-law towards that end in mid-1989. The request was granted and Yanjing received a licence to sell 50 per cent of its output itself. The Yanjing historiography does not provide details as to what channels were used and how the relevant officials have been persuaded. One of the more likely reasons could be that Yanjing had a strong rural character. Even though it was not a so-called Town and Village Enterprise, it was located in a rural region. A city like Beijing consists of a number of districts (*qu*) and counties (*xian*). The difference between the two is that districts are regarded as urban and counties as rural. People living in a district are urban residents, while those of counties are not. A Chinese citizen with a rural ID cannot easily settle down in an urban region. This measure is to contain a rush of rural inhabitants to the urban centres, looking for a job that pays better than the work they can get in their home regions. In order to promote the creation of job positions in the rural area, rural enterprises have always had more economic freedom than their urban counterparts. Above, I pointed out that many people doubted at first that a 'rural state-owned enterprise' would be able to survive in the brewing world, as it was deemed unable to build up a sufficient critical mass. Yanjing had already attained a market share of 30 per cent in the Beijing region, so this doubt had already been proven unfounded. I presume that this circumstance has at least played a significant role in honouring Yanjing's request for a higher sales quota.

On the basis of this feat, Yanjing's historians describe their company as a 'state-owned enterprise full of life'. This is once more a statement laden with symbolic power. Yanjing uses its status as a state-owned enterprise in its identity construction. Even during the stage that the establishment of a new brewery in the Beijing region was conceived, a number of state-level organizations were involved. Attention from two state councillors, Wan Li and Chen Muhua, is mentioned as a source of pride. This self-written history celebrates the fact that Yanjing proved that a rural state-owned company can be successful in the brewing industry. This specific mentioning of its legal status is rare in current self-descriptions of Chinese enterprises. Most enterprises try to shake off the burden of being state owned, which is regarded as highly restrictive of operational freedom. For Yanjing, being owned by the state is a symbol of national pride.

Another expression for state-owned enterprise in Chinese political parlance is 'owned by the entire people'. Yanjing is owned by all Chinese and its success is a success of the Chinese nation. The visits of high officials to Yanjing indicate that it is a genuine identity construct in terms of my model, it is a bidirectional process. Yanjing's behaviour stimulates the visits and the visits reinforce the pride of being a state-owned enterprise.

Moreover, it is a very active construction process. When Yanjing contacted the relevant government organizations to enlarge its freedom in selling its own products, it was on one hand trying to push the limits of what was considered appropriate at that time in the Marxist perception of economy. On the other hand, it also specifically wished to retain its status of state-owned enterprise. In doing so, the Yanjing managers not only constructed their own unique identity of state-owned enterprise full of life, but also 'enlivened' the sense-making of the concept of state-owned enterprises in general.

Another issue related to this period in the historiography of Yanjing is the company's branding policy. Two guidelines for its branding strategy are mentioned:

- the Yanjing brand = essence of national industry;
- the Yanjing brand = major sign of state economic strength.

This positioning of the Yanjing brand again suited the identity of Yanjing as a proud state-owned enterprise. Yanjing is once more linked to the national (*minzu*) industry, calling on the nationalist sentiments that are common among the Chinese. A strong Yanjing brand is positioned as the symbol of a strong national economy. An interesting aspect of this parlance is that the industry is linked to the Chinese nation, the people, while the economy is linked to the state, the institution. Of course the state and the people are closely linked. After all, a state-owned enterprise is 'owned by the entire people'. The reason for the difference is probably cognitive: the industry refers to physical plants, while the economy is a much more abstract concept. Physical firms are linked to physical people, while the abstract economy is linked to the abstract notion of the state.

Yanjing was awarded the designation 'Beijing famous brand' in 1993. A survey performed in that year showed a brand awareness of 98.5 per cent among Beijing residents; 80.1 per cent of Beijing citizens had purchased Yanjing Beer at least once and 55.4 per cent would prefer it in a restaurant, when available.

Some diversification was initiated as well in this period. The construction work of a ginseng beverage plant started in September 1992.

Period 3, 1994 to 1998: 1 million hl/year

This period starts with the designation of Yanjing Beer as the official beer served at state banquets in the Great Hall of the People in February 1995. It is an honour of symbolic value, which once more suits Yanjing's identity of state-owned enterprise that is proud of that status. This was the time in which a company like Five Star, which had also been served, was fighting a losing battle to survive in the new competitive environment created when the command economy was forced to give way (partly) to a market economy. Qingdao, still a source of national pride, was engaged in a fierce competition with Yanjing that had in that year replaced Qingdao as China's number one brewery. Yanjing was number one and therefore deserved this honour, while its closer proximity to the national state organizations probably also played a positive role in gaining it.

Yangjing was reorganized into a limited stock company in 1997. In the same year, the company sought listings at the stock exchanges in Hong Kong and Shenzhen. I will first briefly introduce the listings and then examine these activities in detail.

* May 1997; Yanjing was listed at the Hong Kong Stock Exchange with Beijing Holding, a consortium of eight Beijing-based companies;
* June 1997; Yanjing was listed at the Shenzhen Stock Exchange in a consortium with the Xidan Department Store and the Niulanshan Distillery, under the name of Beijing Yanjing Brewing Co., Ltd.

Some background information is needed to understand this information properly. China opened its first stock exchanges in Shanghai and the Shenzhen Special Economic Zone (near the Hong Kong border) in the beginning of the 1990s as part of the endeavour to align the Chinese economy with international practices. However, as is often the case in Chinese imitations of Western institutions, while these organizations were called 'stock exchanges' and showed many similarities with such well-known counterparts as the New York Stock Exchange, their functioning and role in the national economy was not the same. This would have been impossible, as part of the Chinese economy was, and still is, functioning as a command economy. Everything is 'regulated' in China, so one cannot expect to find a genuinely free market. The nature of Chinese stock exchanges is a topic that exceeds the scope of this study and I will not go into details here. However, as the Chinese government was wary of losing too much control through a completely free and open exchange of shares of companies deemed vital to the national economy, ways were developed to protect such enterprises from being taken over completely or going bankrupt due to a depreciation of their stock.

One frequently used ruse is that a state-owned company isolates part of the company and transforms it into a stock company. The other old Chinese brewery, Qingdao, provides a good example of this practice. Qingdao was one of the first Chinese companies listed on the Hong Kong Stock Exchange (known as Red Chip Stock). However, the Qingdao Brewing Co., Ltd whose stock was offered for sale was actually only a part of what was then already known as the Qingdao Brewing Group. The first subscribers, who proudly pronounced that they owned part of the famous Qingdao Brewery, in fact only owned a part of that subsidiary. In the case of Qingdao, someone who took the trouble to investigate the company would have been able to find this information in the publications. However, through private communication about a Shanghai chemical company that also ranked among the earliest Red Chip companies, I learned that a similar organizational arrangement was made, but that the company in question had gone to great lengths to hide this situation.

The listing of Yanjing at the Hong Kong Stock Exchange proceeded in a slightly different way. The government of Beijing organized a number of companies into an ad hoc holding company. It was the holding that was listed in Hong Kong. Yanjing teamed up with that consortium. This is quite a different way of 'going public' than we understand the term in Europe. However, the working of the stock exchange and the way Chinese companies are attempting to maximize income from their listing, while minimizing the risks, is not the concern of this study. What we can learn from the way Yanjing was 'listed' in Hong Kong is that the company associated itself with other Beijing-based state-owned enterprises under protection of an umbrella company set up specially for this purpose by the Beijing government. Yanjing's identity of a state-owned company full of life was enacted again, by Yanjing and by parties in its environment, in other words it was a bidirectional process of identity construction.

When we then move to the Yanjing listing on the domestic Shenzhen Stock Exchange, we can see a repetition of the pattern, but without the protection of the Beijing government. Yanjing associated itself with two other Beijing-based state-owned enterprises, Xidan Department Store, one of the few old state-owned retailers that managed to re-invent itself in the new market economy and Niulanshan Distillery, an enterprise from the same region as Yanjing. Judging by the name of the consortium, Beijing Yanjing Brewing Co., Ltd, we can conclude that Yanjing was regarded as the core company of the three. Apparently, listing on a domestic exchange was regarded as less risky than on a foreign one and therefore the protection of the Beijing government was not needed. However, the risk was still large enough to resort to a hiding behind one another's back type of construction. Also in this case, Yanjing's partners were both state-owned enterprises.

By this time, Yanjing ranked among China's major enterprises. The Chinese government keeps a number of lists that are updated annually. In this context, Yanjing was regarded as:

- one of 520 Large Enterprises recognized by State Council;
- one of 300 enterprises supported by the State Economic Committee.

Being included in lists like these is more than just honourable. It is an indication that an enterprise has access to funds that are out of reach for others. It also means that an enterprise is more likely to obtain support from the government for ambitious plans. Lists like these are often slighted by foreign investors looking for partner organizations in China. If two or more potential partners are being considered of relatively equal size, level of technology, etc., but one of them is included in such a list, it is usually advisable to look into the consequences and how they can be turned into an advantage.

Period 4, 1999 to 2004: 3 million hl/year

Yanjing received a foreign trade licence, which allowed the company to engage directly in import–export business without the use of a foreign trade company in March 1999. In the old command economy, production enterprises were just established for that purpose: production. The distribution of the products inside China was in the hands of distribution enterprises under the Ministry of Internal Trade and export was part of the tasks of the foreign trade corporations under the Ministry of Foreign Trade and Economic Cooperation. We already saw earlier in this historiography of Yanjing that the company successfully enlarged the part of its production that it could sell outside the state-controlled distribution system in the first years of its existence. By the time this period started, this system had already been reformed and most manufacturing companies were responsible for their own sales.

The control of import–export business through foreign trade corporations remained in operation longer than the domestic distribution system. However, in the course of the 1990s more and more larger enterprises were granted the right to engage in foreign trade directly with foreign parties without the obligation to go through foreign trade companies. Contrary to its pioneering role in domestic trade, Yanjing seemed less eager to gain such a foreign trade licence. This is no surprise, as beer was not really a major export product of China. Yanjing exported its first batch of beer to the USA in 2001. Export to Europe started in 2005.

The main issue of this period is the expansion of Yanjing into various regions of China. Yanjing had been using the name Yanjing Group since 1993. However, the company really only consisted of one brewery, the old mother plant. The first expansion by acquisition took place in 1995, when Yanjing took over the bankrupt Huasi Brewery. Huasi was also based in Shunyi and included capital from a Hong Kong investor. Very little is known about the background of this company, but according to Yanjing's historians it was located right on Yanjing's doorstep.

The story about this takeover resembles the formation of the Gucheng Group in Shanyin County as described in the previous chapter. There, the local government ordered a number of dairy companies in its region to merge into a larger conglomerate, as a means to regulate the market. Again, although no details are provided regarding the background of the acquisition, it seems likely that the local government played a regulating role.

Moreover, this move also meant that a brewery which was partly foreign funded became part of a state-owned enterprise. In other words, Yanjing once more confirmed its identity of (protector of the) national industry. The Chinese brewing industry was at that time still recovering from the turbulent China Strategy incident. Earlier in this chapter, I mentioned that the Beijing Brewery had been unable to adapt to the market economy and was acquired by an Indonesian investor. This Indonesian of Chinese descent had set up an investment company called China Strategy in Hong Kong. This company acquired a large number of Chinese companies in a few selected markets, including brewing, in the years 1992–1994. China Strategy promised to revive those companies by investing in them and putting professional managers in charge of them. In reality, the newly acquired assets were left untouched and China Strategy listed its stock on the Hong Kong stock exchange, thus attracting considerable investments in a period when foreign investors were eager to invest in newly available Chinese stock. Many of the assets were sold to other foreign investors at a profit. This way of operating, while in principle not illegal, was heavily criticized by Chinese economists and became known as the China Strategy phenomenon (Liu *et al.* 1997: 325–347). It is not unlikely that the rapid expansion of Yanjing, and a number of its competitors, during the years following this incident was at least partly inspired by an attempt to save the national brewing industry from such short-term profit-taking behaviour.

After Huasi was acquired, it was quickly consolidated into Yanjing. Yanjing's historians devote some space to describing how the production facilities, personnel, finances, etc., of Huasi were gradually unified with Yanjing. It seems as if the acquisition of Huasi was a learning experience to prepare Yanjing for what was about to come. During the following years, Yanjing acquired a considerable number of breweries in various parts of China. Before discussing this acquisition spree, I have drawn up Table 6.2 showing the acquisitions of Yanjing in chronological order. The information has been compiled from a number of sources.

Yanjing has never claimed to have a specific strategy as to the order of regions in which it intended to become active. However, there seems to be a certain pattern in the above list. During the first 18 months of its

Table 6.2   The history of Yanjing's expansion

18/01/1999	Jiangxi Ji'an
18/06/1999	Hunan Xiangxiang
18/12/1999	Hubei Xiangtan
20/01/2000	Hunan Hengyang
18/05/2000	Jiangxi Ganzhou
08/08/2000	Shandong Laizhou
18/11/2000	Inner Mongolia Baotou
18/03/2001	Shandong Wuming
20/03/2001	Shandong Qufu Sankong
10/07/2001	Inner Mongolia Chifeng
18/07/2002	Guangxi Guilin Liquan
16/09/2002	Fujian Nan'an Huiyuan
16/07/2003	Zhejiang Xiandu
26/07/2003	Fujian Huiquan

acquisition spree, Yanjing developed into South Central provinces: Jiangxi, Hubei and Hunan. During the following 18 months, the company aimed its acquisition activities on the Northern coastal province of Shandong and Inner Mongolia, both quite close to its own home region. The period that seems to emerge then is a two-year period in which Yanjing penetrated to the very South and the Southern coast.

If I attempt to interpret this course of action, it seems as if Yanjing deliberately did not start with China's richest, most developed regions, but also avoided the poorest, less developed regions. Instead Yanjing aimed to gain a foothold in regions that were just starting to develop. As I pointed out in the beginning of this chapter, a frequently observed phenomenon in an economy that is starting to develop is a rapid increase in the demand for beer. The existing breweries in those regions are not always able to increase their capacity in time. In particular in the Chinese context, where most of these breweries were state owned or collective enterprises, the government organizations that were in charge of them did not always have sufficient funds available to expand the local beer production. A major brewery from the national capital that comes prospecting for takeover candidates, carrying a big pouch of money, is then regarded as a *deus ex machina*. In such a politico-economic environment a beneficial deal is (relatively) easy to close.

A second pattern that can be extracted from Yanjing's acquisition list seems to corroborate this hypothesis: Yanjing's acquisitions are never located in provincial capitals, but always in second echelon cities in their respective regions. Just as breweries in rich well-developed regions will be harder to approach, or come up with tougher conditions for a takeover, breweries in provincial capitals and their mothers-in-law (these are always involved in an acquisition) are more demanding negotiation partners than their counterparts in smaller cities. Just as Yanjing did not select China's poorest regions, the company also stayed out of the poorest provincial towns. Cities like Ji'an and Ganzhou in Jiangxi are industrial centres in their home province. From a purely economic point of view it could even be argued that the industrial city of Ganzhou, close to rich Guangdong, is at least as important as Jiangxi's capital, Nanchang. However, exactly because Nanchang is the capital, it is the seat of the provincial government (see Chapter 4 on the identity of a Chinese provincial capital). This adds significantly to the perceived authority of Nanchang. Of two breweries of a similar size and level of technology, but one located in Nanchang and the other in Ganzhou, the one in Nanchang is most likely turn out to be the toughest negotiation partner for an acquisition. On the other hand, being able to attract investment from a Beijing-based company like Yanjing, which at that time was already China's top brewer, would bestow tremendous honour on Ganzhou. In terms of identity construction, Yanjing's takeover of the Ganzhou Brewery gave Ganzhou a little Beijing identity. This is more than an emotional matter, it will give a city like Ganzhou a little extra political clout that could be put to good use in future dealings with the provincial government.

Finally, we can have a look at what we feel is missing. I already observed that Yanjing, so far, has not developed into China's poorest Western regions. However, I still seem to miss three regions: the Southwest (Yunnan, Sichuan, Chongqing), the Northeast (Heilongjiang, Jilin, Liaoning) and the North Central region (Tianjin, Hebei and Henan). The last is the most prominent, as Yanjing's earliest statement regarding regional expansion put Hebei third. Yanjing first intended to develop its home region Beijing, followed by Beijing's twin city: Tianjin. The third step in that process was Hebei. If I once more try to make sense of this from a Yanjing perspective, it is very well possible that Yanjing has drawn an imaginary circle around its mother plant, marking the region that can be served from its Beijing location. This would cover Tianjin and the major part of Hebei. Henan, like Hebei located in the North China Plain, can be served from Beijing and Shandong Qufu. However, it is equally possible that Henan has been prospected by Yanjing, but that no acquisition has (yet) been finalized. The same may apply to the other two regions.

Adding so many subsidiaries in such a short span of time is bound to have a major impact on the identity of a company. A special management company was established to deal with non-Beijing companies in June 2001. This decision seems to corroborate my periodization of Yanjing's acquisition programme. This management company was established at the end of the first period, in which Yanjing penetrated the South Central provinces. This decision indicates that Yanjing at that time perceived its companies as consisting of two parts:

1 Beijing (Yanjing and Huasi);
2 non-Beijing (five plants in Jiangxi, Hubei and Hunan)

This distinction is reflective of the traditional way in which inhabitants of Beijing perceive the world; there is Beijing and there are the 'outer territories' (*waidi*). In a previous paragraph I already pointed out that being from Beijing meant something when a company like Yanjing went on a buying spree in second echelon cities in second echelon provinces. This authority was recognized by the hosts and thus constructed a genuine, bidirectional, process of identity construction. The term used by Yanjing's management office for non-Beijing breweries contained the term 'outer prefectures' (*waifu*), which is merely a more literary equivalent of the term *waidi* used in everyday Beijing speech. This is a further indication that Yanjing had a strong Beijing identity.

In October 2003, Yanjing established a South China Office, replacing the management office for non-Beijing subsidiaries. Following the same line of analysis, we can conclude that this decision indicates a change in the geographical perception among Yanjing's management. I will devote the rest of this chapter to the significance of 'the South' in Yanjing's identity constructs. Here, I will concentrate on the important symbolic feature of establishing such a South China Office, as it indicated that Yanjing was shifting from a Beijing identity to a China identity. It was becoming a truly national company. While the term 'outer prefecture management company' still had a strong Beijing flavour, the term South China Office implicated that Yanjing in the sense of the mother company was cognitively located in North China, and no longer in Beijing. This analysis is corroborated by the fact that the non-Beijing subsidiaries were good for more than 57 per cent of Yanjing's turnover of 2003.

Yanjing's largest acquisition was the 31.8 per cent State share in the Huiquan Brewing Co., Ltd. Although Huiquan at that time was not performing well, it ranked in size among China's top breweries. Huiquan generated a turnover of RMB 760 million. The brewery was reorganized from a state-owned production plant to a limited stock company in 1997, with the State retaining a minority share. Following this reorganization, Huiquan sought to attract more capital by a public listing. This proved to be a bad move, on the eve of the Asian financial crisis. The takeover was celebrated with a ceremony in the Great Hall of the People. Yanjing was celebrated as the saviour of the state's assets. This was yet another event confirming the state-owned identity of Yanjing. Although it has never been confirmed, this official state-level celebration seems to indicate that Yanjing was requested by the State to take over the financial burden of Huiquan. Years before, when Yanjing took over the almost bankrupt Huasi brewery, the company positioned itself as the protector of state assets against the encroaching foreign investors. When Huiquan became an ideal target for a takeover, the State seemed to prefer this to be done by a domestic rather than a foreign party.

After the acquisition of the State's share in Huiquan, Yanjing started buying up more shares of that company. It became the majority shareholder in March 2004 and Huiquan was consolidated into the Yanjing Group in July of that year.

Yanjing's road to the South

Although Yanjing's expansion to the South is the incident in this chapter, I need to revert to the construction of Yanjing's identity as envoy of the central government from a more theoretical perspective first.

I derive my conclusion from the interaction between Yanjing and various parties in various contexts. I do not intend to state that THE Chinese government ever decided to designate Yanjing as its representative. I do not conclude such a situation either, because it is not attested by any narrative. However, it would be irrelevant for an understanding of Yanjing's current identity constructs to try to investigate the 'veracity' of this construct. Yanjing's identity as representative of the central authorities is a construct that has emerged during ongoing social interaction of a number of actors. Moreover, it is still continuously reconstructed in what I refer to as social-cognitive contexts [cognate to Weick's enacted environments (Weick 1979: 131) and (Weick 1995: 30–38)].

The original Shunyi Brewery was established with the intent to alleviate the need for beer among Beijing residents. This idea co-creates an identity of the existing breweries in the region, in particular Five Star and Beijing, of not being able to fulfil the local demand. Moreover, as the Shunyi Brewery would be operated as a state-owned enterprise, an approval from the State Planning Committee was required. This could explain that a Vice-Minister found it useful to visit the plant in 1981, even though it was a relatively small project of a county government. However, once such a visit had taken place, which involved considerable interaction between a number of parties (arranging the Vice-Minister's security alone would be an enormous task), the Vice-Minister did more than just honour the plant with a visit. He suggested that the brand name should be changed from Shunyi Beer to Yanjing Beer. In Weick's terms of retrospective sense-making (Weick 1995: 18–24), the creation of Shunyi Beer as the brand name took place almost automatically. A brewery established in Shunyi was called Shunyi Brewery and its beer sold under the Shunyi brand. Even though we do not know exactly what triggered it, the suggestion to switch the county-related name to a name linked to the municipality indicates a strongly heightened state of sense-making. It again stands to reason that, as the new project was to supply beer to the thirsty citizens of Beijing, the brand name should be broader in geographic scope. However, just like the idea itself, this suggestion for Yanjing as the brand name (and a few years later as the company name) reinforced the negative identity of the existing local brewers, in particular Beijing Brewery. Suggesting Yanjing as the brand name was almost like saying that the new brewery would replace Beijing Brewery. It actually did; Beijing Brewery is currently a subsidiary of Asahi.

Visits by State Councillors in 1982 and 1986 further strengthened the 'central authorities' identity of Yanjing. Identity is a process, a product of social interaction. The behaviour of state leaders took place in interaction with local leaders of Shunyi county and later managers of Yanjing. The behaviour of the state leaders therefore affected the behaviour of the Yanjing-related actors. The latter started acting as favourites of the central authorities, first in their interaction with the leaders, but then also in their interaction in other contexts. This explains why so many of the events of Yanjing were reported in media close to the central government, like the *People's Daily*. Reporters of those media will tend to visit Yanjing to interview managers, who will therefore have more frequent interaction with the government-controlled media than other, 'less important', competitors. Yanjing managers brainstorm about the importance of the South Chinese market, which makes the journalists report that Yanjing's acquisition of a brewery in Ji'an is actually only the prelude to conquering the South. These reports will play a role in the strategic sense-making of Yanjing managers and the mothers-in-law of Yanjing, etc. In the midst of all this interacting (= sense-making = organizing), Yanjing was also designated as the beer to be served during state banquets in the Great Hall of the People.

By the time Yanjing made its first acquisition outside the Beijing region, it was included in a context in which it was made sense of as a strong symbol of the central government, a protector of the national industry, etc. The behaviour of Yanjing, a number of central government organizations, the centrally controlled media, etc., was tightly coupled.

When analysing Yanjing's expansion activities, the notion 'South' seems to play a major role. Although Yanjing has never made explicit statements regarding the order of regions in which it acquired new subsidiaries, the company spent the first 18 months of its acquisition spree on buying up breweries in the South Central provinces: Jiangxi, Hubei and Hunan. After a second 18-month period in which Yanjing expanded in regions closer to its home region, another move to the South started, including Guangxi, Zhejiang and Fujian.

The division of China into two major regions, North and South, is very old. Allusions to it can be found in ancient works of literature. The division is not only a geographic one. An imaginary border, often localized in the Yangtze River, has been perceived to divide the people in the North from those in the South. The people in the North are struggling with the harsh continental climate, constantly threatened from invading barbarians. They are, on the other hand, the speakers of Mandarin and most Chinese imperial families have been of Northern descent, while some of them actually were barbarians, including the last dynasty, the Qin. The staple of the Northerners is wheat. The Southerners live in a milder climate, although Northern officials often did not appreciate a post as local magistrate in the South, complaining about the hot and humid summers. The Southerners grow and eat rice. They speak many, mutually not intelligible dialects. Although also mainly farmers, many of them have switched working the soil for trading. Most Chinese who emigrated to start a new life abroad were Southerners.

That most Chinese imperial families originated from the Northern half of China and that the various capitals of the Chinese empire have mostly been located in that area has probably been a product of a number of causes. First of all, Chinese civilization, based on archeological findings, started in the North(west) (see Fairbank *et al.* 1973: 17 ff. for an excellent introduction). Then, during the ages, most threats to that Chinese civilization had come from the North. The Northerners had to take the first blows, but by doing so also became the rulers of China. In terms of organizing processes, the recurrent behaviour of the Northern Chinese as the protectors of the nation constructed an environment in which the dynastic families were typically Northerners. Moreover, this also explains the continental inclination of most Chinese dynasties, with a high regard for the tilling of the land, but with a dread for sailing out to sea; a fear re-enacted by the Communist rulers until the 1980s.

The Northerners thus were the rulers and the Southerners the ruled. However, the Southerners have learned how to live a life of their own without too much interference by the rulers (the federalist tendency in Chinese culture introduced in the beginning of this chapter). The rulers through the ages have realized that and, in turn, have devised ways to maintain a basic level of control in the South, without antagonizing the Southerners too much. One typical way for the Emperor to establish his influence in a far away region that was (reported to be) rebellious was the special envoy, who was given the Emperor's sword as a token that he enjoyed the undivided trust of the Emperor. Such an envoy could decide over life and death.

Yanjing's decision to establish a South China Office in October 2003 can be interpreted as a continuation of this tradition. By that time, Yanjing was operating breweries in nine administrative regions of China, equally divided over the North and the South. However, the company's head office was located in the capital, as was the Forbidden City in imperial times. It seems as if Yanjing, steeped in Northern culture, felt that it could operate the Northern subsidiaries sufficiently from Beijing, but that those in the South needed to have an office of their own. This would give the Southerners the feeling that they were to a certain extent in charge of their own affairs.

I have already pointed out that Yanjing has so far not been reaching out to a number of regions, including the very North of China. The very South, on the other hand, in particular the rich province of Guangdong, is frequently mentioned as a major objective. However, instead of directly acquiring a suitable brewery in that province, Yanjing attempted to attack Guangdong by means of a siege from its neighbouring provinces first.

Yanjing's first acquisition outside the Beijing region, in Jiangxi's Ji'an, was directly linked to a move South by Chinese analysts. A commentator in the *Market Daily* (Ding 1999) described the deal in Ji'an as a guarantee and condition for increasing market share in the South. He then continues by stating that it is 'actually nothing more than a prelude to Yanjing conquering the entire Chinese market'. This statement shows remarkable insight into Yanjing's strategy. When this article was published, Yanjing had only acquired two breweries outside the Beijing area. It seems that this reporter was being used as a mouthpiece of Yanjing's management. The *Market Daily* is a publication of the *People's Daily*, the national newspaper published by the Communist Party. Further in the article, Yanjing's Vice-Party Secretary is cited as the main source of the 'news' published in this article. In a Chinese context, it is easy enough to perceive Yanjing as the tool of the central authorities in Beijing. Yanjing was served at the official state banquets in the Great Hall of the People; it was the new Emperor's favoured brew. The role of Yanjing as the Party's envoy to the South is then only one step away, the sword being traded for a bag of money.

Another analyst more directly related Yanjing's acquisition activities in the South as aimed at Guangdong (Ke 2003). In this article, Yanjing's subsidiaries in Ji'an (Jiangxi), Hengyang (Hunan), Guilin (Guangxi) and Hui'an (Fujian) are grouped together as each taking care of part of the Guangdong market, apart from their respective home regions. It reports that a Vice-General Manager of Yanjing has spent the period of December 2002 to March 2003 forging this circle of breweries into a chain around Guangdong. This Vice-General Manager is referred to as 'holding a flying office' (*feixing bangong*), yet another expression that seems to allude to the office of special envoy of the Emperor; who has traded the traditional horse for a modern plane.

The same article reports that Yanjing had been shopping around in Guangdong and has held negotiations with the Qiangli Brewery in Sanshui (near the border with Hong Kong) and the Doumen Brewery in Zhuhai (near the border with Macao). The talks with Qiangli failed, because Qiangli insisted on continuing the Qiangli brand, which was not performing very well at that time, while Yanjing did not want to link its strong brand name with one with a bad reputation. The reason for not acquiring Doumen was not given, but the article cites a Yanjing spokesman stating that the company was not considering an acquisition in Guangdong any more, because the exorbitant price required by any Guangdong brewery exceeded the cost of a greenfield plant.

During the time that Yanjing was preparing itself for the attack of Guangdong, a peculiar incident occurred in Nanchang, the capital of Jiangxi. In late February 2003, a number of unidentified people purchased 400 000 bottles of Yanjing beer at more than 3600 retail outlets in Nanchang. Some of them offered a price higher than the actual retail price, while others offered to trade one bottle of freshly produced Yanjing beer for three bottles of Nanchang beer dating November 2002. Reporters investigating this matter found an abandoned warehouse with approximately 100 000 bottles of Yanjing beer piled up. The incident was never further reported, but after the short article appeared in a local paper, it was also published in Guangzhou (*Guangzhou Evening News* 2003) and even the national *People's Daily* (2003b). Especially the latter fact seems to corroborate once more that even such a, seemingly, minor incident is a matter worth reporting in the 'throat and tongue of the Party' (*dang de houshe*; a slang term for the *People's Daily*).

This incident indicates that, although Yanjing had already been active in the region for more than two years, it had not yet been accepted as a local beer. Regardless whether the 'raid' on Yanjing beer in Nanchang was an initiative of the local brewer of Nanchang beer, or that it was an act of local popular protest, the offer to substitute one bottle of recently brewed Yanjing beer for three bottles of the local brew that had been produced four months earlier is highly symbolic. Even though the campaign was apparently directed against Yanjing, the attackers subconsciously still attached a higher value to Yanjing than to their local Nanchang beer; three time higher to be precise. The alternative deal, offering a price higher than the regular retail price, has a similar symbolic value.

This incident also fits in with the identity of Yanjing as the envoy of Beijing, the central government, the Communist Party, etc. In the old days, the imperial envoys, in spite of the power invested in them by the Emperor himself, had to deal with suspicion and even a downright display of dislike from the local people, including the local gentry. We should never forget the enormous symbolic power of the Yanjing brand. As Yanjing is a literary equivalent of Beijing, protest against Yanjing can be likened with protest against Beijing, and from there everything 'Beijing' stands for. I will revert to this mechanism in the final chapter, in which I will integrate the findings of the case chapters with the theoretical framework laid out in Chapters 1 and 2.

Then finally, still unexpected, Yanjing decided to build a brewery in Guangdong after all. Beijing Yanjing Brewing Co., Ltd and Beijing (Industrial) Brewing Co., Ltd, two Beijing-based daughter companies of the Yanjing Group, had entered into a joint venture in December 2004 to build the Guangdong Yanjing Brewing Co., Ltd. The location selected was the Nanhai District of Foshan, a city close to Guangzhou, the capital of Guangdong. The objective was to start production in June 2005.

A Yanjing spokesman motivated this move with three reasons (*Southnet* 2005):

1 Foshan was an excellent location, offering favourable investment conditions;
2 Foshan was an economically developed region, with a pool of affluent consumers;
3 Yanjing still did not have its own production facilities in Guangdong, which was a burden for the mother company in Beijing, as it had to ship the Yanjing beer all the way to Guangdong.

The latter is the most intriguing of the three. While Yanjing had been carefully siting a chain of breweries in adjacent provinces to attack the Guangdong market from four sides, now the establishment of a brewery of its own in the region was motivated as a means to lighten the burden of the mother plant. It seems as if the consumers in Guangdong had never really accepted 'Yanjing beer' that was not produced by the real Yanjing (the one in Beijing). While the acquisition of Huiquan was even celebrated by a party in the Great Hall of the People, yet another act that constructed the 'central government' identity of Yanjing, it was never able to penetrate the Guangdong market as hoped. Major competitors of Yanjing on the other hand, in particular Qingdao, were more successful in this region through local subsidiaries.

Actually, Qingdao acquired Doumen, after Yanjing broke off its negotiations with that brewery. Apparently Guangdong consumers do accept beer from other regions, but only if it is produced by the mother company, or brewed in their own home province. Yanjing then realized what it had exclaimed in despair a couple of years before: it is cheaper to build a greenfield plant in Guangdong than to acquire an existing one.

With a brewery in Guangdong on the way, Yanjing now seems to have ended its journey to the South. Yanjing = Beijing = the central government rules in the South, be it through an entity with a Southern identity.

7 Food Components Asia – China – Shanghai – ?

Trade fairs as organizations

With the theme of this final case chapter I intend to be a little more provocative. I have selected a trade fair as its core case. It can, and probably will by many readers, be argued that a trade fair is a service, rather than an organization. However, a successful trade fair is the result of combined effort by a number of organizations. Although each edition of a trade fair usually lasts only a few days, three in this case, it is held for a prolonged period, with regular intervals. Our example trade fair is held every year. Moreover, the interaction between the organizers of a trade fair and various other parties (exhibitors, visitors, government organizations, regulatory organizations, venue managers, etc.) is an ongoing business. The organization of the next edition of a trade fair has already started before the current edition has even opened its doors. In a similar fashion, while the current edition is being held, some unfinished business related to the previous one, like the collection of payments, may still be pending. The result is a social-cognitive structure, an aggregate of actors who rather frequently interact on a certain theme. One of the constructs resulting from this interaction is the concept of the trade fair, symbolized by its name. The cognitive element of this social-cognitive structure includes a construction rule that makes them convene at an agreed place and time each year. Their behaviour is coupled rather tightly: one party books and prepares the venue, while a number of other parties book parts of that venue from the former. Yet others just visit that venue to check out what is new, etc.

What I just described in the previous sentences fits my definition of a cognitive space. The jargon related to trade fairs also substantiates the idea that we are dealing with something recurrent. Each physical event is called an 'edition' of that trade fair. This is a term derived from the publishing industry. A monthly magazine is not regarded as something that is reinvented every month, but as a long-term activity that crystallizes in a concrete edition once a month. Analogously, the use of the term edition in the organization of an annual trade fair constructs a permanent abstract formula that crystallizes once a year as a physical exhibition in a certain venue. For the particular case of this chapter, the comparison with the publishing business is even more suitable, as the organizer of this trade fair is also a publisher of the major business publication in that industry, a bimonthly magazine called 'Global Food Components'. Indeed, most of the world's leading organizers of trade fairs are also active in the publishing business.

There are as of yet no studies on the organization nature of trade fairs. Most of the existing academic publications on trade fairs focus on their management or the most ways for potential exhibitors to draw up an exhibition plan that is most suitable for their individual needs. An interesting article that at least attempts to define the nature of trade fairs is that of Maskell *et al.* (2004). They define trade fairs as 'short lived, often periodical events for the exchange of commodities, information and ideas and the initiation and maintenance of contacts' (op. cit.: 8). The phrasing of Maskell *et al.* is highly interesting, it reveals that they are struggling with the temporal nature of trade fairs. Their definition starts with the phrase 'short lived', but after a short pause (represented by the comma) they add 'often periodical'. The final function of trade fairs in their definition is 'maintenance of contacts', a phrase that implies contacts are not one-time events, but something that needs to be maintained over a prolonged period of time. This definition then starts with a temporal connotation, moves on to periodical, and ends with ongoing. Later in their article, the authors construct a typology of what they regard as 'organizational configurations of knowledge creation' (op. cit.: 11). Within that framework, trade fairs are typified as temporary, broad focused. In their sense-making of trade fairs, Maskell *et al.* seem to reify the temporary nature of trade fairs.

In our contemporary Internet age, many trade fairs have permanent web sites. These sites offer data of previous editions, like lists of exhibitors, and detailed information of the upcoming edition. Many of the sites offer channels to communicate with the organizers and even with exhibitors. They thus become a (semi-)permanent forum of interaction and therefore of sense-making. In fact, one could even argue that the web site of a trade fair is a (semi-)permanent representation of that trade fair, or in terms of organizing: that these web sites are a (semi-)permanent part of the cognitive element of the trade fair space. A certain prospect, for example, may base its decision to exhibit at the coming edition of the trade fair only if one or several of its competitors participate as well. The web site is then one of the sources for such information. We could even argue that the physical edition of a trade fair is just that: a physical representation of the concept and that the web site, provided it is (literally) attractive to a sufficient number of actors, is a similar representation but using another medium. However, this calls for a separate study.

There are more occasions for stakeholders of a particular trade fair to interact. First of all there are other trade fairs. Participants, or subsets of participants, of trade fair A meet on trade fair B. Trade fair A can and usually will be a topic of discussion. Companies that operate in the same business like to compare their respective plans for participating in trade fairs. Participating can be a costly matter and companies want to spend their promotion budgets as effectively as possible. Trade fairs actually are an area in which enterprises that are otherwise fierce competitors like to co-ordinate their activities. Companies like to exhibit at those trade fairs at which they are likely to see the highest number of their competitors. Further in this chapter, we will see that this propensity is affecting Exposure's business in China. Exhibitors of the same trade fair, even competitors, regularly join forces to lodge collective complaints at the organizer of a trade fair, as a combined action will give them more clout. This process of interaction is ongoing enough to construct a cognitive space. From an organizing point of view we can then conclude that trade fairs are cognitive spaces.

From a management perspective, the relationship between trade fairs and the services connected with them is different from that between, for example, a bank and its services. The bank, as a service-oriented enterprise, offers its services to its customers. Formulated more precisely in terms of the theoretical framework used in this study: banks produce their services during the interaction with their customers. Companies that organize trade fairs first produce trade fairs, in interaction with the other stakeholders, and then, through those trade fairs, produce related services, still in interaction with the exhibitors, visitors, etc.

The various trade fairs organized by such an organizer show traits of very low level subsidiaries. They are vehicles through which their 'mother companies' offer their services. Many organizers of trade fairs create communication co-ordinates for each of their trade fairs, in particular e-mail boxes, to channel their interaction with their relations. Exhibitors, visitors, etc., can always reach the organizer through the same telephone number. Organizers of trade fairs typically have a matrix structure, in which employees of the functional departments are assigned to the various trade fairs. Each trade fair has an organizing team, but each member of a specific team can be a member of two or more of such teams. Most larger trade fairs have Event Managers that are dedicated to a single trade fair. On the financial side of the organizer, each individual trade fair is usually treated as a separate profit centre.

When we try to place them on the imaginary scale of cognitive spaces as introduced in Chapter 1, trade fairs are too large to be regarded as 'configurations', but are not compliant with all typical traits of 'organizations' either. They seem to suit a position quite close to that of 'organizations'. As in-depth research into the organization-like nature of trade fairs would go beyond the scope of this study, I would like to end with the following statement. Within the theoretical framework of the present study, trade fairs can definitely be considered as cognitive spaces. These cognitive spaces show a number of traits of the cognitive spaces that are referred to as 'organizations'.

Trade fairs are commercial activities. This means that, as a consequence of my assumption that trade fairs have an organization-like status, they should have identity constructs similar to those of companies. This argument is also valid, when turned around: if evidence can be found that trade fairs have company-like identity constructs, this would corroborate the hypothesis that trade fairs are a type of enterprise.

The case of this chapter is based on ongoing business, which offers unique first-hand and very recent research material. However, unlike the case histories of the previous chapters, I have altered a number of company names, etc., to protect the interests of the parties involved. Moreover, this case is probably one of the most complex ones in this study, as it involves a number of enterprises, some of which are highly intertwined as members of the same international group. This case also offers a possibility to observe the co-operation between a European and Chinese company belonging to the same international group. The case further involves a competitive trade fair organized by two Chinese organizations that used to be the partners of the foreign party. Both groups of organizers claim that the other party is imitating its respective trade fair. I intend to show that either claim is irrelevant.

Case history

Exposure Ltd is an organizer of business-to-business trade fairs in a wide range of markets. It has subsidiaries in a number of countries spread over three continents. Most of these subsidiaries had been independent companies until they were acquired by Exposure.

Exposure B.V. in the Netherlands is a subsidiary of Exposure Ltd, specialized in trade fairs in the field of food components. For the sake of convenience, I will use 'Exposure' in the remainder of this chapter when referring to Exposure B.V. The first food components exhibition was held in 1985 and FC Europe (FCE) gradually developed into the leading trade fair in this field in the world. The acquisition of Exposure by the current British mother company provided the resources to grow even further, including expansion to other parts of the world. By the time this case study starts, 1995, annual exhibitions were organized in Europe, the USA, South America and Asia, the European event being the largest in scale.

An important factor leading to the success of Exposure was the unique formula of its food components concept. Food components can be categorized according to dosage rate from bulk components to micro-additives (dosed in ppm units). For example, a soft drink like Fanta mainly consists of water, followed by orange juice and sugar and some small amounts of colourants, flavours, preservative, etc. In this case water is a common bulk component, which is not commercially manufactured but provided by governments as a public service. Orange juice, usually purchased in the form of concentrate, is regarded as a component by some manufacturers, while others regard it as a bulk commodity. This difference in the sense-making of fruit juice is reflected in the fact that some fruit juice manufacturers are regular exhibitors at Exposure's trade fairs, while others prefer to present their products on a forum like Anuga, the large biannual food fair held in Cologne. Sugar is an industrial product, but hardly any sugar manufacturer exhibits at Exposure's trade fairs. Apparently the sugar world does not perceive the need to market its products through trade fairs. All major manufacturers of colourants, flavours, preservatives, etc., on the other hand, can be found at all of Exposure's exhibitions. Later we shall see that this formula, although not protected by any law as intellectual property, is not easy to copy, because it is embedded in the daily routines (construction rules) of Exposure.

Exposure's trade fairs are named after the region in which they are organized. Each exhibition rotates between a number of major venues within its own region. For example, the European exhibition rotates between Frankfurt, Paris, London, Amsterdam, etc.

The development of Exposure's business in Asia progressed less smoothly. A trade fair was started in Japan, but had to give way to a competitor. Another trade fair in South-East Asia was attempted in Hong Kong. However, in spite of Hong Kong's fine reputation as a venue for conferences and trade fairs, FC Asia (FCA) was not a success in that region. When FCA was moved to Singapore, it proved viable, though still a lot smaller than FCE, and organized biannually.

The China Food Components Association (CFCA) is the leading government organization in this business in China. CFCA had been organizing a domestic trade fair since 1990. This trade fair was a great success and expanded every year. Moreover, CFCA started organizing delegations of Chinese exhibitors to FCE in the mid-1990s. These delegations were regarded as very important, as they were extensively reported on by CFCA in the Food Additives section of each Food Industry Yearbook.

The reason for this success was the high costs of participating in FCE. Exposure worked with a minimum requirement of 20 square metres, which was considered excessive by quite a number of smaller international companies, especially by the emerging Chinese exporters of food components. In some countries subcontractors booked a certain exhibition space with Exposure, which they then sold in smaller segments to companies in their home country that would otherwise not be exhibiting at Exposure's major trade fairs. This group of exhibitors from the same country, led by a subcontractor is known as X Pavilion, where X stands for the group's home country.

A complicating legal matter for CFCA in its role of organizer of the Chinese delegations was that it lacked the licence to do so. CFCA has therefore sought the co-operation of the China Light Industry Chamber of Commerce (CLICC).

Through participating in FCE and FCA, CFCA and its member companies grew interested in reorganizing their domestic trade fair into an international one. For organizing international trade fairs in China, a similar special licence is required as well by Chinese law. Therefore, CFCA once more linked up with CLICC for their new venture, for which CFCA would be responsible for attracting domestic exhibitors and CLICC for the international promotion. The new trade fair was given the, obvious, name: Food Components China (FCC). It was originally designed as a biannual event. After a kind of pilot edition in 1995, the first trade fair with the FCC name was held in 1997.

CFCA's activities attracted Exposure's attention at an early stage. Following an 'if you can't beat them' spirit, Exposure sought contact with CFCA to suggest alternating in Singapore and Shanghai, just like FCE was rotating between a number of European venues. When organizing FCA in Shanghai (FCA-Shanghai or FCAS), Exposure would do so by co-locating its own trade fair with FCC, where FCC would exclusively attract domestic exhibitors and FCAS international ones. In years that Exposure would hold FCA in Singapore or other South-East Asian venues, FCC would be held by CFCA/CLICC alone in Beijing (or any other Chinese venue).

CFCA/CLICC were interested in starting negotiations and after some deliberations an agreement was reached to hold FCAS in Shanghai in 1998. Apart from the more common issues, like division of revenues, a more specific conflict during the negotiations of this deal was that the Chinese side originally insisted on Beijing as the venue, while Exposure would not hear of any other venue but Shanghai. The Chinese side gave in and Shanghai was selected.

Exposure's fixation on Shanghai was caused by an enquiry held by Exposure of a selection of its clients in 1995. The enquiry consisted of one single question: 'if we were to organize a Chinese edition of our FC formula, what would be your venue of preference?' Most votes went to Shanghai, which constructed the perception that Shanghai was the only venue to be considered. However, the flaw in this enquiry was that it presumed that the clients had sufficient information available to make such a judgement. It would need to be corroborated by research, but if an enquiry were made with this question: 'what is the first Chinese city that comes to mind?', the odds are that more than 80 per cent would reply with Shanghai; the remaining 19 per cent+ mentioning Beijing. People do not know that many Chinese geographic names.

Moreover, regional preference for foreign investment, or setting up representative offices, is influenced by a strong propensity for fads. If the same enquiry had been made a decade earlier, the outcome would almost certainly have been Guangzhou, which has been China's primary gateway to the outside world for more than a century; again with Beijing in second position. Although Beijing is the national capital and therefore the seat of the central ministries and ministry-like organizations and also the city with the foreign embassies, it also has a strong political, bureaucratic connotation. The cognitive calculation of foreign businesses was then: we know of Beijing and Guangzhou (Shanghai), but then opt for the less bureaucratic one: Guangzhou (or later: Shanghai).

Holding this enquiry by itself was not a mistake. On the contrary, it is an essential part in the regular interaction between the organizer of trade fairs and its exhibitors. The problem is the fact that the outcome of the enquiry was interpreted as an imperative that did not leave any room for variation. In terms of my theoretical framework, the outcome of the enquiry was reified almost instantaneously. Later in this chapter we will see how this reification has had dramatic consequences for the strategic choices of Exposure and CFCA.

FCAS1998 was an overwhelming success. Exposure's then CEO was so taken by the success that he decided on the spot that FCAS should be organized as an annual event rather than biannual. The new situation would then be that in one year (like 1998) Exposure would only co-organize FCC/FCAS, while in the following year it would be involved in FCA and FCC/FCAS. The Chinese side was again willing to go along, but there was a major problem: the venue for FCC1999 in Beijing had already been booked for dates only one week after FCAS1999 in Singapore. CFCA/CLICC were willing to accommodate and try to postpone FCC1999 for a few weeks, but they needed a confirmation from Exposure that it was willing to join them in Beijing within two weeks. This event is pivotal in the case history and therefore deserves to be told in great detail. Exposure's CEO held such reified ideas regarding Beijing as a venue for 'his' show that he kept postponing the decision. Daily communication took place with Exposure Asia, which was based in Hong Kong and also involved in the organization of FCA(S). In the course of this communication Exposure and the expatriate managers of Exposure Asia engaged in a vicious circle of reduction of meaning, until it was cognitively impossible for Exposure to decide. After two weeks passed by without any signal from Exposure to CFCA/CLICC, the latter fixed their original dates for FCC1999.

Negotiations for an annual FCC/FCAS started. The Chinese side was afraid that in the years that Exposure would also organize FCA, FCA would cannibalize FCC/FCAS. Moreover, they still wanted to keep Beijing and other cities, in particular Guangzhou, open as possible venues for the combined event, while Exposure insisted on Shanghai as the exclusive venue. Exposure insisted on Shanghai and the Chinese side gave in once more. A three-year agreement was signed, for the years 2000–2002.

Meanwhile, FCC1999 held in Beijing without Exposure was another overwhelming success. The fact that it was held only a week after FCA in

Singapore did apparently not deter major international companies from exhibiting in Beijing as well, as was originally feared by Exposure. Exposure's CEO realized his mistake and booked a stand at FCC1999 to promote Exposure's various trade fairs, including FCC/FCAS2000 for the coming year. CFCA invited him to participate as a guest in the opening ceremony. He also organized an Exposure Courtesy Reception in an international hotel near the exhibition centre to confirm the impression among the international exhibitors at FCC1999 that Exposure was somehow part of this event as well.

FCC/FCAS2000 went on smoothly and the market seemed to acknowledge the event as useful for the business. Though not as large as FCE, FCAS had the potential of growing into Exposure's second largest trade fair. Then another pivotal event took place.

CFCA's management group was changed almost entirely in the spring of 2001. Moreover, the change took place rather suddenly, without any announcement to partner organizations like Exposure. In addition, Exposure Asia started to spread rumours that owing to this abrupt change of leaders, CFCA had lost the confidence of the Chinese food components industry. The industry indeed was as surprised about the events as Exposure, but in a Chinese context this does not automatically mean that the food components industry and CFCA's members would 'lose confidence' in CFCA, let alone stop supporting that organization and its trade fairs. CFCA as a typical Chinese sector association is a semi-government organization that has a number of tasks, like participating in relevant legislation, the registration of new food components, collecting and spreading market information, etc. After such an abrupt change of management, the new leaders, in particular the de facto leader, the Secretary General, would need to make an extra effort to gain respect. However, being placed in that position would, again in a Chinese context, already give such a person sufficient respect to make a good start. It was surprising that this insight into Chinese practice was not available at Exposure Asia in Hong Kong.

Exposure's CEO lost his nerve completely this time and, on advice from Exposure Asia, even signed an agreement with another Chinese party, notifying CFCA/CLICC that the co-operation would be discontinued. This was a downright breach of contract, as there was still one FCC/FCAS to go: 2002. CFCA moved quickly and booked the venue for 2002 in Shanghai as planned for FCC2002. This decision revealed a detailed insight into Exposure's beliefs on the part of CFCA. They knew that Exposure would not consider moving to another Chinese city, so by planting their flag in Shanghai first, which was not even their primary choice of a venue, they forced Exposure to renege on the statement to discontinue the co-operation.

FCC/FCAS2002 was once more a great success and, despite the concatenation of conflicts, both sides still started negotiations for a continuation of the co-operation. Exposure added another complicating issue to their relation with CFCA. It decided to change the South-East Asian FCA into an annual event as well. Even though the experience of 1999 had shown that the cannibalization of FCA to a following trade fair in China was only limited, CFCA/CLICC still feared that this would decrease the number of foreign companies to be attracted by Exposure for FCAS. When Exposure changed the biannual status of FCA into an annual one, CFCA reacted by creating an Autumn Fair, a national trade fair organized in smaller interior venues, without international exhibitors and therefore not co-organized with CLICC. While this move was caused by Exposure's initiative, it further escalated the mutual suspicion between the two parties. Although foreign companies were not allowed to exhibit at CFCA's local trade fair, Chinese subsidiaries of such companies were fully acceptable. This means that CFCA's domestic show had the potential of growing into a quasi-international trade fair, cannibalizing on FCC/FCAS. However, by this time a third and much larger crucial event had taken place in Exposure's organizational environment.

Exposure Asia had embarked on a localization strategy. This strategy aimed to let trade fairs be managed as much as possible in the country of the venue. Trade fairs in South Korea should be managed by Exposure Asia's branch in that country, etc. Exposure Asia had been exploring possibilities for a similar partner in China. So far, the company had offices in Shanghai and Guangzhou, but these were not real companies capable of organizing trade fairs independently. Exposure Asia's single largest trade fair was an annual furniture show in Shanghai, which was co-organized with a privately owned local company. The owner of that company, Mr Zhang, a former army officer who had made a fortune in the furniture business, was an astute business man with a good nose for opportunities. He realized that by partnering with Exposure Asia, recognized as a top player in its business in Asia, he would be giving up part of his independence, but would also gain a tremendous influence in the Chinese exhibition market. He negotiated an arrangement in which he would become the CEO of the joint venture. Exposure Asia had a majority share in the venture, but as the managers in Hong Kong completely trusted their local partner, Zhang became the person who decided what to do in China, where, with whom, etc.

The appearance of the joint venture in Hong Kong, even though it was one with Exposure Asia, rather than Exposure B.V., brought a new group of actors into the organization of FCAS Exposure Ltd. The London-based mother company stipulated that, as the organization had its own regional company in China, all activities by Exposure subsidiaries in China should at least involve Exposure China. While this will strike most people as a matter of course, this decision was bound to have significant consequences. New actors bring in their own inclusions and interests. When they start participating in the interaction, both the existing actors and the newcomers will need sufficient time to make sense of the new situation. Moreover, to make sure that this process unfolds smoothly, managers will be needed with the ability to steer these processes. Exposure lacked such management.

In mid-2001, it was decided that Mr Zhang would be involved in the negotiations with CFCA. During the following months the negotiations virtually came to a standstill and in the autumn of that year the CEO of Exposure sent a message to CFCA proposing to stop the negotiations for co-operation and 'continue with a competitive relation' (sic). What Exposure (apparently) failed to see was that Exposure China was a direct competitor of CFCA as a potential partner of Exposure in organizing FCAS. Mr Zhang believed that his company could take over this role entirely, thus earning commissions for the square metres sold. Zhang claimed that he would be able to bring CFCA in by going through the superior organization (mother-in-law) of CFCA, with which he claimed to have good relations. However, he never even tried and Exposure never reminded him of his claims. Even when, occasionally, Exposure questioned some of Mr Zhang's doings or statements, Zhang was always able to silence them through his associates in Exposure Asia, who would in turn take the matter up through Exposure Ltd, the mother company. The fact that the CEOs of all Exposure subsidiaries involved, except for Exposure China, were British, was conducive of creating a tightly coupled configuration that held Exposure's CEO in a strong grip.

As a result, FCAS and FCC continued as separate, competitive, events. FCAS2003, the first edition without CFCA, was not unsuccessful, but left much to be desired. However, Exposure received help from a (super)natural source: right after the event the SARS epidemic broke out and although FCC2003 was held in the very early period, the trade fair did suffer, especially by losing some foreign exhibitors and visitors. Exposure tried to cash in on this setback for CFCA by starting a final round of talks aimed at persuading CFCA to join in the organization of FCAS. CFCA refused.

FCAS2004 was quite a success, in the sense that by being slightly larger than FCAS2003, it proved that it was able to survive in a fierce competitive environment. The same can be said about FCAS2005, held a few weeks before the writing of this chapter. It was again slightly larger, but more in terms of square metres than number of exhibitors. The domestic exhibitors especially were gradually reaching a stage in which their booths showed few differences with those of the international exhibitors, both in size and appearance. Moreover, the same development was affecting FCC, which was also expanding, at an even faster rate than FCAS. FCAS2005 and FCC2005 were held with only ten days in between, in exactly the same venue and with a considerable number of companies participating in both.

This historic account of FCAS contains only a fraction of the organizational complexity. However, it should be sufficient for the reader to understand the following analysis of identity constructs of FCAS. I have opted to approach this topic from the various parties involved. Some of those parties are companies (organization spaces), others are larger groups of stakeholders like visitors. I will analyse how each party constructs its own edition of FCAS. In the final section of this chapter I will attempt to integrate these editions of FCAS.

To all their own trade fair

Exposure

It stands to reason to start with Exposure, the owner of the intellectual property of FCAS, as it is called in legal terms. Exposure is also the information carrier of the FC concept. A large body of literature has been written on organizations as information carriers. Daft and Weick (1984) describe in great detail how organizations can be regarded as interpretative systems. Walsh and Ungson (1997) have studied the same topic from the perspective of organizational memory, i.e. the capability of organizations to retain information. Hodgkinson and Sparrow (2002) describe the entire process of strategy formulation in companies as a cognitive process. A basic common element in all these studies is that knowledge is stored in the ritualistic symbolic behaviour of actors. Actors try to make sense of what they are doing while doing it (enactment). One of the consequences of this process is the appearance of social-cognitive structures of people who more or less frequently interact about more or less specific topics. The social element of these structures are the actors, while the cognitive element consists of a number of aspects, including a set of 'ways we do things', typical language (jargon), symbols, etc. The cognitive aspects are stored in the behaviour of the actors. New actors (e.g. new employees of a company) will acquire them through the process of socialization. Socialization can then be defined as the transfer of organizational knowledge by coupling the behaviour of the newcomers to that of the old hands through social interaction. After a successful socialization the new actors will behave in the same way, interpret information in the same way, speak in the same way, etc., as their older colleagues.

The concept of food components was born at and developed by Exposure, when it was still an independent company. Even after it became part of the Exposure organization, the FC trade fairs were organized from this Dutch subsidiary. Employees left the company and new ones were hired, but through the process of socialization, the newcomers became acquainted with the FC concept in all its finesses, without often completely understanding it from a rational point of view. On the other hand, Exposure Ltd cashed in on the success of these trade fairs and Exposure subsidiaries in countries where FC shows were organized did participate in the preparation. However, the unique identity of FC trade fairs remained a product of the interaction between Exposure and its customers.

Probably the best proof of this statement occurred in the period 1996–1997. It was a few years after Exposure became part of the British group when the then Dutch CEO left and was replaced by the first British manager. A rumour started to circulate among a considerable number of stakeholders, including exhibitors, external consultants, etc., stating that the mother company intended to organize the FC trade fairs from London, closing the Dutch subsidiary. This was a major blow to confidence among those stakeholders in the continuity of the FC concepts. It was as if the viability of FC was linked to the Netherlands, or the Dutch employees, even though some of the Dutch employees at that time had only been hired recently. These rumours affected the Dutch employees as well, as the rumours became part of their interaction with exhibitors, visitors, consultants, etc., and a more than usual turnover of managers could be observed during this period. This behaviour then in turn reinforced the belief among the other stakeholders that the disappearance of Exposure from the Netherlands was imminent.

Exposure Ltd in the end decided against the closure of the Dutch subsidiary and appointed a British CEO in the Netherlands. The fact that the new CEO was British did not affect stakeholder confidence; that immediately went up again, after it became clear that the FC trade fairs would continue to be organized by the same staff, from the same location. Investigating the relationship between Dutch culture and the FC concept is not part of the scope of this study. For understanding this particular case study, it will suffice to know that Exposure's location in the Netherlands is an aspect that matters. The Dutch employees have stored knowledge of the FC concept in their day-to-day behaviour. Exhibitors, visitors and other professional stakeholders recognize this, intuitively, as well. Marketing and sales people of food components manufacturers, as organizational actors, also have stored the knowledge of their organization in their daily routines, the way they speak, etc. They feel comfortable in booking exhibition space with Exposure sales people, because the way they are dealt with by Exposure people is in accordance with their expectations. To state this in more precise organization terminology: the booking of space at an FC trade fair is an interaction; it is not A acting on initiatives by B or B reacting after openings from A, but A and B interacting. It is a complex combination of 'way we do things', symbolic language, etc.

It was in this organizational environment that FCAS was conceived. FCA was a replication of FCE in Asia. It was started in South-East Asia, as Exposure believed that that was the most promising market (after Japan, where it had been defeated by a competitor). FCAS, hence the name, was regarded as originally conceived as a special edition of FCA. However, right after the first, very successful, FCAS in 1998, it was decided to hold FCAS annually. It thus became a separate trade fair; to be precise: the Chinese rendition of the FC concept.

In the initial configuration, Exposure's FCAS would attract international exhibitors, including companies with majority joint ventures in China and FCC domestic exhibitors. The consequence of this way of coupling behaviour was that FCAS was almost literally a small-size replica of FCE. The group of exhibitors at FCAS was a subset of the exhibitors at FCE, the mother trade fair. The activities for Exposure employees to attract exhibitors for FCAS were not that much different than for other FC trade fairs. There was some assistance from Exposure Asia, including for the logistic work in Shanghai. They did not have to deal with the Chinese exhibitors, which was the task of CFCA, for their own FCC show.

This situation changed considerably after Exposure and CFCA discontinued their co-operation. The two major changes were:

1   now there was a major competitor, while before competitors were not really an issue;
2   now the Exposure staff in charge of FCAS had to deal with Exposure China, whose sales staff was responsible for the sales among domestic prospects.

A major cognitive problem was posed by the question of whether the domestic exhibitors were the customers of Exposure or those of Exposure China. In the context that FCAS was a trade fair organized by Exposure, the Chinese exhibitors were the customers of Exposure. However, in terms of sales activities, the domestic exhibitors were attracted by the sales people of Exposure China and were therefore the cognitive clients of Exposure China.

The same situation applied to Exposure China. The international exhibitors were regarded as the relations of Exposure. Exposure China sales people would refer to the international companies at FCAS as 'your clients', when talking with Exposure people. The CEO of Exposure China was not satisfied with the number of international exhibitors and therefore repeatedly urged Exposure to get in more international customers.

On the other hand, Exposure felt that Exposure China was not making enough effort in a number of sectors included in the FC concept. Exposure China sales people were mainly approaching prospects during trade fairs organized by CFCA. As a consequence of this behaviour, the domestic part of FCAS was bound to be a subset of that of FCC. From an organization theoretical point of view, this is the result of the fact that the FC formula resided in Dutch staff of Exposure. Exposure China was also familiar with organizing trade fairs, but not with this particular sector.

As a result of the processes described in the previous paragraphs, FCAS was actually a hybrid trade fair, of which the international section was the Chinese edition of the FC formula and the domestic part an imitation of FCC. We could even conclude, again from an organizing point of view, that FCAS after Exposure and CFCA had parted was still a replica of the previous FCC/FCAS, with FCC not being organized by CFCA, but by Exposure China.

CFCA

CFCA is a so-called sector association. In the Chinese context this means that it is a semi-governmental organization consisting of member enterprises in a certain sector. Those enterprises pay an annual fee, which is the main source of income. While sector associations are managed by a small professional staff who perform their task on a full time basis, the board of an association also includes representatives of so-called 'member enterprises'. Chinese subsidiaries of foreign companies in the sector are Chinese legal persons and therefore qualify as members of their respective associations. CFCA already has a number of foreign members and even has a few of them appointed as 'managing members', which means that they can influence the activities of the association.

Sector associations are usually linked to the relevant ministry or ministry-like organization and the people that are directly employed by the association are often on the payroll of that supervising organization (mother-in-law). For CFCA the mother-in-law was the Ministry of Light Industry, which was later downgraded to the China Light Industry Council and then further to the China Light Industry Commission.

Sector associations have a number of tasks. Some of those tasks, like assisting in drawing up legislation, are shared by all, while others are more sector related. The main activities of CFCA are the following:

- assisting in drawing up quality specifications for food additives;
- helping companies, Chinese and foreign, with the registration of new products;
- scanning the international publications related to food additives and spreading this information through the Chinese industry;
- assisting member companies that encounter legal problems abroad, like dumping accusations;
- organizing academic conferences;
- publishing a bimonthly magazine;
- organizing an annual international (FCC) and national trade fair;
- organizing Chinese delegations to trade fairs abroad.

Knowledge of these activities of CFCA is necessary to understand the various inclusions of (the staff of) CFCA. Any one of the activities listed above (and the list is not exhaustive) involves social interaction with a number of parties. This interaction will take place in different social-cognitive contexts and will also be (potentially) creative of new contexts. One example will suffice. The second activity, assisting suppliers of food components with the registration procedure, alone implies that connections with CFCA are deemed necessary to succeed in the Chinese food components market. When we link this to the first activity, CFCA's involvement with drawing up specifications, an activity typically reserved for government agencies, we can see the identity appear of CFCA as the ideal gateway to the Chinese food components market. This identity is created as soon as a sufficient number of manufacturers and/or traders of food components use CFCA in this matter.

CFCA held its very first exhibition in Beijing in October 1990. The venue was a side hall in the Beijing Military Museum. The 'stands' were actually wooden tables on which companies placed samples of their products. Still, this event drew considerable attention. A national conference was held as well and the opening was televised on the evening news. I participated in the conference as a representative of a Dutch company.

This trade fair developed quickly into the main event at which buyers of food additives would meet suppliers and at which they would place their orders for the coming year. Its dates were moved to spring, soon after Chinese New Year, which marked the beginning of the new production season for many food and beverage product groups, in particular soft drinks and ice cream, which are major consumers of additives.

In the mid-1990s CFCA started organizing delegations of Chinese exhibitors to foreign trade fairs, in particular Exposure's main show: FCE. CFCA was impressed with the formula and its success and the idea arose to recreate FCE in China. The national trade fair was reorganized as an international one. The Chinese law stipulates that a licence is required to organize trade fairs involving foreign exhibitors. As CFCA did not have such a licence, it needed a partner to organize the envisioned international event. A logical candidate was CLICC, as CLICC was the international chamber of commerce of the Light Industry hierarchy. A pilot of FCC was launched in 1995. The first fully fledged FCC was held in 1997. By that time, CFCA had already been contacted by Exposure to discuss co-operation.

Co-operating with Exposure had advantages and disadvantages for CFCA. The major advantage was that it allowed CFCA to attain its goal of creating a food components trade fair that had the potential of growing into a size comparable with that of FCE. The main disadvantage was, as Exposure was in charge of attracting non-Chinese exhibitors, CFCA ran the risk of weakening its contacts with the international market. CFCA was willing to accept that risk in exchange for the opportunities offered by the co-operation.

The current situation, FCC and FCAS organizing separate competitive trade fairs, has been advantageous to CFCA in any perspective. FCC2005 attracted 750 domestic exhibitors and 117 international ones. The exhibition halls were not even large enough to accommodate all exhibitors and a temporary hall had to be constructed on the pavement adjacent to the exhibition centre.

A useful insight to gain into CFCA's sense-making of its competition with Exposure is to look at what is missing, or more precisely in this case, what we could expect CFCA to do to make life difficult for Exposure, but failed to do in practice.

Although CFCA is a semi-governmental organization, it is not in a position to request the relevant authorities to withhold an exhibition licence to FCAS, solely on the basis that Exposure is a foreign company competing with a government-related organization. However, there is regulation in China that discourages organizing two similar trade fairs in the same city closely after one another. This has certainly been the case in 2004 and 2005. The relevant authorities in Shanghai apparently did not have a problem with it, judging by the fact that no attempts were made to stop or move either of the trade fairs. However, CFCA also did not make any initiative towards the regulating authorities to report this 'irregular' competitive situation. The Secretary General of CFCA has stated during a number of discussions that it is not CFCA's aim to put Exposure out of business in China, as long as it does not resort to unfair competition. The latter remark refers to the fact that Exposure China is concentrating its sales activities for FCAS to CFCA's exhibitors at FCC and other CFCA-supported trade fairs or Chinese Pavilions. This seems to indicate that CFCA at least tolerates the existence of FCAS as a competitive trade fair to its own FCC.

As a sector association, CFCA cannot cease to exist, unless the central authorities decide on drastic changes in the way the Chinese economy is organized. FCC will therefore always be there. It is not a commercial enterprise, like Exposure's FCAS, but a typical service organization to the Chinese food components world. One of these typical services that the Chinese food components market would expect from CFCA is organizing trade fairs. FCC is the event in China at which suppliers and users of food components meet and discuss their business for the coming season. I already described above that CFCA has a problem providing all the space requested by its customers. Some exhibitors at FCC2005 had to be placed in a temporary hall, while, according to CFCA, still a number of slow deciders missed the boat completely and were unable to exhibit at FCC2005. To CFCA, as the organization responsible for the smooth operation of the Chinese food components market, FCAS is a blessing in the sense that it offers the additional exhibition space CFCA needs.

A recent note sent by CFCA to its major member companies corroborates this analysis (private communication). The note states that the average size of the stands of domestic exhibitors has been increasing each year. This has now reached the stage that FCC no longer fits in its current venue. CFCA is not (yet) willing to move to a larger, but more expensive, venue, as its objective is to be the low-price no-frills organizer of food components trade fairs in China. CFCA therefore requests its exhibitors not to book excessive space. Moreover, it suggests that those who have already booked space at 'other similar' trade fairs should consider not exhibiting at FCC. This is an interesting message. It could be explained, and is explained as such by Exposure, as an attempt to frighten domestic exhibitors that consider exhibiting at FCAS as well as FCC. Such companies may then refrain from booking space at FCAS, lest they will find the doors to FCC closed to them. However, in view of CFCA's relaxed behaviour towards FCAS described above, this message can also be interpreted as a way of stating that FCC is in principle there for all food component suppliers that want to exhibit, but that it would like to give priority to the smaller companies that cannot afford large costly stands. Those that insist on building elaborate stands are welcome to do so at FCAS, the only event that fits the description 'other similar trade fairs'.

Indeed, FCC2006 will remain at the current venue, while FCAS2006 will be held in a newer larger exhibition hall in Shanghai's newly developed Pudong New District. In spite of the fact that CFCA and Exposure are competitors, they are, from an organizing point of view, making sense of that competition in a similar way, which is reflected in a perfect coupling of their behaviour: CFCA remains at the older cheaper venue and requests its exhibitors to show restraint in the booking of space; Exposure is moving to a more expensive venue and is now contemplating increasing the minimum stand size from nine to 12 square metres. Both decisions have been made without mutual consultation. That such a perfect coupling of behaviour is still taking place is for me the most powerful support I have come across yet of the theoretical framework on which this study is based.

Exposure China

Exposure China is a young enterprise, established as a joint venture between Exposure Asia in Hong Kong and a local organizer of trade fairs in China. Moreover, Exposure China has only been involved in FCAS since 2002. Exposure China is itself an organizer of trade fairs that organizes a large number of events in a number of markets. It is not set up to assist Exposure subsidiaries with business in China. However, Exposure China is performing such a role when Exposure companies from outside China bring out editions of their trade fairs in China. This is based on the belief that an Exposure China will always provide the most efficient access to the Chinese market, regardless of the scope of the trade fair.

At the time that Exposure China was established, Exposure was still co-operating with CFCA. As CFCA was running its own FCC and also taking care of most of the logistic work for the combined FCC/FCAS in China, there was not much to do for Exposure China. However, as FCC/FCAS was such a tremendous success, it was obvious to Mr Zhang, Exposure China's CEO and former owner of the Chinese partner in the joint venture, that taking over the role of CFCA as Exposure's domestic partner would pose a great opportunity. When he was put in charge of renegotiating the co-operation with CFCA, it was as if Exposure had already decided against renewal of the co-operation. The negotiations did not only fail, they were hardly held and the contacts between CFCA and Exposure decreased to virtually zero.

I already mentioned the complaint of CFCA that the sales people of Exposure China are aggressively deploying sales activities at trade fairs organized by CFCA or Chinese delegations at foreign trade fairs headed by CFCA/CLICC. This indicates that Exposure China perceives (the domestic section of) FCAS as similar to FCC. A consequence of this sales behaviour is that the domestic section of FCAS is a subset of FCC.

This perception runs counter to Exposure's plans with FCAS, as laid out earlier in this chapter. While Exposure is concentrating its efforts for the development of FCAS to distinguishing it as much as possible from FCC in terms of product scope, Exposure China is reconstructing the domestic section of FCAS as FCC. As a result, the current FCAS, seen from an organizing perspective, can be regarded as two co-located trade fairs: a domestic one, very similar to FCC, organized by Exposure China and an international one, organized by Exposure, as the Chinese rendition of its proprietary FC formula.

The exhibitors

The total group of exhibitors of FCC and FCAS shows such large variety that it is not at all clear at first sight that they constitute a cognitive space. The first distinction is that between domestic and foreign companies. This distinction is first of all created by the fact that both trade fairs have special sections for international companies, located at a prime location near the main entrance of the exhibition hall. Foreign companies are still virtually always charged a higher price per square metre and are therefore regarded as entitled to such a prime location. Moreover, seeing the larger foreign stands upon entering the hall creates a better impression of the trade fair on the part of the visitors. Even when the foreigners do not pay a premium price, Chinese organizers of international trade fairs still prefer to use the foreign exhibitors as the façade of the show.

The second distinction that I would be inclined to find is that between patrons of FCC and those loyal to FCAS. Those companies indeed exist. However, one of the striking aspects of exhibitor behaviour in the competition between FCC and FCAS is that a considerable group of companies exhibit at both. I have combined the exhibitor lists of FCC2005 and FCAS2005 and sorted them. From the resulting list, the companies that exhibited at both can easily be detected, as they appear twice. The list of exhibitors thus extracted consists of 82 Chinese and eight foreign exhibitors. It is not surprising that the number of domestic doubles is so much larger. Chinese companies pay less per square metre on both shows and their other expenses, like travelling expenses, are much lower. However, eight international companies participating in both trade fairs is still peculiar for the trade fair business. Such companies can be expected to work according to international management standards with tightly controlled promotion budgets. Exhibiting twice per year in the same country would itself be out of the question, let alone in the same city with only ten days in between.

This customer behaviour indicates that the market is still going through a period of intensified sense-making that has resulted from the break up between Exposure and CFCA. Companies are still trying out the various options to make a final choice later.

On the other hand, against this background, it then strikes me that of the 90 Shanghai companies that exhibited at FCC and/or FCAS, only 13 (21 per cent) participated in both events. One would expect this ratio to be higher, as Shanghai-based companies would have even lower costs. The people in the stands would not even need hotel accommodation. Apparently, CFCA and Exposure China have a group of customers of their own that are loyal to their respective trade fair.

Among the domestic companies that exhibited at both shows we can observe a number of regional clusters. Ten per cent of all Shandong companies that exhibited at one trade fair or the other participated in both. Perhaps there is a forum in that region, e.g. the provincial counterpart of CFCA, the Shandong Food Additive Association, at which some companies have launched the idea that it would be better to take part in both. Shandong is China's main food province, good for 14 per cent of the total national turnover in that industry. It would make sense for the Shandong food components industry to invest in showing itself to the outside world.

Apart from observing exhibitor behaviour, I have had contacts with a number of international exhibitors during various editions of FCAS. Moreover, I have worked for some of Exposure's exhibitors as a consultant. One of the more common expectations of the foreign exhibitors is that they want to participate in a trade fair at which they can also find their main Chinese competitors, which is even more important for them than sharing a trade fair with their international competitors, whom they already meet at a number of similar forums. FCC is organized as *the* Chinese buying and selling trade fair for food components. The foreigners wish to develop the Chinese market and would like those flows of buyers to visit their stands as well. A number of foreign companies have switched trade fairs and opted for participating in FCC because more of their Chinese competitors were there.

A small, though influential, group are the multinationals with Chinese subsidiaries that are member organizations of CFCA. The mother companies tend to delegate all matters related to the China business, including the selection of trade fairs, to the Chinese companies. We can even observe a snowball effect among exhibitors from the same home region.

Two important foreign members of CFCA are Danish companies. Those two have not only opted to exhibit at FCC right after the break up between Exposure and CFCA, but also seem to have dragged two other important Danish food component players with them. This has created a configuration of Danish companies at FCC, which are not organized as a 'Danish Pavilion', but behave as such. This is a similar type of organizing process as the process mentioned earlier in this section that may have led to so many Shandong exhibitors participating in both trade fairs.

At FCC2005, I have made the rounds of the Chinese companies that have exhibited at both trade fairs. I asked them to name the strong sides of each trade fair, while refraining from using negative vocabulary like 'which is the best', or 'which do you prefer', etc. The replies showed great consistency. Most exhibitors perceived FCC as more Chinese and FCAS more international. When trying to find the reasons on which this perception was based, the replies were also surprisingly consistent: there was a considerably higher number of foreign visitors at FCAS than at FCC. While CFCA/CLICC perform quite well in attracting foreign exhibitors, Exposure is in a much better position to promote its Chinese trade fair among international visitors.

This perception of the difference between FCC and FCAS among Chinese exhibitors that participated in both shows coincides with the way Exposure China promotes FCAS among the domestic prospects. Exposure China stresses that FCAS is a more foreign trade oriented trade fair, while FCC is more geared to the domestic market. However, this perception does not agree with the objectives of Exposure and CFCA. These two partners-turned-competitors both strive to organize a comprehensive trade fair that serves importers, exporters, domestic buyers, foreign buyers, etc. I will return to the consequences of all of these perceptions and objectives in the conclusive section of this chapter.

Others

There are other parties involved whose sense-making of FCAS matters. However, in order to contain the size of this chapter I need to make a selection of the most significant parties. Others have been mentioned as well in the sections above and do not require an analysis as elaborate as that of Exposure, CFCA, etc.

CLICC's role has been explained in the analysis of CFCA. Although CLICC is the party that officially handles CFCA's dealings with foreign organizations, in actual negotiations, CFCA representatives always act as the main negotiators of the Chinese side. CLICC does not seem to have significant political clout.

On the Exposure side there are Exposure Asia and Exposure Ltd in Hong Kong and London respectively. They matter in the battle between Exposure and Exposure China over influence in the organization of

FCAS. However, this role has been sufficiently explained in the earlier sections of this chapter.

Another influential group of stakeholders in the organization of trade fairs are the visitors. There is no study of the perception(s) of FCC and FCAS among Chinese visitors. The foreign visitors (some consultants, mainly traders, etc.) are usually annoyed about the fact that as a result of the split between Exposure and CFCA there are now two trade fairs that they ought to visit. Doing so does not always fit in with their diaries and so far most of them have been loyal to Exposure and visited FCAS. However, there seems to be a growing awareness in this segment that FCC is bigger in terms of square metres as well as number of Chinese exhibitors. Visiting Chinese exhibitors tends to be the main objective of foreign visitors. This is a paradox: Exposure has the edge in attracting foreign visitors, but most foreign visitors would be more satisfied by visiting FCC.

There are a number of (semi-)governmental organizations involved in the organization of both trade fairs. Some act as sponsoring organizations literally participating in name only, while others assist in attracting exhibitors. Some help organize the technical seminars that are part of both shows.

Making sense of a trade fair

In the final section of this chapter I will make an inventory of the identity constructs of FCAS that can be observed at the time this part of the text was written (April 2005). I will point out two types of conflicting identities:

1   conflicts within the ways a party makes sense of FCAS;
2   conflicts between the ways two parties make sense of FCAS that affects their interaction.

Exposure

For Exposure, FCAS is the Chinese edition of the FC with the company's FC concept. This perception triggers the construction rule that the Exposure sales staff will try to persuade as many of their pool of FC clients as possible to exhibit at FCAS. As a consequence of that activity the actual exhibitors booked by the Exposure sales staff are a subset of that pool. To Exposure the identity of FCAS has not changed after their divorce from CFCA. Before that moment, Exposure took care of the international section, while CFCA handled the domestic one. In the current situation, Exposure employs exactly the same activities based on exactly the same perceptions.

CFCA

FCAS's identity vis-à-vis CFCA is that of complement to its own FCC trade fair. CFCA's primary task is to optimize the Chinese food components market. Organizing FCC is one of the key activities in attaining that goal. FCC is currently not capable of fulfilling this task completely, but FCAS can absorb most of what FCC has left behind. CFCA has not actively supported FCAS since the co-operation with Exposure was discontinued, but it still does so passively by not undertaking any possible action to make life difficult for Exposure. This analysis is further corroborated by the fact that the FCC editions of 2004 and 2005 were both held in the same venue. In 2006 FCAS will move to a different venue, but still in the same city. This facilitates parties that wish to participate in or visit both.

Exposure China

To Exposure China, FCAS is business as usual. It is a trade fair organized by Exposure, their own company. The subtleties between Exposure B.V., Exposure Asia, Exposure Ltd, etc., do not play an important role in the sense-making of the Exposure China sales staff. For them FCAS is a replica of FCC and Exposure China is the replacement for CFCA after CFCA and Exposure broke up. As a result of that perception, Exposure China employs its sales activities for this trade fair mainly at trade fairs organized by CFCA or including Chinese Pavilions organized by CFCA. This in turn produces the result that the domestic section of FCAS is a subset of the client pool of CFCA.

For Exposure China's CEO, FCAS is a business opportunity generating income without having had to go through the process of developing a formula from scratch. However, in the context of Exposure, FCAS is an important symbol in the sense-making of his position as the person any Exposure member company should turn to if it intends to develop business in China.

Foreign exhibitors

The foreign exhibitors are plagued by ill-compatible expectations. On one hand they expect to exhibit in China at a trade fair together with the maximum number of their Chinese and international competitors, in that order of importance. On the other hand, they tend to believe that Exposure, with its reputation of the world leader in food components trade fairs, will be able to offer the level of service they expect. The first expectation leads a number of them to participate in FCC, while the second belief makes others decide to exhibit at FCAS. A few have exhibited at both in 2005, which is extraordinary in this business and therefore a strong signal that the process of identity construction between the foreign exhibitors and FCAS is still in a state of heightened sense-making.

Chinese exhibitors

Chinese exhibitors are also torn between two tendencies. On one hand all of them need to see the flow of domestic buyers. The Chinese food components market is highly cyclical in nature, with a peak in purchasing activities in early spring. On the other hand, those who are, or wish to be, active on the global market expect to see a sufficient number of foreign buyers at their stand. Most of the Chinese exhibitors are curious about what is happening in the world and hope to be able to visit a sufficient number of foreign stands during the trade fair. FCC foresees best in the first need, while FCAS performs better for the second. Regarding the third wish, FCAS2005 still had the edge, but FCC is closing in. This analysis is corroborated by the behaviour of more than 80 Chinese exhibitors that participated in both events in 2005. Although budgeting is less strict in Chinese corporations, it is still rare for a Chinese company to exhibit at such similar trade fairs in the same city in the same month. In this respect the identity construction of FCAS among the Chinese exhibitors is also in a state of intense sense-making.

Who saved FCAS?

The major conflict between identity constructs of FCAS is that between Exposure and Exposure China. While Exposure is constructing FCAS as much as possible along the same line as its generic FC formula, with the successful FC Europe as the typical example, Exposure is reconstructing FCC.

This situation is by itself not necessarily a fatal problem. The direct threat to the existence of FCAS is posed by the expectations of a major stakeholder group: the foreign exhibitors. The success or failure of FCAS is determined by the question of whether Exposure will still be able to attract a sufficient number of international exhibitors. As long as they are, Exposure China will have no problems matching that with a sufficient number of Chinese exhibitors. If not, the Chinese will change sides too.

Exhibitors have expectations. Expectations are not perceptions, but function as attractors. The majority of Chinese exhibitors still believe that their expectations can best be met by CFCA and its FCC. This expectation is shared by the bulk of the domestic buyers. As a result FCC attracts the largest number of domestic exhibitors and visitors.

Exposure China is promoting FCAS among Chinese exhibitors and visitors as a typical foreign trade event. This promotion strategy reinforces the belief that domestic exhibitors who are not or only slightly interested in exports are better off at FCC. Domestic buyers who prefer to buy domestic components, unless no domestic alternative is available, are triggered by these signals and also frequent FCC.

In other words, Exposure China's promotion strategy runs counter to what Exposure needs to safeguard the continuation of FCAS.

The saviour of FCAS seems to be not Exposure or Exposure China, but CFCA. For CFCA FCAS has a dual identity:

1   FCAS is a convenient vehicle for solving FCC's capacity problem;
2   FCAS helps CFCA to fulfil its primary task of regulating and developing the Chinese food components market.

CFCA therefore not only did nothing to hinder FCAS after it broke up with Exposure, but has now also started to refer some domestic companies to FCAS, in particular those that wish to exhibit with oversized stands. CFCA guarantees its patrons that FCC will always be organized with the lowest possible cost (unpublished internal CFCA note). CFCA has, for example, discarded such expensive activities as the opening ceremony, first day banquet, press conference, etc. This statement is constructive of FCAS with an identity of high cost, high price. In this respect, CFCA also contributes more to realize Exposure's expectations of organizing FCAS as a world class trade fair, with a high level of service. CFCA feels comfortable with FCC as the large low-cost low-price average-service trade fair, complemented by FCAS as the high-cost high-price high-service niche trade fair. Finally, CFCA accommodates FCAS by maintaining Shanghai as the venue of FCC. CFCA is very well aware that Exposure is horrified by the idea of holding its Chinese edition of the FC formula in another Chinese city and, primarily to accommodate the exhibitors and visitors, holds its own FCC in Shanghai as well. This behaviour in turn subconsciously confirms the belief at Exposure (or in terms of my framework: in the Exposure space) that Shanghai is the only conceivable venue for their Chinese FC event. I have showed throughout this chapter that the reified results of the enquiry held by Exposure among a number of its largest customers in 1995 has affected its activities and interactions with other parties in China a number of times. CFCA's decision to fix Shanghai as the venue for FCC is the last, and probably the most spectacular, example. For me as a researcher of organizing process it has at least generated the perfect example of two companies coupling their behaviour, which still continues as these words are typed, almost two years after their last negotiation.

8 Chinese corporate identity
Summary and integration

Integrating incidents

Chapters 3 to 7 contain detailed descriptions and analyses of identity constructs of five enterprises. Although each chapter has been written around one core enterprise, the stories also feature a host of other organizations and many more individual actors. As identity is constructed in interaction, any study of identity needs to start with observing a sufficient number of interactions. Furthermore, as identity is a construct, a product of sense-making, it is linked to a certain social-cognitive context in which the sense-making takes place. Individual actors or a group of actors, as the enterprises that are the theme of this study, will construct different identities in the different social-cognitive contexts (cognitive spaces) in which they are included. Different contexts are linked through the multiple inclusions of actors, which means that an identity construction process in one context can be influenced by similar processes in other contexts in which one of the actors participating in the process is included. An example will help.

Two actors, a university professor and a student of that professor, are also members of the same political party. In the university context they enact their role identities of teacher and student, which can be reflected in behaviour (the teacher stands in front of the classroom talking to an audience of students, the student sits in the classroom listening to the teacher, etc.), typical language (the teacher speaking rather formally, the students interrupting with rather informal questions), symbols and artefacts, etc. During a party meeting, the same two actors will enact their identities as equal party members, in which their ways-we-do-things, jargon, symbols, etc., will be more or less the same. However, it is highly likely that the processes of identity construction in both contexts affect one another. This would already be the case if one of the actors were included in both contexts and is even more so when, as in this example, both actors are included in both contexts. When the professor was addressing the student about an academic topic in his room at the university, he would be simultaneously addressing his fellow party member. At that particular moment, the inclusion in the academic space would be stronger than the one in the party space, but both contexts would play a role in their ongoing interaction. If, for example, the student's academic performance left much to be desired according to the professor, the student may opt to invoke his shared inclusion in the party space to ward off the threat to their relation in the academic space. A fellow student without such a shared inclusion in that party space would not have this opportunity and would need to search for an alternative context. McCall and Simmons have phrased this in slightly different terms, using the term audience. Actors are constantly seeking audiences for supporting their points of view. An actor 'has alternative audiences to whom he can, in imagination, appeal ... when the audience present does not confer to the required support' (McCall and Simmons 1966: 100). My framework goes one step further by stating that all actors always have such alternative audiences available, but this availability is sometimes blocked by reifications. More-over, my term 'inclusion' does better justice to the equality between actors and their audiences.

This phenomenon of mutual influencing of interaction in different con-texts through multiple inclusions of actors is the core mechanism of a healthy organizing process. Actors interact in a specific context, but do so with the possibility of bringing in cognitive matter from any of their, theoretically indefinite, other inclusions. On the other hand, the blocking of access to other inclusions, be it by the actor him/herself or by an act of another actor, is the main threat to a sound organizing process (Van Dongen *et al.* 1996: 253–263).

The case chapters are mainly descriptive in nature. I have attempted to describe the main contexts in which the core enterprise of a chapter appears to make sense and how each of those sense-making processes take place, what parties are involved, etc., using the general model introduced in Chapter 1. In doing so, I found it necessary also to describe identity con-struction processes in other inclusions that I presumed to be influencing the processes under description. As a result, each chapter is so packed with actors, inclusions, interactions and other information that it may not always be easy to extract the recurrent guiding principles governing these processes. In this chapter I will attempt to retell the stories of the case chapters in a more abstract fashion, emphasizing what each story can teach us about the construction of corporate identity in general and Chinese corporate identity in particular.

My methodology will be to concentrate on the major incident in each chapter. At the end of Chapter 2, I introduced 'incident-driven case history' as an experimental alternative for the classical type of business case study. The incident-driven method starts with a general description of the company, its market and its place in the market, more or less similar to that in classical case studies. Then the company is described in terms of the theoretical theme, which in our case is the construction of corporate identities. Finally, the findings of the theoretical section are applied to an incident, an event, period, etc., in the history of the core company that called for a heightened degree of sense-making.

In this chapter I will start retelling each case story starting with the incident and concentrate on the main identity constructs that affected the cause and development of the incident. In the final section I will then attempt to make another cycle of concentrating the findings of this study to see what common aspects of the case histories can tell us about the most salient aspects of Chinese corporate identity.

Lukang

Lukang's incident was the conflict between its CEO, Mr Zhang, and the manager of one of Lukang's subsidiaries, Mr Wu, on the integration of that subsidiary in the conglomerate. The incident started within Lukang and proved difficult to win for either party. Mr Wu turned to an inclusion outside Lukang, the State Securities Supervisory Commission in Beijing, for a solution. However, this move had repercussions for the identity of Lukang in the Ji'ning space, thus escalating the conflict to that space as well. Mr Zhang countered that with a similar move, invoking his inclusion in the Communist Party space. Mr Zhang's route proved strongest and Mr Wu disappeared from the scene.

As I already indicated in the graphic representation of the conflict history at the end of Chapter 3, this incident involved (at least) three identities of Lukang:

- Lukang = Lukang;
- Lukang = Ji'ning;
- Lukang = CCP.

Lukang = Lukang

The Lukang = Lukang identity is most difficult to describe, as little information is available. Lukang is a *danwei*, a Chinese work unit. However, this is not part of Lukang's Lukang identity, but an identity inherited from a higher cognitive space. In the organization of society of the People's Republic of China, all Chinese citizens should belong to a work unit, as explained in Chapter 2. Lukang is such a work unit for all people on its payroll and this aspect will play a role in the process of identity construction of what Lukang is to those people. However, if we want to understand what is unique about Lukang, as a work unit, then we need to exclude such aspects as providing salaries, housing, medical care, etc. The corpus of Lukang texts shows that Lukang in its Lukang identity is strongly linked to the person of its CEO, Mr Zhang Jianhui. Mr Zhang's name appears frequently in the texts on a variety of themes. He led the company from a state-owned and operated 'factory' to a major Chinese corporation, listed on the Shanghai Stock Exchange. Mr Zhang's activities as reported in the corpus show that he is always personally in charge of major actions. For example, he led the Lukang team to Beijing to prepare for the second issue of shares, an activity that many Chinese CEOs would rather delegate to others. Mr Zhang also regularly heads Lukang delegations to trade fairs abroad. The world's largest trade fair for pharmaceutical raw materials is CPhI World Wide, which is held in rotating European venues. Mr Zhang is part of the Lukang delegation to this trade fair almost every year and is present in the Lukang stand personally, at least during the opening day of the show. Lukang's stand is a typical Chinese stand with a counter for the brochures and a table with a few chairs. Mr Zhang usually sits at the table and as long as there are no visitors to talk to, he chats with his staff, apparently, as their equal. Mr Zhang is recognized as the person in charge and therefore has little need to confirm his authority with authoritative behaviour.

In such a corporate culture, it is easy to understand that Mr Wu, who was only recently reorganized into Lukang by an administrative measure, and still in the process of socialization, developed a conflict with Mr Zhang. One of the construction rules of the Lukang space seems to be: you do not openly question a decision by Mr Zhang. Mr Wu did openly question this decision and although the case story does not tell us in detail to what extent Mr Zhang had been personally involved in incorporating Lingzhi into Lukang, what we observe about his behaviour in general leads us to the assumption that he was indeed involved. Moreover, the fact that Lingzhi was a trading company, while Lukang's main business was manufacturing, also constructs differences in corporate cognition. In Peverelli (2000: 143 ff.) I have already indicated that manufacturing and trading, even concerning the same products, can construct striking differences in the perception of time and risk.

Internal corporate identities, or $X = X$ identities, have a propensity to become reificational. The interaction that constructs this identity is interaction between the employees of the company. It tends to centrifugality and therefore is probably the single most important interaction that is constructive of the corporate boundary, the perceived boundary that separates the organization from its environment. It is the sense-making of 'us defined as other than them' (Haslam 2001: 26 ff.).

Lukang = Ji'ning

This identity, what Lukang is to Ji'ning and vice versa, is much easier to describe than Lukang = Lukang: Lukang is one of the Ji'ning's major employers. As such it contributes to the local social stability and therefore is a strong pillar of the municipal government. This is a genuine, interactively constructed, identity. Lukang had gradually expanded and absorbed more and more of the regional workforce. Ji'ning increases its support to Lukang more and more, proportionally to the expansion of Lukang as an employer. These actions from Lukang to Ji'ning and vice versa are two separate, but co-genetic actions.

The identities of Lukang = Lukang and Lukang = Ji'ning are intertwined. Actions in one can have repercussions in the other. One of the consequences of Lukang = Ji'ning is that it creates an obligation of Lukang to retain its position as largest employer. Or, in terms of identity, to retain the conditions under which Ji'ning Municipality makes sense of Lukang as the largest employer in its administrative region. The more Lukang expands, at least in Ji'ning, the heavier this burden becomes.

When the internal conflict between Messrs Zhang and Wu was extended to what we could name the 'listed companies' space, the existence of Lukang, at least the existence of Lukang as of that particular moment in time, was threatened. This also threatened the identity of Lukang as the largest employer in Ji'ning. The threat in the listed companies space was bad enough for Mr Zhang, as it made him make the headlines of the national newspapers in a negative way. However, the threat to Lukang's Ji'ning identity was much more urgent, as it posed a real threat to the very existence of Lukang. If Ji'ning Municipality regarded this conflict as a sign that it should not bet too many of its scarce resources on Lukang and should instead divert some of them to other major enterprises in the region, it would be difficult for Lukang to regain its favoured position in the future. Mr Zhang was a key actor in this conflict for two reasons: in Chinese legal terminology he was the representative of the legal person of Lukang and therefore personally responsible, and he had established an image as the strong man behind the success of Lukang and would therefore automatically be regarded as the key person in its demise if the conflict escalated. It was imperative for Mr Zhang to look for a solution that would confirm his personal strength in the Ji'ning space.

Lukang = CPC

The search revealed that the best inclusion was Mr Zhang's position as Party Secretary of Lukang. Lukang's identity of CPC cell is a similar type of identity to its identity as work unit; it is derived from the general politico-economic organization of the PRC. However, while Lukang = *danwei* only played a minor role in this conflict, Lukang = CPC turned out to be a crucial identity, because of the strong inclusions of Mr Zhang in both Lukang = Lukang and Lukang = CPC. As the CEO of such a large corporation he was one of China's better known entrepreneurs and being the Party Secretary of Ji'ning's largest employer made Mr Zhang a person with considerable authority within the Ji'ning CPC space. Through the latter inclusion, Mr Zhang was able to mobilize the party officials of a number of municipal government organizations to break the resistance of Mr Wu against the reorganizations and to prevent officials from the State Securities Supervisory Commission from investigating Mr Wu's allegations. Mr Zhang's power was such that, in spite of the fierce criticisms of his handling of this conflict in the national press, no actions were taken against him. At the next CPhI trade fair after the incident, held in Frankfurt, he headed his delegation to Europe as usual and was the same amiable person who enjoyed chatting with his staff in the stand.

A crucial condition for Mr Zhang to get away with this stunt was that Mr Wu was a party member as well. This 'double confinement' measure is only possible in extreme circumstances and under the condition that the person to be confined is a party member.

Here once more, we can observe a situation in which happenings around one identity pertaining to certain cognitive space can have repercussions for another identity in another space. Before, we could see that a change in the identity of Lukang = listed company affected the identity Lukang = Ji'ning. Mr Zhang then took action based on the Lukang = CPC identity, which neutralized the threat to the Lukang = Ji'ning identity and also made him win his conflict with Mr Wu in the Lukang = Lukang space.

More

Even this strict attempt to analyse the incident in the Lukang chapter in terms of the most crucial identity constructs of the core company involved shows that it is impossible not to refer to a number of other identities as well. The identities of an enterprise are mutually linked through the multiple inclusions of the key actors involved in the incident. I already mentioned the Lukang = listed company identity on which Mr Wu based his strategy to get back at Mr Zhang. However, Mr Wu's inclusion in his family in Ji'ning and hence also his Ji'ning identity played a role in the sense that it determined his return to Ji'ning, even though he should have known that he was putting himself at the mercy of his, then, worst adversary.

Zhengzhou dairy

Although the core company of Chapter 4 is Huahuaniu, this case history cannot be told without constantly involving another dairy company in the same city: Shanmeng. This constructs a highly interesting type of competitive relation. Their relation seems to be almost co-genetic in the sense of the relation between concepts like 'correct' and 'incorrect', 'good' and 'evil', etc., as described by Van Dongen (1991). Van Dongen explains that one cannot discuss a notion like 'correct' without simultaneously referring to 'incorrect'. Something can only be designated as incorrect because there is something else that is correct. That which is correct defines what is not and vice versa. Between the two there is a boundary marking the areas of what is correct and what is incorrect. This boundary is not fixed, its position is determined during social interaction. Its position is a result of sense-making. What is considered correct is therefore linked to the social-cognitive context that regards it as correct. What is regarded as correct in one such context, can be considered incorrect in another context.

Huahuaniu and Shanmeng as proper nouns are designations of enterprises and can therefore not be completely compared with opposite pairs of adjectives like 'correct' and 'incorrect'. I would like to focus my attention in this section on the interaction between Huahuaniu and Shanmeng to see if I can substantiate the impression expressed in the previous paragraph.

I will start with reproducing the sense-making of both companies in the provincial and municipal spaces in Table 8.1. For ease of understanding, I will use the proper nouns Henan and Zhengzhou for the names of the province and the municipality respectively.

In the sense-making of the two companies in the Henan space, Huahuaniu and Shanmeng are clearly separated. Huahuaniu is *the* provincial dairy company, while Shanmeng is a regional dairy company linked to Zhengzhou. In the sense-making in the Zhengzhou space, both enterprises are regarded as one of the two leading dairy companies in their own region. Zhengzhou also makes sense of Shanmeng as a key industrial project, but this does not make Shanmeng different from Huahuaniu to the same extent as the sense-making in the Henan space.

The situation revealed by this table seems to corroborate the co-genetic nature of the relation between Huahuaniu and Shanmeng. However, this relation is now narrowed down to the Zhengzhou space. In Henan, Huahuaniu is provincial and Shanmeng regional (Zhengzhou). In Zhengzhou, Huahuaniu and Shanmeng are members of one construct: 'the two leading dairy companies in Zhengzhou'. Huahuaniu cannot be made sense of without Shanmeng and vice versa.

Positivists will now point out that Huahuaniu 'existed' before

Table 8.1 The sense-making matrix of Huahuaniu and Shanmeng in the Henan and Zhengzhou spaces

Company	Henan	Zhengzhou
Huahuaniu	The leading manufacturer of dairy products in Henan	One of the two leading dairy companies, together with Shanmeng
Shanmeng	One of the major regional dairy companies of Henan	Key industrial project; one of the two leading dairy companies in Zhengzhou, together with Huahuaniu

Shanmeng and that this justifies the conclusion that Shanmeng was established by Zhengzhou to compete with Huahuaniu. I do not contend with this way of expressing by itself, but regard it as not a complete explanation of all the subtleties of the relation between the two companies. In the positivist concept there are two companies, Huahuaniu and Shanmeng. One was established by Henan at a certain time and Zhengzhou set up Shanmeng later to compete with Huahuaniu. In my model, there are (at least) two Huahuanius at the time the research was conducted:

- Huahuaniu = Henan;
- Huahuaniu = Zhengzhou.

The same holds for Shanmeng. Before the establishment of Shanmeng, Huahuaniu = Zhengzhou did not exist. This sense of Huahuaniu was constructed by the sense-making process that led to the establishment of Shanmeng. My conclusion is therefore that Huahuaniu = Zhengzhou and Shanmeng = Zhengzhou are co-genetic in the Zhengzhou space. This sense-making in the Zhengzhou space affected the sense-making in the Henan space, where Shanmeng was made sense of as a 'regional' dairy company, as opposed to *the* provincial dairy maker Huahuaniu.

This model of the competition between Huahuaniu and Shanmeng explains the behaviour of Shanmeng, which seems to copy every major strategic move by Huahuaniu. I will summarize them here:

- *Establishment*
  Huahuaniu was established in 1999. Zhengzhou formed Shanmeng in late 2000.
- *Foreign funding*
  Henan signed the SIDDAIR agreement in March 1999. Zhengzhou officially incorporated Shanmeng Dairy Co., Ltd including EU funding in mid-2001.
- *Local partner*
  Huahuaniu and Shanmeng both sold part of their equity to a national leading dairy company in late 2003, with Shanmeng doing so only two months after Huahuaniu.

The cognitive element of the Zhengzhou space includes the concept 'the two leading dairy companies in Zhengzhou'. This is perceived to consist of two other constructs: Huahuaniu and Shanmeng, of which Shanmeng is further perceived as a key industrial product (of Zhengzhou), while Huahuaniu is neutral in this respect. In the sense-making calculus, the fact that within the Zhengzhou space the sense-making of Shanmeng is more complex, more precise, implies that Shanmeng is more closely linked to Zhengzhou than Huahuaniu.

In the Henan space, the appearance on the scene of Shanmeng required additional sense-making of the provincial dairy industry. Shanmeng became part of the list of major regional dairy companies, with Zhengzhou as its home region. The arrival of Shanmeng did not alter the sense-making of Huahuaniu as *the* provincial dairy company. It also did not affect the perception that Huahuaniu = Henan was located in Henan, not in Zhengzhou. When discussing the competitive situation in Zhengzhou, Huahuaniu officials do include Shanmeng in their narratives, but also a number of national companies that try to get a piece of the Zhengzhou market. In the Henan sense-making there is no counterpart of the construct: 'the two leading dairy companies in Zhengzhou'.

Armed with this insight, we can return to the Dutch venture in Zhengzhou and see how it can clarify some of the mysteries that puzzled the Dutch involved in the project even at the time the appraisal was made, a week before the end of the five-year co-operation.

The Dutch entered the Zhengzhou dairy industry from the Henan space. They exclusively dealt with Huahuaniu = Henan. According to their West European cultural programming, they fixed the identity of SIDDAIR in one single cognitive space, which made it extremely difficult to observe other identities of SIDDAIR. It will be illuminating to place SIDDAIR in the identity matrix drawn earlier in this section (see Table 8.2). I have placed SIDDAIR only in the Huahuaniu = Henan quadrant, indicating that SIDDAIR was only made sense of in that context. This does not mean that SIDDAIR did not make sense at all in the other contexts, but I have not been able to find any trace of cognitive matter that can be linked to any of those three contexts. This justifies a provisional conclusion that SIDDAIR only made sense in those contexts as 'the partner of Huahuaniu = Henan'. This conclusion is corroborated by the fact that the existence of SIDDAIR in that identity had no consequences for the behaviour of any party but Huahuaniu = Henan. Shanmeng, for example, did not purchase raw milk from SIDDAIR.

SIDDAIR's set of identity constructs should be considered as deficient. Companies in any part of the world construct several identities in different social-cognitive contexts. However, this process is even more apparent in the Chinese environment, where identity is less fixed to one 'core identity' as can be observed in Western countries. SIDDAIR therefore did not behave like a Chinese company, it did not play the identity game in the

Table 8.2 SIDDAIR's affiliation with the various identities of Huahuaniu and Shanmeng

	Henan	*Zhengzhou*
Huahuaniu	SIDDAIR = our foreign partner	None
Shanmeng	None	None

same way as Chinese enterprises. In terms of requisite variety, we could conclude that SIDDAIR was considerably less complex than its environment, which gave it little foundation for sustainable existence. SIDDAIR, a year after it was handed over to the Chinese side in March 2004, is at the time this analysis was written (April 2005) nothing more than a subsidiary of what is now known as the Huahuaniu Group, the new name of Yawei.

This is not the proper place to make conjectures as to what SIDDAIR could have been if it had been defined in multiple identities from the start. Organizing processes can be calculated and predicted in a mathematical fashion. However, the analysis in Chapter 4 and the further exploration of the identities of its partner Huahuaniu provide sufficient information to realize that the Dutch have lost opportunities with great potential during the period that the project has been in operation. There is a valuable lesson to learn here for future similar projects, both government-subsidized projects like SIDDAIR, or commercial investment.

Mengniu in Shanyin

The history of Mengniu's establishment and its astonishingly rapid development as a kind of clone of Yili is by itself a highly interesting case of Chinese corporate identity construction. However, the most important aspect of corporate identity exposed in Chapter 5 is that (Chinese) enterprises tend to re-enact the identities constructed in their home region when expanding to other regions.

Before turning to Mengniu's activities in Shanyin, I will review its identity constructs in Huhhot.

Mengniu = Yili

In the context of the local dairy market, Mengniu was established by Niu Gensheng and a few hundred of his former colleagues who he had been able to extract from Yili. In terms of organizing, we can observe that even before Niu was 'removed' from the top management of Yili, he had formed a configuration of loyal followers around him by sharing his earnings with them liberally. He regarded himself as a self-made man who owed everything he was to a number of people. This started with his foster parents and continued to all his direct colleagues. Later, when he was given various management positions, he still shared bonuses, etc., with his subordinates. Instead of one single configuration, it is also conceivable that Niu and his 'allies' within Yili constructed a number of configurations that together formed a cognitive space. As soon as Niu set up Mengniu in his one-room office and started contacting his acquaintances in Yili, the entire 'Niu Gensheng space' left Yili for Mengniu. Doing so, all of the actors involved could basically continue their daily activities, with the only difference that they enacted another enterprise space: Mengniu.

Niu's behaviour when he was still with Yili already showed a keen insight in the value and workings of building configurative networks. He did not behave simply as a doer of good deeds, but deftly used the Chinese inclination to understand relations in material terms by literally investing in his network. Moreover, he continued this behaviour during the more than two decades that he was employed by Yili. Niu's 'generosity' became an important part of what we could refer to as the 'Niu space' within Yili.

This analysis is corroborated by the behaviour of the top management of Yili in trying to rid their organization of Niu. Niu's fellow managers were acting in the same social-cognitive structures as Niu himself and we therefore can expect that they would be aware of Niu's strong networks within Yili. While on one hand wishing to release Niu from Yili, they realized that they could not simply send him home with a nice bonus. This may have met with severe protests from Niu's friends in Yili. Instead, he was sent away to study. He still held his position in Yili, but was no longer physically present.

However, the coupling between Niu Gensheng and his Yili companions proved too strong for the Yili management to break. Niu received the returns on his investment after the establishment of Mengniu in two ways:

1   the entire Niu space left Yili for Mengniu;
2   Niu's former Yili friends readily invested their savings in Mengniu and even mobilized their relatives and close friends to do the same. Due to Niu's behaviour of the past two decades, they had no reason to believe that Niu would not repay them generously.

As a result, immediately after setting up Mengniu, even before the company was officially registered as such with the proper authorities, Niu has capital and a staff of dairy specialists, accountants, personnel officers, clerks, secretaries, workers, etc., with experience in the dairy industry. Moreover, the entire staff of Mengniu at that moment consisted of actors who were already interacting in existing social-cognitive contexts. The only thing that had changed was the name of the enterprise they were enacting: Mengniu instead of Yili.

Even Niu Gensheng's policy of the Three Don'ts that he issued to prevent direct confrontations with Yili reinforced the Mengniu = Yili identity: all three were defined in terms of Yili. Or, more precisely, both what Mengniu did and what it did not do were defined in terms of Yili.

Mengniu = a good second

This identity construct has been derived from the identity Mengniu = Yili, but has developed into a separate identity, involving a larger number of (organizational) actors. In the sense-making of Mengniu as the new player in the Huhhot dairy market, Niu actively positioned Mengniu as a loyal follower of the leader. Mengniu was competing with Yili, but without obstructing Yili's own development. Yili was frequently mentioned as the great example for what Mengniu strived to become. Later, in slogans like 'The vast grasslands have given birth to: Yili, Xingfa and Mengniu Dairy', Niu started to include third parties. Mengniu and Yili, as well as other famous local enterprises, were positioned as co-operating to put Inner Mongolia on the map. Rephrased in terms of the theoretical framework of this study: by including third parties in the relationship between Mengniu and Yili, Niu incorporated cognitive matter from a space in which Mengniu and Yili were not competing. It invoked a reality in which both were coupling their behaviour with other parties for a goal exceeding that of their mutual competition.

In his strategy development for Mengniu, Niu also constantly let Yili experiment with various new possibilities offered by the evolving politico-economic environment. Mengniu could then follow suit with activities that seemed to work for Yili and do things at which Yili failed differently. The same follower behaviour was extended to other companies. Mengniu became a company that did better what others did well.

Finally, Mengniu enacted this identity of good second so well that it actually became the example of others to follow. This included even Yili, Mengniu's primary example. This is most evident in the way these two Inner Mongolian dairy giants expanded to other parts of China. Mengniu sometimes followed Yili's initiative towards a certain region, but Yili sometimes also followed Mengniu's first step to another region. The incident of the Mengniu case, Mengniu's setting up shop in Shanyin, however, shows that even when Mengniu entered a region before Yili did, it still enacted its identity of good second.

Other identities

As an enterprise, certainly and enterprise of that size, Mengniu has a large number of other identities, some of which are essential to understand if one wishes to understand Mengniu's behaviour. One of the more typical identities of these is: Mengniu = Niu Gensheng. Up to the moment that this final chapter was being written, it seems to be virtually impossible for the Chinese media to report on Mengniu without mentioning Niu Gensheng at least once. While Mengniu is not the only example of a strong relation between a young enterprise and its founder who is still acting as CEO, Mengniu is certainly one of the most telling examples.

The Mengniu = work unit identity, the identity construct shared by all Chinese enterprises, also played a strong role in the birth of Mengniu. One of the motivating forces for so many of Niu's former colleagues at Yili to leave Yili for Mengniu is that they made sense of Mengniu as a more attractive work unit than Yili. This is related to the Mengniu = Niu Gensheng identity, as the reason for the sense-making of Mengniu as a more attractive work unit than Yili was based on their experience with Niu as colleague and/or superior when at Yili.

However, as this chapter is concentrating on the role of corporate identities in specific incidents, I will restrict my analysis of Mengniu's activities in Shanyin to its identity constructs that are related to Yili.

Shanyin was known as a major traditional dairy region that was also quite close to the Huhhot region, the home region of Mengniu and Yili, only separated from it by a mountain ridge. It was therefore only a matter of time before the Inner Mongolians expanded their activities to Shanyin.

When Mengniu was the first to start looking for possibilities in Shanyin, the company had to start interacting with different (groups of) actors in the region. As Mengniu had not yet constructed any Shanyin identity, it started out with its existing Huhhot identities of Mengniu = Yili and Mengniu = good second. Both identities appear to have played crucial roles in Mengniu's choices in that region.

A consequence of the Mengniu = Yili identity seems to be that Yili is part of Mengniu's sense-making, even when Mengniu is not directly interacting with Yili. Phrased differently, we could pose that because Yili has a place in Mengniu's sense-making of its environment and its place in it, when Mengniu appears in a new region, even if it is the first to do so, it also cognitively brings along Yili. Weick's properties of sense-making includes 'enactive of sensible environments' (Weick 1995: 30–38). It seems that enterprises construct markets in interaction with their competitors. Within the large scale cognitive space of a market, an enterprise will develop competitive relationships with a varying degree of coupling with each competitor. In the case of Mengniu, it is included in the rather large scale space of the Chinese dairy market and simultaneously in the smaller space of the Inner Mongolian dairy market and the still smaller space of the Huhhot dairy market. Moreover, Mengniu is also included in the geopolitical space Inner Mongolia, etc. Within the Huhhot dairy space it has constructed a tightly coupled competitive relationship with Yili. This relationship is apparently so tightly coupled that it is difficult for Mengniu to make any strategic decision without not taking account of the consequences of that decision for Yili. Yili's behaviour, on the other hand, seems to corroborate that analysis, as Mengniu appears to have a similar position in Yili's sense-making of its own strategic decisions. The identity of 'good second' is co-creative of the identity of 'good first' of Yili (see Van Dongen 1991 for the co-genetic relationship of such pairs of opposites).

This understanding of the relationship between Mengniu and Yili explains the peculiar behaviour in new regions of both companies: the first, while seeking a suitable position (local partner, geographic location, etc.) for itself, will also cognitively prepare one for the other. Mengniu needs Yili to be around, if not physically, then at least cognitively, in order to enact its other important role identity: a good second. Although these are separate identity constructs, they are related because the Mengniu = good second identity started out as Mengniu = good second to Yili.

I will refrain from retelling Mengniu's investments in Shanyin, as that can be read in Chapter 5. I will summarize them here, in terms of Mengniu's identities. The Mengniu representative can be expected to have contacted a number of parties in the Shuozhou region. For example, they would have visited Gucheng, the local leading dairy company, a number of times to chat and seek them out as potential partners (CEO of Gucheng, private communication). That Mengniu finally started out in Huairen, in the periphery of the Shuozhou region, completely coincides with the identity constructs observed above. Huairen is the ideal partner and location for 'a good second' like Mengniu and it leaves the political centre, Shuozhou Municipality, for its cognitive partner Yili.

Mengniu's activities in the region made Yili follow suit soon and indeed it partnered with a party related to Shuozhou. Yili's partner was physically located in Shanyin, which in turn triggered Mengniu to follow once more. But then as well, Mengniu enacted its role identity as 'good second' by forming an alliance with a Shanyin-based partner, rather than a Shuozhou-based partner.

At that moment Mengniu and Yili were neighbours again (Mengniu = Yili), with Yili linked to the municipal level and Mengniu to the county level (Mengniu = good second).

Yanjing's symbolic road to Guangdong

A number of the case enterprises in this study are conglomerates (*jituan*, literally 'groups'), but Chapter 6 takes a detailed look at the way a company established and firmly rooted in a suburb of Beijing expanded to different regions of China and how this affected its identity constructs.

But Yanjing's case illuminates another aspect of (Chinese) corporate identity as well: the symbolic value of the company name. As Yanjing is a synonym of Beijing, the company name can be regarded as a metaphor for Beijing, thus constructing a Beijing identity for Yanjing. Here 'Beijing' does not only refer to the geographic location, but more so to Beijing as the symbol of the national government. The facts then that Yanjing is located in Beijing and that its name is a synonym of Beijing mutually reinforce the various Beijing identities of this company. Yanjing's Beijing identity played an important role in the way its Southward expansion affected its identity constructs. Whenever Yanjing entered a new region, it did not simply come as Yanjing the brewer, but also as Beijing, the central authority.

Symbols are important aspects of the cognitive element of social-cognitive structures. The construction of symbols is a powerful means to reduce equivocality. Symbols have a semantic aspect, but also an action aspect. This aspect has been phrased strongest by McCall and Simmons: 'If a gesture elicits the same response from the actor and his audience, it is said to be a "significant gesture", or a *symbol* (McCall and Simmons 1966: 53). Beijing in the sense of central authorities is not just that, a sense, but also elicits a response. This response can be a state of mind (varying from a feeling of pride 'the Middle Kingdom', to resentment 'those Beijing bureaucrats'), but also actions derived from that state of mind. In the Lukang case, for example, we could observe that security officers from Beijing (= central authorities), visiting Ji'ning to investigate the allegation that Lukang was cooking the books, were met with almost complete collective resistance.

The history of Yanjing's expansion in Jiangxi province also shows different actions based on different ways of making sense of the symbolic power of Yanjing's arrival. Yanjing's first investment in that province in Ji'an was welcomed by the local government as a major boost to the local economy (Ding 1999). However, the attempt to buy all Yanjing beer available in Jiangxi's capital Nanchang that took place in February 2003, when Yanjing had already been active in the region for more than three years, indicates that the adverse reaction, Yanjing as threat, still existed, simultaneously with the positive reaction. Both reactions were triggered by the same symbol: Yanjing = Beijing = central authorities. Again, I need to stress that Yanjing was interacting with all those parties in all its identities all the time. For example, Yanjing = China's top brewer also played a role in the Nanchang incident. However, the identity Yanjing = central authorities apparently reinforced the sense-making of Yanjing as a threat. Qingdao, still China's second brewery, was also active on the Nanchang market, but was never a target of the same type of attack as Yanjing. This is another example that 'what we do not see' is as important as what we do see, while engaged in the research of organizing processes.

Before summarizing Yanjing's road to Guangdong, I will list a number of events that corroborate the Beijing identity of Yanjing.

Yanjing, the company name

The name Yanjing was first suggested by a vice-minister of the Ministry of Light Industry in 1981, only one year after the Shunyi Brewery had been established. Such a high visit from a central ministry is rare and therefore has by itself immense symbolic power. Second, the choice of the name, a synonym of Beijing, suggested by a vice-minister, is not a coincidence in a Chinese context. It symbolized that the central government was stamping the company as its favourite brewery.

State Council visits

Yanjing received visits from members of the State Council, China's highest government body in 1982 and 1986. Especially the first visit, by

Wan Li, again only two years after the brewery, then still a Town and Village Enterprise, had been founded, is rare and hence symbolic by itself. It could still be argued that the brewing industry is a matter of Light Industry in the Chinese classification of industrial sectors. This could explain the visit by a vice-minister of Light Industry, even though this should still be regarded as rare. However, a visit from the State Council as early as 1982 is extremely significant.

State banquets

Yanjing was selected as the beer served at state banquets in 1995. This event by itself is strongly constructive of its identity as representative of the central authority. Moreover, it coincided with the transformation of Yanjing as one of the three pillars of the Beijing brewing industry to one of the three pillars of the national brewing industry. By 1995, Yanjing also became China's top brewery. Finally, it was the year in which Yanjing took over Huasi, its bankrupt neighbouring brewery, and was reorganized into a conglomerate. By 1995, Yanjing was China's number one brewery and designated by the state as its official representative. It was ready for the conquest of Guangdong.

Yanjing's march to Guangdong can be divided into four periods.

January 1999 to August 2000 occupying the South Central

Regions: Jiangxi, Hunan and Hubei

August 2000 to July 2001 consolidating the North Central

Regions: Shandong and Inner Mongolia
No information has been found shedding light on why Yanjing stopped its quest to the South for a while to direct its acquisition efforts to the regions surrounding its home region. One explanation could be that it had to consolidate the mother company from encroachments of other brewing groups like Qingdao in its own home region. This would explain why Shandong was included in the acquisition activities of this period. It is reflective of that typical Chinese 'follow your competitor' way of competing that was also visible in the competition between the dairy companies Huahuaniu and Shanmeng in Zhengzhou, and Mengniu and Yili in Huhhot. Although Yanjing had beat Qingdao as China's number one brewer in 1995, the two remained engaged in fierce competition. I will revert to this in the second half of this chapter.

At the end of this period (June 2001), Yanjing established a special Management Office for Non-Beijing Subsidiaries. At that moment, Yanjing still made sense of the Chinese brewing market in terms of home region versus non-home region.

July 2001 to December 2004 occupying the South Coast

Regions: Fujian, Zhejiang, Guangxi

At the end of this period (October 2003), Yanjing established its South China Office. This marked a change in the company's sense-making of the Chinese brewing market in terms of North and South. By that time 57 per cent of Yanjing's turnover was generated by its subsidiaries outside its home region. During the period December 2002 to March 2003, Yanjing was forging a chain of subsidiaries around Guangdong as a preparation to attack that region from four neighbouring provinces.

December 2004 to the present

Region: Guangdong

Yanjing did not succeed in conquering the Guangdong market through its subsidiaries in other regions. It established a subsidiary in Foshan, a suburb of Guangzhou in December 2004. Here again, we can observe the influence of Yanjing's competition with Qingdao. Qingdao had acquired the Doumen Brewery a couple of years earlier; a company that Yanjing had considered to acquire as well, but had declined because of the excessive price. As both Yanjing and Qingdao are large brewing conglomerates, it is not surprising that both will be found investing in the same regions of China. Sometimes Yanjing will be the first to enter a region, while Qingdao will beat Yanjing in others. The development of both companies does not show such a strong coupling as in the case of Mengniu and Yili. However, as both management teams can be expected to watch one another closely, some similar, even imitative, activities are bound to take place. Yanjing had a hard time entering Guangdong, a major objective of its expansion strategy. When Qingdao acquired a local brewery, Yanjing realized its earlier suggested option to build a greenfield plant, which it deemed cheaper than buying an existing company.

Summarizing: Yanjing development, from its establishment in a Beijing suburb in 1980, to the start of the construction of its plant in Guangdong, shows a remarkably straight and clearly visible line from Beijing, the seat of the central government, to the rebellious region of Guangdong that has always been so hard to rule by the same national government. The foundation of Yanjing's success is the strong symbolic power of Yanjing's Beijing identity based on the similarity of 'Yanjing' and 'Beijing'. Much older and stronger, at least during the initial years of Yanjing's existence, breweries like Qingdao interfered with this straight line occasionally, giving it a few bends here and there. However, this competition has always been marginal. An emperor cannot be beaten easily by a single adversary in China. It requires a popular uprising and such an uprising is currently not in sight.

FCAS2005 – who is/are its organizers?

The final case chapter of this study, Chapter 7, presents probably the most confusing case of all. A number of aspects contribute to this perception:

1   I have taken the experimental stand of regarding a trade fair as a social-cognitive structure very close to the 'organization' on the scale of such structures.
2   The core trade fair of the case and its main competitor are so close, in scope and in name, and their behaviour is so tightly coupled, that it is difficult to tell them apart for an observer who is not familiar with the business (and even for many who are).
3   The social-cognitive structures involved in the organization of the trade fair and that competitor make sense of their respective events in terms of the other. It is not always immediately clear who is competing with whom, or, phrased differently, who is imitating whom?

Most readers will start to recognize the recurrent theme of competitors making sense of their business in terms of one another. I will revert to that in the comprehensive section at the end of this chapter, but this section on the core incident of the FCAS case offers highly interesting material for studying this phenomenon.

I will recapitulate the history of FCAS in one paragraph here for the sake of convenience, but refer to Chapter 7 for the details. The development of FCAS can be divided into three periods. I will indicate the main identity of FCAS vis-à-vis Exposure in the header of each period.

1995–1999 FCAS = Chinese edition of FCA

Exposure's initial idea was to let FCA rotate between China (Shanghai) and a venue in South-East Asia. FCA then would be held in Shanghai in 1998, in combination with FCC and the following year in Singapore, etc. After the enormous success of FCC/FCAS1998, Exposure decided to hold the Chinese trade fair annually.

2000–2002 FCAS = Chinese edition of FC

Although the symbolic value of the name FCAS still indicated a link between FCAS and FCA, the fact that it was held annually, separately from FCA, indicated a change in the sense-making of FCAS by Exposure. This is corroborated by the decision to make FCA into an annual event as well. Both shows were organized by Exposure, with the aid of the local Exposure organizations in or near the respective venues. Moreover, Exposure was not involved in attracting domestic exhibitors and visitors, a task taken on by CFCA and its own trade fair FCC, which was co-located with FCAS.

2003–present FCAS = Chinese edition of FC +

Since FCAS2003, the show has been organized by Exposure and Exposure China, where Exposure performs more or less the same activities as during the previous period and Exposure China the activities previously executed by CFCA. I have added a + to the main identity of FCAS to indicate that the ways Exposure and Exposure China make sense of FCAS is different, which constructs distinct identities.

In this section, I will concentrate on identity construction as a process, embedded in the general sense-making (organizing) process. To this end, I will divide this section over the three main organizations: Exposure, Exposure China and CFCA. Other parties, like visitors, exhibitors, etc., will play a role in the analysis.

Exposure

Social

Exposure is a company that has developed into the world's leading organizer of food components trade fairs. It has been so successful that it has been instrumental in the construction of the food components market as a cognitive space. The FC concept was a creation of Exposure and was adopted quickly by manufacturers, traders, publishers, etc., related to this business. Exposure has been bringing the FC formula to a number of other geographical locations and has started a bimonthly magazine to which companies can contribute company 'news'.

Cognitive – general

The strength of the FC formula lies in the fact that it is strict enough to protect the integrity of the FC trade fairs, but still leaves sufficient space for elasticity. A number of clients are present at virtually all FC events. Their participation is almost an automatic act. Those companies book space for the 2006 edition during their participation in the 2005 edition, etc. This behaviour constructs a configuration of Exposure + regular participants with a very strong coupling. There is also an aggregate of companies that could be regarded as fitting the FC scope, or not. Some of those participate regularly, others once every few years, etc., but will always participate as visitors. Actually, a salient feature of a business trade fair is that one can exhibit as a visitor as well, but this is not the proper place to explore that aspect of trade fairs. The coupling between Exposure and this group of relations is also quite tight.

Cognitive – construction rules

A typical feature of tightly coupled organizing is a relatively large set of relatively precise construction rules. Instead of presenting here a long list of examples of such rules, I will restrict myself to analysing one very basic rule more elaborately: sales of exhibition space. Sales of exhibitions are formulated in terms of square metres rather than stands. This is a rule that Exposure inherits from the larger cognitive space of 'organizing trade fairs'. However, as a result of the exhibitor behaviour of booking most space for the next edition of a trade fair during the current one, Exposure tends to concentrate its sales activities during FC events. A large sales staff is present on each FC trade fair, in particular the core event, FC Europe. During FC Europe virtually the entire staff of Exposure is present on the floor to assist in sales activities. As social constructionists, we will immediately see the other side of the interaction between Exposure and its exhibitors: Exposure will be strongly inclined to rely on the existing hard core of exhibitors that will sign up automatically anyway, while too little energy is left for attracting new exhibitors or convincing the hesitant ones.

This is a perfect moment to introduce an important construct in sales activities: customer loyalty. A company like Exposure will be inclined to define the automatic participants as 'loyal'. However, if we asked the sales staff to define the term 'loyal', they would reply in terms of those exhibitors being content with Exposure's trade fairs and other services. They would use emotional terminology. From an organizing perspective, however, we can observe that most of these exhibitors exhibit owing to a blocking of the sense-making process. Booking space on the next edition is a matter of 'what worked in the past will work in the future as well', or in terms of Weick's model: retrospective sense-making (Weick 1995: 24–30). This is not to say that customer loyalty does not exist. However, I would like to reserve that term for the situation in which exhibitors sign up for the next edition as a result of a decision that signing up for that trade fair would be more beneficial than for any other. The behaviour of the customers is the same in both situations, but the sense-making of which that behaviour is a consequence is not.

Cognitive – symbols

The interaction between Exposure and its relations is laden with symbols. I will once more select only one and treat it in more detail: the annual FC awards. The annual FC awards are another powerful instrument with which Exposure constructs the FC space in ongoing interaction with the other parties involved. The awards are announced during an official banquet usually held on the evening of the second day of the European edition, Exposure's main event. A short list of contestants is selected by a committee of experts. This committee itself is also a powerful symbol, as it means something to be a committee member. However, that is nothing compared to what it means to an exhibitor to be selected for one of the awards. I have personally attended such a ceremony once in Paris. I shared a table with employees of a Belgian multinational, with its CEO sitting opposite me. These gentlemen spent most of the first half of the evening making sarcastic remarks about Exposure and their attempts to 'position themselves as the godfather of food components' (sic). Observing the change in attitude of that man after he learned that his company had won the Gold Award of that year was one of the most telling examples of jumping from one inclusion to another that I have ever personally watched. I would be the last to deny him his pride for winning the award and praise for Exposure for granting it to his company, but his behaviour, or better, his response to the award, in his ongoing interaction with Exposure corroborated that Exposure was indeed 'the godfather of food components'. This man was literally hooked for the rest of his career on that company; that company joined the ranks of the exhibitors that automatically sign up for the next edition of a trade fair during the current one.

FCAS

Exposure makes sense of the international part of FCAS as one of its FC shows, applying all construction rules, symbols, etc., to FCAS as to any other FC trade fair. Exposure has a floor plan of the next edition of FCAS ready before the start of the current edition. Sales for the next edition will therefore start on the opening day of the current one. The sales behaviour for FCAS proceeds in exactly the same way as at FCE. Moreover, Exposure also offers FCAS for sale on other FC trade fairs, although there the interaction regarding FCAS is usually initiated by exhibitors. Exposure's use of the same cognitive matter to FCAS as to other FC trade fairs works with the international exhibitors in the sense that they also interact in the same way. Phrased differently, Exposure starts by doing 'what worked well in the past' and the exhibitors seem to follow suit.

Exposure China

Social

Exposure China is a joint venture between a private company in Shanghai and Hong Kong Exposure Asia. As an organizer of trade fairs, Exposure China interacts with similar parties as Exposure: exhibitors, visitors, venues, etc. Exposure China is active in more diverse markets than Exposure and therefore their coupling with these parties is considerably less tight. Exposure China is also a Chinese working unit (*danwei*) and as such the relation between Exposure China and its employees is also different from that between Exposure and its staff. This working unit identity also causes differences between the ways Exposure China and their Dutch counterpart interact with government organizations.

A special relationship exists between Exposure China and Exposure Asia that is reflected in a rather tightly coupling of behaviour and frequent interaction.

Cognitive – general

Exposure China is set to behave in accordance with what is expected by the various key parties involved in trade fairs: exhibitors, visitors, government agencies, etc. Exposure China is made sense of as an organizer of trade fairs, rather than as an organizer of trade fairs in a certain market. This difference in sense-making is usually not noticed by employees of either or other Exposure subsidiaries involved in the organization of FCAS.

Cognitive – construction rules

As the coupling between Exposure China and its interaction partners is less tight than in the case of Exposure, the construction rules followed by Exposure China are fewer in number and less precise, but each rule is invoked more frequently (Weick 1979: 112–117). I will follow the line of analysis of the previous section by concentrating on the sales activities. As an organizer of trade fairs, Exposure China inherits the construction rule pertaining to that larger space of selling most of the next edition of a trade fair during the current one. This rule is complemented by another rule: determine the most important competitive trade fairs and send a couple of salespeople there to sell our own trade fair. This way of working is not completely absent in Europe, but would be regarded as less correct. However, it complies with the tendency of copying what others do well, introduced at the beginning of Chapter 6. We have already seen in a number of the case chapters that imitating competitors is so inherent in Chinese-style competition that it includes symbolic matter like logos, advertising phrases, etc. When I walked around FCC2005, I did not only see salespeople of Exposure China promoting FCAS, but also representatives of other Chinese organizers of (cognate) trade fairs.

Cognitive – symbols

The most salient symbol that Exposure China tries to construct is its relation with Exposure, the holder of the intellectual property of the FC formula. This aspect is most conspicuous on Exposure China's web page introducing FCAS. Exposure China introduces Exposure as its 'sister company'. This is probably not completely correct from a genealogical point of view. Exposure Asia is the sister company of Exposure, while Exposure China, as a daughter of Exposure Asia, should be regarded as a niece of Exposure. Another symbol included in Exposure China's web site of FCAS is that is specifically mentions that FCAS is an edition of FCA, rather than the FC formula in general. The latter seems to be a product of the interaction between Exposure China and Exposure Asia. Exposure China is a daughter company of Exposure Asia and therefore also has an 'Asian' identity. This company-related identity construct is paralleled and therefore probably reinforced by the geographic identity of China being part of the continent Asia. This in turn can explain the use of sister company when referring to Exposure, as Exposure China is speaking in its identity as Exposure China = Exposure Asia.

FCAS

Exposure China makes sense of FCAS as a domestic trade fair. This is the consequence of the strict separation of the international and the domestic sections of FCAS, in which Exposure China is responsible for the promotion and sales of the domestic segment. Exposure China started selling FCAS during the last co-located edition of FCC and FCAS, FCC/FCAS2002. Exposure also allowed salespersons of Exposure China to sell FCAS to Chinese exhibitors at FC trade fairs outside China, most of which were participating in those events as members of CFCA delegations. As a result, the domestic section of FCAS2003 was a subset of the relations of CFCA and an imitation of FCC.

CFCA

Social

As the sector association in the Chinese food components market, CFCA is interacting with a wide range of parties and individual actors in that sector. These include foreign organizations and individuals. The role of CFCA in the construction and ongoing reconstruction of the Chinese food components market can be compared with Exposure's role in the global market of the same industry. CFCA's role is slightly stronger, as it is a semi-governmental organization. This identity would make CFCA the typical Chinese partner organization for Exposure and indeed this has been the case for a few years. Breaking off this relation would not automatically mean that Exposure's activities in China are doomed to fail, but the company should actively try to build up a network of relations in China to restore at least part of the access to the market offered by CFCA.

In the organization of FCC, CFCA is included in a configuration with CLICC.

Cognitive – general

Organizing trade fairs is but one of the many activities of CFCA. However, it is one of the most important activities. Moreover, in its configuration with CLICC, the most tightly coupled type of cognitive space, CFCA has to take into account that for that partner FCC is the single most important event of the year (private communication from a CLICC official). The initiative to organize FCC was mainly an initiative of CLICC, proposed to CFCA. CFCA then picked up this idea positively, after which the interaction between the two resulted in the configuration that is currently supporting FCC.

Cognitive – construction rules

CFCA hardly needs to do any sales activities for its domestic part of FCC. Sales activities for the next edition of FCC also take place during the current edition, but exhibitors tend to turn up themselves. CFCA typically 'sends a document down' (*xia wenjian*), a typical phrase used by secretaries of Chinese sector associations referring to the written reminder about the upcoming trade fair. So far, every year the demand for square metres has exceeded the available space, so no active sales activities are called for.

Cognitive – symbols

FCC is the event of the year at which all market parties meet. CFCA therefore also uses that momentum to organize its annual meeting, usually one or two days before the opening of FCC. Several exhibitors at FCC organize technical seminars to introduce their new products in the hotels in the vicinity of the venue (exhibition halls tend to attract hotels, yet another organizing process typical of the trade fair space).

FCAS

CFCA makes sense of FCAS as a source of irritation for the visitors who are forced to visit two trade fairs since CFCA and Exposure broke off their co-operation. CFCA is annoyed by Exposure China, which does not come as a surprise, as Exposure China almost exclusively performs its sales activities at CFCA's trade fairs in China or CFCA-led delegations to trade fairs abroad. However, CFCA does not regard Exposure China as a threat. This has been repeatedly stated during private discussions with

CFCA managers, but is also corroborated by the fact that CFCA has so far not undertaken any action to attempt to create problems for FCAS, even though they would be able to so. The recent internal document issued by CFCA to its member companies reveals that CFCA even makes sense of FCAS (although FCAS is referred to as 'similar trade fairs') as an outlet for the demand for space that it cannot completely satisfy itself. This means that CFCA will be de facto starting to act as a co-organizer of FCAS once more.

Summary

I will summarize the identities constructed of FCAS by its various organizers. I will concentrate on the latest edition, FCAS2005.

Exposure:	the Chinese edition of the FC formula
Exposure China:	their own version of FCC
CFCA:	a relief for the excessive demand for space at FCC

Although Exposure China and CFCA both define one another as adversaries, their frequent competitive interaction seems to make them couple their behaviour more tightly each year. The same appears to hold for CFCA and Exposure, although the two instances of coupling seem to take place in two configurations:

CFCA–Exposure China:	domestic relations
CFCA/CLICC–Exposure:	international relations

CLICC seems to play a rather passive role, but is a necessary partner for CFCA in its dealings with foreign companies, like foreign exhibitors and visitors.

It seems that these processes are heading towards a reconstruction of the FCC/FCAS formula. What I see appearing is a combined event in which FCC and FCAS take place in the same city with a very small time-span in between, allowing the visitors to visit both. The organizers of both will still be pulling separately on the pool of international prospects, but the domestic prospects will be divided between both, where FCAS will be the trade fair for the larger, more export-oriented, domestic exhibitors. Some symbolic competitive behaviour will remain between CFCA and Exposure China, but this will be more of the type of competition between Mengniu and Yili in their home region. To quote Mr Niu Gensheng, the CEO of Mengniu: 'a bit of you in me and a bit of me in you'. This development of FCAS is represented graphically in Figure 8.1. The right half of each picture refers to the international exhibitors, the left half to the domestic ones.

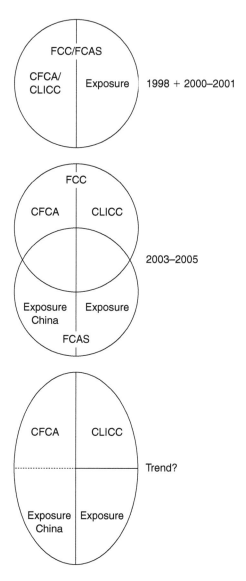

Figure 8.1   Graphic representation of the development of FCAS.

Chinese corporate identity

This study has been written in a style compliant with the basic thought of naturalistic research (Lincoln and Guba 1985). After an introduction of the theoretical framework, I have provided the case stories as a large set of only basically ordered data. Each time cognitive matter like construction rules, symbols, typical language, etc., was introduced, it was also necessary to introduce the actors and their occasions for interaction that constructed this cognitive matter. Providing a large pool of data is a consequence of the theoretical point of view taken by me as the researcher. Moreover, as I would like to make this study equally accessible to readers who are less familiar with China, I needed to provide sufficient information on such typical Chinese occasions for sense-making like administrative levels, industrial sectors, Chinese sense-making vis-à-vis home region, etc.

In the first sections of this final chapter I took out the incidents of each case chapter and retold that part of story, on one hand in even more detail, but on the other hand transforming those details into more abstract principles behind the construction of corporate identities. Now I have finally arrived at the stage that I feel comfortable to extract a number of recurrent themes in the case story and present them as salient features of Chinese corporate identity.

A bit of you in me

The title of this section has been quoted twice as a statement by Mr Niu Gensheng the founder and CEO of Mengniu, the Inner Mongolian dairy company, referring to his competition with Yili. He meant to say that the nature of the competition between these companies was on one hand extremely fierce, but on the other hand the companies also had so much in common. Indeed, the central incident of that chapter showed that their competitive interaction had created a relation in which a move by one would very often be followed by a similar move by the other. Mengniu and Yili even re-enacted their relation as 'follower' and 'leader' respectively in their activities in other parts of China.

I have made a search of the Chinese expression 'a bit of you in me' (*ni zhong you wo*) using the Chinese version of Google and was told that it had approximately 41 400 instances of this phrase in its database (acessed 30 April 2005). A quick glance over the first 20-odd links reveals that a major part of the texts found involved some sort of Sino-foreign co-operation. However, examples referring to competition between Chinese companies can also be found.

This leads me to the first general observation regarding Chinese corporate identity: although competitors will always be an aspect contributing to the identity constructs of companies in any culture, it seems to play a crucial role for Chinese enterprises. The cases in this study seem to point out that this is related to the Chinese propensity to imitate, to do what others do well rather than doing something unique. Western textbooks on marketing and strategic management teach us that companies need a Unique Selling Proposition (USP) to survive. If you are unable to show the market how you differ from your competitors, you will not be able to survive. While not denying that Chinese enterprises also pay attention to unique features, they do seem to be keen to describe their position in the market in terms of others that they deem equal or better. I will make an inventory of instances of such behaviour from some of the case chapters. I will no longer strictly separate the different case stories, as the focus now is on common traits.

I already cited Mr Niu's famous statement, but he said and did much more. Especially during the initial years of Mengniu's existence it was hard to find an advertisement or other form of promotion from Mengniu that did not directly or indirectly refer to Yili. Even the 'three don'ts', the three guidelines laid out by Mr Niu to avoid a direct collision with Yili, were formulated in terms of Yili. Then there was yet another expression of Mr Niu that Mengniu was 'a good second (after Yili)'. I have put 'after Yili' in brackets, as he tended to leave that part out, apparently presuming that people could guess that he was referring to Yili.

Apart from the Chinese propensity to imitate, the tightly coupled relation between Mengniu and Yili was also caused by the fact that a large group of Yili employees, including managers, left Yili to join Mengniu. As Mengniu and Yili were both dairy companies, those people simply continued to do what they were used to, be it under another corporate name.

Another factor contributing to the you-in-me aspect of Chinese corporate identity is the Chinese regional chauvinism, introduced in the first section of Chapter 6. Companies that are competitors in their home region, like Mengniu and Yili, still share an inclusion in that home region. Such an inclusion constructed a common cause: contributing to the good name of the home region. Mr Niu of Mengniu showed a remarkable cultural insight in this respect, as he used this cultural propensity twice: he placed Mengniu and Yili together with a third Inner Mongolian enterprise, Xingfa, as the three main companies of the grasslands and he created the image of Huhhot as the Dairy Capital of China, the glory of which was shone on Mengniu and Yili alike.

We could observe the same identity constructs, but in different outward appearances in the case of Huahuaniu and Shanmeng in Zhengzhou. Huahuaniu was constructed in Henan, the provincial space. When Zhengzhou wished to cash in on the booming dairy industry as well, it formed Shanmeng. As soon as Shanmeng was constructed, it co-constructed a Zhengzhou identity of Huahuaniu: Huahuaniu as one of the two major dairy companies of Zhengzhou, together with Shanmeng. In Mr Niu's terms: there was a bit of Huahuaniu in Shanmeng, but as a consequence there was also a bit of Shanmeng in Huahuaniu. We could continue on this line and apply another of Mr Niu's metaphors to Shanmeng: Shanmeng behaved like a (good) follower (to Huahuaniu).

Moreover, some of the managers of Huahuaniu and Shanmeng had studied together in the same local college and referred to one another as old school mates, which is at least as significant in terms of social networks as it is in Europe.

Competition was not the core issue in the Lukang case. However, even in that chapter we could observe that on the nation level, Lukang had an identity of 'one of the three large antibiotics manufacturers of China'. These three competed in some contexts, but also coupled their behaviour in others. Moreover, Lukang's CEO had been an employee of one of the other big three, before he was transferred to Lukang.

In the case of Yanjing's road to the South, competition does play a role, although it seems to be a peripheral one. Still, examples of the influence of the you-in-me principle can be found a number of times. When Yanjing started to break through in the Beijing region, Yanjing regarded itself as one of the three main breweries in Beijing, together with Five Star and Beijing Beer. The latter two were still old established and respected brands at that time. Yanjing, a newcomer, was drawing part of that honour to itself with this statement. On the other hand, this status was reinforced in the competitive interaction between these three breweries, as Five Star and Beijing seemed to 'grant' part of that market, common retail outlets, to Yanjing, while they continued to concentrate on their traditional market, the main hotels, restaurants, etc. This in turn helped Yanjing realize its initial goal: relieving the demand for beer among Beijing citizens.

Later, when Yanjing started making a name in the entire country, Yanjing once more placed itself in line with two main competitors: Qingdao and Zhujiang. By this time, Yanjing's Beijing = central authority identity was already maturing and proved an effective means to compete with Qingdao (China's oldest brand, but with foreign roots – German missionaries) and Zhujiang (originating from Guangdong, Yanjing's ultimate goal in China and also with foreign connections – Stella Artois). Yanjing, as the representative of Beijing, was also the defender of the national industry with no foreign roots or connections. However, it was apparently still useful for Yanjing to start positioning itself in terms of its main competitors.

Towards the end of Yanjing's quest, the company even had to follow an example of Qingdao, by establishing itself in Guangdong, after the attempt to attack the province from its neighbouring provinces had failed. This means that in the smaller region of Guangdong, Yanjing is now also heading for a similar one-of-the-top-three situation, once more with Qingdao (which is already producing in Guangdong) and Zhujiang (for which Guangdong is its home region).

This bit-of-you-in-me aspect of Chinese corporate identity is apparently so strong that it is sometimes more important for a Chinese enterprise not to acquire a competitor, even when a possibility to do so appears. Yili got into trouble recently, affecting the value of its stock. However, in spite of the expectations of nearly everyone, Mengniu stated that it did not intend to attempt to acquire a majority share in Yili. Huahuaniu and Shanmeng have been reported at least once to have been on talking terms to merge, but failed to do so. Yanjing and Qingdao, China's top two brewers, compete by acquiring smaller regional breweries, often in the same regions. However, they have so far never attempted to acquire member companies of one another's group. The reasons for not doing so are complex for each example, meaning that the reasons are constructed in more than one cognitive space. However, the common pattern is that Chinese enterprises cannot be completely understood without taking into account the main competitors that contribute to their identity constructs.

This aspect of Chinese corporate identity is very useful for foreign companies that are active, or intend to become active, in China. In my own practice as consultant it appears to me that a large share of the problems Western companies encounter in their interaction with Chinese enterprises can be attributed to a lack of understanding that they are actually dealing with a company of many. Actually, in my theoretical framework all enterprises in any 'culture' are companies of many, but this phenomenon is much stronger with Chinese enterprises than is the case with companies in Europe, North America and similar regions (Peverelli 2000: 52–58 and 123–126).

The Zhengzhou case in this study shows that the Dutch project was co-operating with one of the two players in the local dairy market, Huahua-niu. Moreover, my analysis reveals that the Dutch were cognitively only linked to one of Huahuaniu's identities: Huahuaniu = Henan. This link became so reified, that the Dutchmen regularly involved in the project were unable to notice that there was at least one other, quite different, 'Zhengzhou dairy market' existing simultaneously with the 'Zhengzhou dairy market' in which they were interacting with their partner. When projects like the Dutch SIDDAIR project are initiated, it is essential that the feasibility study, which is always part of the preliminary work, not only pays attention to technical and financial aspects, but also includes the organizational aspects.

The Mengniu case does not really include a foreign party. I have occasionally mentioned that Gucheng Group, the local market leader in Shanyin, included a joint venture with a Dutch dairy company. However, this does not seem to be included in the sense-making of any party involved in the competition of Mengniu and Yili in Shanyin. This by itself is a sign that the Dutch, also in this case, were not aware of the competitive environment of their Chinese partner (Peverelli 2001). However, the period of heightened sense-making that was a consequence of Mengniu and Yili's activities in Shanyin has affected the relation between Gucheng and its Dutch partner. The Dutch share is quite small and hence little influence in the strategy of the company can be derived from it. However, due to the respect that the Dutch enjoyed within Gucheng and the expectations the Chinese side had for the development of the co-operation, the Dutch side was able to have much more influence than its equity was worth. This situation has changed. Gucheng has re-organized its position in Shanyin. It is still the local 'Dragon Head' in the Shanyin space, but in the Shuozhou space, it is one of the top three, a situation Gucheng shares with Huahuaniu/Shanmeng and the early Yanjing/Five Star/Beijing. That the new situation makes sense to Gucheng is corroborated by the recent example to couple behaviour of Gucheng, Mengniu and Yili to fix the purchasing price of raw milk. The Dutch partner is still a partner, but the Gucheng management's current attitude is that the Dutch have to act in accordance with their humble equity share and invest more if they wish to gain more influence.

In cases like this, foreign investors with existing co-operative relations need to be constantly aware of the relations of their Chinese partners. This should also include their partners' main competitors. The Chinese tend to develop a bit-of-you-in-me relation with competitors that they are unable to beat, or unwilling to beat, if they believe that they can gain more from a competitive relationship (like Mengniu). At the first sign of the appearance of Mengniu in the Shuozhou region, the Dutch investor should have heard the alarm bells ringing. Actually, the CEO of Gucheng had given a hint in that direction during a personal meeting with me in March 2003, when he mentioned that the only competitor he really feared was Mengniu. The methodology used in this study can be used to reveal and, to a certain extent predict, such processes. This insight can then be used in scenario planning.

The ultimate example of foreigners struggling with Chinese corporate identity is the FCAS case, in which the foreign party is one of the key players. Exposure had problems with understanding the identities of a number of Chinese parties, in particular CFCA and Exposure China. However, the nature of this misunderstanding is different from both the Zhengzhou and the Mengniu case. Exposure, as a European company, has one fixed self-perceived identity: organizer of trade fairs (see once more Peverelli 2000: 52–58 and 123–126). Looking at CFCA and CFCA's relation to FCC, Exposure also attributes one single identity to CFCA: organizer of FCC. After the establishment of Exposure China, Exposure once more made sense of the new member of their groups in a singular way: organizer of trade fairs.

There is a construction rule in the Exposure Group (as an organization, the Exposure Group is a cognitive space in itself) that 'we do not co-operate in organization of a trade fair, unless it is absolutely necessary'. This has never been written in any medium, nor stated by any Exposure representative, but can be observed in the behaviour of Exposure companies and individual employees.

The initiative from Exposure toward CFCA to co-operate in China was made from the perception that CFCA was a competitor in the sense that CFCA, like Exposure, was an organizer of trade fairs. The negotiation did not result in one single trade fair with two organizers, but a co-location of the existing FCC and Exposure's FCAS. Co-location was made sense of as a looser form of co-operating, suiting Exposure's propensity not to co-operate if not absolutely necessary. From 1998, Exposure started executing the co-operation by doing in China what it was used to doing elsewhere in the world. While the commercial success did come, Exposure did not seem to gain from the co-operation cognitively. CFCA on the other hand, as a Chinese organization, started acting towards a bit-of-you-in-me type of relation. The commercial success also benefited CFCA, but CFCA also gained from the co-operation cognitively. Exposure seemed to be aware of this change in CFCA, but made sense of it as a threat.

It was this sense of threat, reinforced by the new situation in the Asian part of the Exposure Group (the appearance on the scene of Exposure China), that led to breaking off the co-operation between Exposure and CFCA. Again, the situation was complex in the sense that many parties interacting in various social-cognitive contexts were involved. However, the core problem seems to be the different ways in which Exposure and CFCA made sense of their co-operation.

When I read through the huge body of literature, from academic to popular (Clissold 2004 is an excellent example of a popular book with an academic touch), published on co-operation between Western and Chinese companies, it seems to me that the majority of the problems described in these publications can be attributed to a misunderstanding on the part of the foreign party in the way their Chinese counterparts are linked to other organizations, including their main competitors. It is essential to always be aware that your Chinese partners also have 'a bit of their competitors in them'.

Administrative level

Another recurrent theme in the case chapters of this study is the importance of the administrative level in the sense-making of enterprises. In China, all government activities are part of the tasks of each administrative level, but some activities are mainly performed at the lowest level, while others are more relevant at higher levels. Birth control is a typical example of a policy that is delegated to the lowest administrative level, as it is a matter that concerns the individual household. This example is particularly crucial for enterprises as work units, as each Chinese work unit has a quota for the number of babies that can be produced by its employees.

The theme of administrative level is also related to the emotional value the Chinese attach to their home region, as introduced in the beginning sections of Chapters 4 and 6. The Chinese tend to develop a double bind with their local government. On one hand they have the same frictions with the local authorities regarding regulations, taxes, etc., as Europeans have, but on the other hand their local government is also the symbol of the home region. They will be willing to defend their local government in its conflicts with higher administrative layers. This link is especially strong between the lowest level governments and the enterprises in their region.

A common construction rule in Chinese local administrative spaces seems to be: 'we protect one another unconditionally from threats from above' construct which Chinese scholars refer to as 'local policies' (*tu zhengce*) as opposed to the state's policies (Xi 2000).

The Lukang case already provided strong evidence in this matter. The ways Lukang was made sense of in the municipal (Ji'ning), provincial (Shandong) and national (China) levels were very different. After my analysis it feels quite useless to state that Lukang is a major manufacturer of antibiotics in China, located in Ji'ning, Shandong. Such a statement does not reveal that Lukang is Ji'ning's main employer, that it is an important source of hard currency income for Shandong and one of the top three antibiotics producers of China, etc. People with knowledge of China may infer that Lukang is a work unit and a Communist Party cell and if they are told that Lukang is a company with a few thousand people on the payroll, they may further deduce that this makes Lukang an important work unit and influential Party cell. However, regardless of how many cognitive spaces in which Lukang makes sense we add, it is still impossible to grasp the meaning of Lukang until we focus our understanding from a particular identity in a particular space and related to a particular incident. From that position we can gradually move to the various related spaces of sense-making through the inclusions of the key actors involved in the incident.

A key identity of Lukang in the conflict between Mr Zhang and Mr Wu was Lukang = major employer in Ji'ning. The internal conflict did not affect that identity, but as soon as Mr Wu tried to solve the conflict in his favour by moving it to another context, the result of that action started to threaten Lukang's identity in the Ji'ning space. This had potentially massive repercussions for a large number of people. When the inspectors from Beijing came to Ji'ning to investigate Mr Wu's accusations, the conflict invoked the construction rule 'we protect one another unconditionally from threats from above'. This interaction included even the local representatives of the National Securities Supervisory Commission, which indicates that their inclusion in the Ji'ning space was stronger than that in the National Securities Supervisory Commission space, a convincing proof of the power of 'local policies'.

The differences between administrative levels was the main theme in the Zhengzhou case. Huahuaniu was constructed in the Henan space. However, as soon as Shanmeng was constructed in the Zhengzhou space, with Huahuaniu as an element in its sense-making, a Zhengzhou identity of Huahuaniu was created as well. Moreover, Huahuaniu also had to give Shanmeng a place in its sense-making of the Henan dairy market.

Although there is a competitive relation between Huahuaniu and Shanmeng in the commercial sense (space), both companies seem to fare well in their own contexts. It is actually remarkable to observe how these two companies that are located in the same city (geographic space) and active in the same industrial sector can live together in that geographic space without making one another's life difficult. For the foreign researcher charged with drawing up a business plan for a cheese plant in Zhengzhou, Shanmeng was just another competitor of Huahuaniu, with which he was connected through the Dutch dairy project.

The differences between administrative levels were much more conflicting in Mengniu's activities to set up shop in north Shanxi. There we could observe a difference in sense-making of the dairy market in Shanyin county between the county government and the government of Shuozhou Municipality that was one level higher than Shanyin. I summarized the main difference as one between a homogenizing strategy (Shanyin) and heterogenizing strategy (Shuozhou). This is a difference in sense-making that can be observed frequently, as it is a consequence of the reduction of equivocality in ongoing organizing (see Chapter 1). Human actors need to reduce the amount of data they are confronted with before they can start to make sense of it. However, this process can easily be carried too far, resulting in fixations, which block the access to other inclusions and therefore obstruct the process of ongoing interaction. Actors usually are instinctively aware of excessive reduction of equivocality and will seek diversification by surfing through their inclusions.

When groups of actors interact in complex contexts, the propensity towards simplicity can be translated into a strategy of homogenization. In Shanyin, the authorities wished to reduce the number of local dairy plants vying for the same scarce resource (raw milk) by combing a number of them in the Gucheng Group and stimulating Gucheng to acquire as many of the others as possible. Some of these others with inclusions in the Shuozhou government sought protection from that side. This led to a strategy of heterogenizing by Shuozhou Municipality by linking one of their relations in Shanyin up with Yili. This in turn triggered Mengniu to move to Shanyin as well, not through a link with Shuozhou, but as a consequence of its competitive relation with Yili, which included a construction rule 'go wherever Yili goes'.

When Gucheng was confronted with the new competitive situation in Shanyin, it continued with the homogenizing strategy by forging a configuration with Mengniu and Yili. The news that Gucheng, Mengniu and Yili joined forces to control the purchasing price of raw milk is evidence that this homogenizing strategy is working.

Administrative level played a different role in the Yanjing case. There we saw that Yanjing was almost a joint conception of three government levels joining forces: Shunyi County, Beijing Municipality and the central government. The fact that the central government was geographically located in Beijing certainly was an advantage. The relation between Beijing Municipality and the central government can be compared with the relationship between Zhengzhou Municipality and the Henan government.

The strong Yanjing = Beijing identity played a role in Yanjing's entire quest to conquer Guangdong, although the way this identity affected the local sense-making of its arrival differed from place to place. This was even the case in the same province. Ji'an (Jiangxi province) welcomed Yanjing as a boost for the local economy, but Yanjing's arrival in Ji'an and particularly its entering the market of Jiangxi's capital Nanchang, was met with hostile reactions. Perhaps Yanjing would have fared better if it had set up shop in Nanchang, instead of going for a cheap deal in Ji'an. However, 'chose the cheapest option' seems to be a strong construction rule in the Yanjing space, as witnessed by its refusal to pay too much for a brewery in Guangdong, which was subsequently acquired by its main rival Qingdao. Yanjing later decided to build a greenfield plant in Guangdong, which was perceived as a cheaper option.

Administrative level played yet another role in the FCAS case. We have seen that Exposure's decision to ask their exhibitors about their favourite venue in China in 1995 has been affecting their strategy in China up to the present date and, due to the bit-of-you-in-me type aspect of Chinese competition, has also affected the strategy of their main competitor, CFCA.

Exposure and CFCA negotiated for almost a year on one theme: Beijing or Shanghai as the venue for their co-located trade fair. Exposure won and FCAS was born. The case history then shows how the reification of Shanghai as the venue for the Chinese edition of their FC formula led to a major strategic error, resulting in CFCA successfully organizing their FCC without a foreign partner in Beijing in 1999.

Once CFCA had incorporated a-bit-of-Exposure in its sense-making of its own FCC, it had to stay in Shanghai as well, close to FCAS in time and space. However, CFCA had devised a heterogenizing strategy as well by starting a separate domestic trade fair to be held in other venues in the autumn. These other venues included the other two major industrial centres: Beijing and Guangzhou. Each edition of the domestic event includes local parties as well, like local food components associations and local government organizations. In this way, this provides CFCA with opportunities to interact with those parties and construct an identity of *the* organizer of food components trade fairs in China, while Exposure's fixation on Shanghai makes it literally a marginal player. This does not mean that FCAS is not a successful trade fair. It was believed by many parties that FCAS would not be able to survive the break up with FCC. FCAS not only did survive, it has been growing steadily during the past few years. However, as was concluded in Chapter 7, FCAS's survival should be attributed to the way it continues to make sense to CFCA.

Economic sector

The economic sector to which an enterprise belongs will affect its identity constructs in any culture, but due to the hierarchical structure of industrial sectors in China, from the central organization in Beijing down to the level of county, municipal district, and sometimes even lower, sector spaces in China are much more tightly coupled than in, for example, Europe. This aspect of Chinese economy has been introduced in Chapter 6 as one of the mechanisms leading to the often very dispersed character of Chinese manufacturing.

Economic sector did not play a major role in all of the case stories introduced in this study. That Lukang was a pharmaceutical company did not play a role in the core incident of that chapter. The only consequence of being included as a pharmaceutical manufacturer was that Lukang was inspected more often and more strictly by a number of authorities, as the cognitive element of the pharmaceutical space includes sets of rules like Good Manufacturing Practice (GMP), etc. The pharmaceutical industry also tends to be more centrally controlled. This seems to reinforce the strong inclusion of Lukang in Ji'ning as the representatives of the National Securities Supervisory Commission failed to investigate the accusations of fraud committed by Lukang.

Economic sector played a role in the decision of the government of Shanyin to combine a number of dairy industries operating in different sectors into one, locally controlled group. This was a conflict between the attraction of the sector inclusion and the inclusion in the administrative region. Which inclusion will eventually win is again a function of a number of interactions in various social-cognitive contexts. However, the Gucheng case already provides sufficient information to show that sometimes the administration wins and sometimes the sector inclusion. Mengniu and Yili were able to enter the region's dairy industry smoothly because of this ongoing tension between the two types of inclusions.

Yanjing and the other top breweries were all included in the Light Industry space, so difference between sector inclusions did not play a role there. The Zhengzhou dairy case was a relatively straightforward battle between two administrative levels. Sector inclusion did not play a role there either.

Most Chinese parties involved in the FCAS case were included in the Light Industry sector. However, in this case we can observe a foreign party, Exposure, that is occasionally confused, as it is not aware of the consequences of this inclusion. First of all, the combination of CFCA and CLICC is not a coincidence, nor a matter of CFCA having to find a suitable partner and through a process of selection picking out CLICC. For some of its tasks, involving formal contacts with foreign parties, CFCA needs to work with an organization that is licensed to do so. As CFCA = Light Industry, CLICC is the automatic choice for this position.

A more telling example is the turbulent period after the change of management at CFCA. The then CEO of Exposure was inclined to change his Chinese partner and an employee of Exposure Asia had got in contact with, what he believed to be, a suitable alternative. This alternative was another company from the Light Industry space, specialized in foreign economic co-operation. Moreover, it was discovered that some of the ousted leaders of CFCA had formed a configuration with members of that company to take over the role of Chinese partner for FCAS. When CFCA and CLICC learned of these contacts, they immediately started to apply pressure through the top of the Light Industry space. The envisioned new partner very quickly withdrew from the plan and Exposure could not do anything else but repair the co-operation with CFCA/CLICC. Exposure's problem in this matter was that in China the production of food, beverages and their components is almost entirely a matter of Light Industry. It is very difficult to get around that sector entirely. It was a mistake on the part of Exposure Asia to suggest another Light Industry party based in Beijing, like CFCA and CLICC, as they should have known that this almost came down to working with the same partners.

For foreign companies dealing or intending to deal with Chinese partners it is useful to find out in what sector their partner is included and what the typical features (construction rules, symbols, etc.) of that sector are. It is also a useful exercise to investigate if the main competitors of the partner are all included in one sector or whether they are divided over a number of sectors. In the latter case, an inventory of sectors and their distinctive cognitive matter has to be made. Foreign investors also need to make themselves known among the leaders of each of those sectors on various administrative levels. This was one of the actions that the Dutch partner of Gucheng had failed to do. This partner was well known on the Shanyin county level, but hardly at the Shuozhou Municipality level. If the Dutch partner had done so in time, it would have been able to assist Gucheng in its local struggles, which would have strengthened its influence in the management of Gucheng (Peverelli 2001).

Mothers-in-law

It can be argued that a number or all of the aspects of Chinese corporate identity introduced in the previous sections already are examples of mothers-in-law. I do not contend this, but would like to point out some subtle differences.

For example, the administrative level can be regarded as a mother-in-law of the enterprises in its region. However, the real mother-in-law of an individual enterprise is usually the local representative of the sector to which the enterprise belongs. We can take Lukang as an example. In Lukang = Ji'ning we could say that Ji'ning Municipality is the mother-in-law of Lukang, but in fact the section of Ji'ning Municipality with which Lukang will interact on a certain topic depends on the nature of the topic. If that topic is related to its business, the mother-in-law would be the Ji'ning Pharmaceutical Bureau, but in case of labour disputes, it would be the Ji'ning Personnel Bureau, etc. When I state that problems within

Lukang threatened its identity Lukang = Ji'ning, then I am pointing out that the threat will affect Lukang's interaction with all Ji'ning municipal organizations. The identity Lukang = Ji'ning is therefore a rather general identity and so is Lukang = pharmaceutical industry. The case story of Lukang shows that some pharmaceutical matters involved interactions with Shandong province and others were even at state level.

Corporate identity construction in general takes place in a huge multi-dimensional matrix. A difference between the Chinese corporate identity construction process and similar processes in regions like Europe is that Chinese corporate identities tend to be constructed at a lower level, resulting in a significantly higher number of relevant identities per enterprise. Moreover, Chinese corporate identities are more tightly coupled to those of related organizations, which is reflected in the typical Chinese jargon of mother-in-law.

Mothers-in-law did not play a prominent role in the Zhengzhou case. They were always there of course, but in the background. In the Mengniu case, Mengniu and Yili were able to find a place of their own in Shanyin, because Gucheng failed to monopolize the entire local dairy market. Some of the Shanyin dairy companies belonged to sectors that were not compliant with the homogenizing strategy of the Shanyin government. Although never actually mentioned, this indicates that those companies were actively aided by their respective mothers-in-law. Yili was introduced to its partner in Shanyin through that partner's mother-in-law on the Shuozhou level.

The entire Yanjing case story is about Yanjing's powerful mothers-in-law. These were at times perceived to be so powerful that it got Yanjing in trouble, as it aroused suspicion from local parties. The Yanjing case shows that it is not always the best strategy to hide behind a powerful mother-in-law. Sometimes it is better to show that you are one of them, which is what Yanjing did, when it decided to build a brand new brewery in Guangdong.

Exposure is once more an example of how difficult it is for Western companies to make sense of Chinese corporate identity. In the previous section I already introduced the attempt by Exposure to switch local partners after the entire management team of CFCA had been changed quite suddenly. Their newly found partner went back on its decision to co-organize FCAS owing to pressure from their mother-in-law, the State Light Industry Bureau. Exposure could have foreseen this problem if they had realized that their new partner and CFCA shared the same mother-in-law. They had indeed switched one daughter for another one of the same family. The first daughter immediately turned to mummy and daddy for help, which they got.

In general foreign companies have to become aware of the most important mothers-in-law of the companies that matter in their China business. This applies to partners in joint ventures, but also to more loose relations like Chinese agents, distributors, consultants, etc. The best method to deal with this aspect is to make an inventory of all major

Chinese relations and all relevant mothers-in-law of each relation. The next step is to make an inventory of the cognitive matter (construction rules, symbols, etc.) for each configuration of relation and mother-in-law. Once such an inventory has been made, it is relatively easy to keep it up to date. It will be an extremely useful source of information for both the day-to-day dealings with the Chinese relations and for crafting a long term strategy for that market.

The outcome of such an exercise can also be used as a point of departure for an intervention. I will list a few possible outcomes that would call for such an intervention.

Too few mothers-in-law

The FCAS case is which the key participating companies are operating under only a few mothers-in-law. The mother-in-law of CFCA and CLICC is the State Light Industry Bureau and so was the short term replacement for CFCA. Exposure, being a European company, does not really have a Chinese-style mother-in-law. However, we could say that, as Exposure, Exposure China and Exposure Asia were all members of the Exposure Group, they were also controlled by the same mother company.

From the perspective of the theoretical framework used in this study, this could be indicative of too low a level of variety and complexity. This conclusion seems to be corroborated by a number of facts from the case history and my analysis in this chapter:

- Exposure and its pool of exhibitors are a tightly coupled space;
- Exposure China concentrates its sales activities on CFCA trade fairs.

Several interventions could be suggested to repair this deficiency. One could be to find other domestic parties that could assist in promoting FCAS in China that were not included in the Light Industry sector.

Unknown mothers-in-law

An inventory of the situation in Shanyin made before the arrival of Mengniu and Yili showed that the Dutch partner of Gucheng was unaware of the importance of the Shuozhou level for its joint venture in Shanyin. A necessary intervention here would be to include a visit to Shuozhou in the next visit by representatives of the Dutch partner to China and establish relations with useful parties there.

Work unit

Being a work unit (*danwei*) is a function of all Chinese companies and is therefore not a real identity by itself. However, it does play a role in many identity constructs. I have introduced the term *danwei* extensively in Chapter 2 and will not repeat it here. I will mention a few examples of identity construction from the cases of this study and show how the work unit status played a role there.

The reason that a threat to Lukang had such a heavy impact in the Ji'ning space was directly related to Lukang's status as the largest work unit in the city. If Lukang really were to go bankrupt (a scenario that was not very likely, though), it would have put thousands of people out of work, who would become a burden for the municipal government. This is the reason why I have paid so much attention to the identity of Lukang = largest employer in Ji'ning. It is at least as important to the day-to-day operation of the company that it is the largest hard currency earner of Shandong, etc.

That Mr Niu Gensheng of Mengniu was able to lure such a large number of people from his former employer, Yili, to his newly established company was remarkable from a work unit perspective. Western readers may not readily appreciate why this step was so remarkable. It happens very often in Western economies. Moreover, the step would probably be attributed to a emotion of loyalty. Yili was a state-owned enterprise and, in spite of the economic reforms, working at a state-owned enterprise was still considered to provide a more stable livelihood than a private company, let alone one that was not yet more than a single rented room. Even the best of friends would be unlikely to bet their protected livelihood that easily on such an endeavour. Niu's behaviour in the past had created a firm belief that Mengniu would succeed and that it would become a better work unit than Yili. Niu's former colleagues were attracted by the belief that it was a good investment to move over to Mengniu.

In general foreign companies, in particular foreign investors, are ill aware of the consequences of the work unit system. Even though that system seems to be going through a period of revision, there are no signs that it will disappear. Some aspects of the old type work unit system reappear in a different way. State-owned enterprises are responsible for the housing of their employees. This is currently regarded as not only a tremendous financial burden, but also in terms of management. However, successful private enterprises often try to lure employees by offering free or cheap housing. The work unit system apparently has created a certain expectation of the employer, part of a Chinese type of psychological contract (Rousseau and Schalk 2000), in which the employer is expected to be involved in the housing of employees.

Another consequence of the work unit system that can get foreign investors into trouble is that a work unit is expected to take care of employees even after their retirement. Foreign-invested companies can decide on ways to circumvent these problems, but when a foreign company is invited to acquire an existing Chinese enterprise it is necessary to take this aspect of the company into account during the feasibility study.

Many others

The construction of corporate identity is a consequence of ongoing inter-action. This study has attempted to reveal the most salient aspects involved in Chinese sense-making processes underlying the construction of identities for Chinese enteprises. It is theoretically impossible to make and provide an exhaustive inventory of all aspects of Chinese corporate iden-tity, as the only aspect there is the ongoing social interaction. As the processes leading to the construction of Chinese corporate identity are embedded in processes that contain traces of thousands of years of ongoing interaction, it is useful to study a number of cases in depth to try to discern a number of recurrent processes.

This chapter could be extended to any length. However, I would be pre-senting more and more of the same. Whenever we try to analyse a particu-lar incident of a particular Chinese company, we would find a large number of company- and incident-related issues, but the processes along which they construct identities would be similar to the ones introduced above.

An example of such a theme is the identity of a Chinese company as a Communist Party cell. This actually is a derived identity, a consequence of the work unit status of each Chinese enterprise. The analysis of how the Party identity of Lukang and its CEO played a role in the solution of the conflict was useful, but it is an example of the basic pattern of 'mothers-in-law'. Once you understand the principle of mothers-in-law, you will be able to grasp the Party cell identity of Chinese companies as well. The same applies for organizations cognate to the Communist Party (Youth League, etc., see Chapter 3).

The sections above contain a comprehensive framework of patterns with which one can start analysing any instance of Chinese corporate iden-tity construction.

This is the end of this book on Chinese corporate identity. However, it is by no means the end of my interest and research in the topic. I sincerely hope that those readers who have withstood the inclination to throw this text away in despair and have reached this last paragraph would like to join me in continuing to dig into the mechanism of Chinese corporate identity construction. It will help to make Chinese and international com-panies co-operate more effectively and may even help the international companies understand themselves better.

Bibliography

Not all texts used for this study can be found in the bibliography. As introduced in Chapter 1, part of my methodology for studying the identity constructs of the example enterprises in the case chapters has been to compile a corpus of narratives for each company. Narrative can be any text, including: texts produced by the company itself, like annual reports, brochures, etc., reports on the company in the media, written private communication, etc. The corpus also includes useful material on the cognitive spaces in which the company is interacting. For the Zhengzhou case in Chapter 4, for example, the corpus also comprises recent reports on the dairy industry of Henan province. Only a few of these sources are mentioned in the text of this study. In that case they are also listed in the bibliography. However, most narratives have only been searched electronically using concordance software. The number of all texts in all corpora is not known, but will be close to a thousand.

Albert, S. and D.A. Whetten (1985) Organizational identity, *Research in Organizational Behavior*, 7: 263–295.

Alibaba (2004) The history of Mengniu's creation', online, available at: info.china. alibaba.com/news/detail/v5003000-d5294029.html (accessed: 21/11/2004).

Allan, J., G. Fairtlough and B. Heinzen (2002) *The Power of the Tale – Using Narratives for Organisational Success*, Chichester: Wiley.

Ashforth, B.E. and F. Mael (1989) Social identity theory and the organization, *Academy of Management Review*, 14: 20–39.

Beamish, P.W. and L. Speiss (1993) Foreign direct investment in China, in: L. Kelly and O. Shenkar (eds) *International Business in China*, London: Routledge.

Bergsma, A. and K. van Petersen (2000) *Psychologie*, Utrecht: Spectrum.

Birkigt, K. and M.M. Stadler (1986) *Corporate Identity, Grundlagen, Funktionen, Fallspielen*, Landsberg am Lech: Verlag Moderne Industrie.

BJSSE (Beijing School of Science Education) (2003) Classical Chinese MBA Cases – First Collection (*Zhongguo MBA dianxing anli – diyiji*), Beijing: China Pricing Publishing House.

Boje, D.M. (2001) *Narrative Methods for Organizational and Communication Research*, London: Sage.

Boje, D.M., R.C. Alvarez and B. Schooling (2001) Reclaiming story in organization: narratologies and action science, in: R. Westwood and S. Linstead (eds) *The Language of Organization*, London: Sage.

Chinabroadcast (2004) 'A story of capital – there is no winner among Mengniu's

Niu Gensheng and Yili's Zheng Junhuai', online, available at: gb.chinabroad cast.cn/7212/2004/12/30/405@408162.htm (accessed: 10/2/2005).

China Daily (2004) Mengniu Dairy expects Hong Kong flotation', online, available at: www.chinadaily.com.cn/english/doc/2004-03/05/content_312129.htm (accessed: 10/2/2005).

CEW (*China Economic Weekly*) (2005) The secret of the intellectual property of the Old Niu Fund', online, available at: www.zgjjzk.cn/more.asp?TN_NID=2005-01-30-1002 (accessed: 12/2/2005).

China Food Industry Yearbook 2002 (2003), Beijing: Zhonghua Shuju.

Clissold, T. (2004) *Mr. China*, London: Robinson.

Cray, D. and G.R. Mallory (1998) *Making Sense of Managing Culture*, London: Thomson.

DAC (2003) Yili Group raises its China dragon head high', online, available at: www.dac.org.cn/showarticle.php?id=3145 (accessed: 2/2/2005).

Daft, R. and K. Weick (1984) Toward a model of organizations as interpretative systems, *Academy of Management Review*, 9.

Derrida, J. (1976) *Of Grammatology*, Baltimore: The Johns Hopkins University Press.

Dijk van, N.N.H. (1989) *Een methodische strategie van organisatie-verandering (A Methodological Strategy for Organizational Change)*, Delft: Eburon.

Ding Chongli (1999) Life of an innovating enterprise – impression of the Yanjing Brewing Group', *Market Daily* (*Shichangbao*), 23/7/1999.H.

Dongen van, A. (1997) *Culture as Method – Homogenizing or Heterogenizing Strategies of Change: The case of the International NGO Forum on Indonesian Development (INFID)*, Delft: Eburon.

Dongen, H.J. Van (1991) Some notions on social integration and steering, in: R.J. In t Veld, L. Schaap, C.J.A.M. Termeer and M.J.W. Van Twist (eds) *Autopoiesis and Configuration Theory – New Approaches to Societal Steering*, Dordrecht: Kluwer Academic Services, pp. 47–54.

Dongen, H.J. Van, W.A.M. de Laat and A.J.J.A. Maas (1996) *Een kwestie van verschil (A Matter of Difference)*, Delft: Eburon.

Dutton, M. (1998) *Streetlife China*, Cambridge: Cambridge University Press.

Fairbank, J.K., E.O. Reischauer and A.M. Craig (1973) *East Asia Tradition and Transformation*, London: George Allen and Unwin.

FIF (Food Ingredients First) (2002) Foreign Firms Invest US$26 MLN Into China's Dairy Industry', online, available at: www.foodingredientsfirst.com/newsmaker_article.asp?idNewsMaker= 2617&fSite=AO545&next=pr (accessed: 31/12/2004).

Gu Jingdun (2003) The development strategy and scientific measures for the Chinese dairy industry' (*Zhongguo naiye fazhan zhanlue yu keji duice*), Beijing: China Academy of Agricultural Sciences.

Guangzhou Evening News (*Yangcheng Wanbao*) (2003) Yanjing Beer encounters mysterious buy out', online, available at: www.ycwb.com/history/gb/2000/02/29/xkb/home.html (accessed 25/3/2005).

Han Furong and Xu Yanmei (1997) *The Stability and Life Cycle of Joint Ventures (Heying qiye de wendingxing yu shouming zhouqi)*, Beijing: China Development Publishing House.

Haslam, S.A. (2001) *Psychology in Organizations – The Social Identity Approach*, London: Sage.

Hatch, M.J. and M. Schultz (2002) The dynamics of organizational identity, in: M.J. Hatch and M. Schultz (eds) *Organizational Identity*, Oxford: Oxford University Press, pp. 377–403.

HAU (2004) Huahuahniu Dairy', online, available at: www.henau.edu.cn/sj/sxjd4.asp (accessed: 29/8/2004).

Hendrischke, H. and Feng Chongyi (1999) *The Political Economy of China's Provinces – Comparative and Competitive Advantage*, London: Routledge.

HNXMY (2004) Henan Huahuaniu Sanlu Dairy', online, available at: www.hnxmy.gov.cn/asp/showdetail.asp?id=10420 (accessed: 29/8/2004).

Hodgkinson, G.P. and P. Sparrow (2002) *Competent Organization: A Psychological Analysis of the Strategic Management Process*, Buckingham: Open University Press.

Hogg, M.A. and G.M. Vaughn (1995) *Social Psychology – an Introduction*, London: Prentice Hall.

Hu Changyi (2003) Interview with the General Manager of Zhengzhou Shanmeng Dairy Co., Ltd.', online, available at: www.tjkx.com/resource/42/2003-06-10/0000257390.html (accessed: 11/6/2004).

Huang Weiding (1996) *China's Hidden Economy* (*Zhongguo de yinxing jingji*), Beijing: China Commercial Publishing House.

IDC (International Dairy Consultants) (2002) '*Feasibility Study Business Diversification into Milk Processing SIDDAIR, Henan, P.R. of China*', Dronten.

Ke Bin (2003) Yanjing Brewing going South, beseiging Guangdong from four sides, Southern Urban Daily', online, available at: www.fsi.com.cn/stock600/point604/604_03033003.htm (accessed: 11/4/2005).

Keister, L.A. (2000) *Chinese Business Groups – The Structure and Impact of Interfirm Relations During Economic Development*, Oxford: Oxford University Press.

Lash, S. and J. Urry (1994) *Economies of Signs and Space*, London: Sage.

Leu, O. (1994) *Corporate Design, Corporate Identity*, Munich: Bruchman.

Lincoln, Y.S. and E.G. Guba (1985) *Naturalistic Inquiry*, Beverly Hills: Sage.

Liu Lisheng, Shao Dongya and Pang Mian (1997) *Foreign Capital Acquires State Owned Enterprises – a realistic analysis and study of countermeasures* (*Waizi binggou guoyou qiye – shizheng fenxi yu duice yanjiu*), Beijing: China Economic Publishing House.

Lu, X. and E. Perry (1997) *Danwei: The Changing Chinese Workplace in Historical and Comparative Perspective*, New York: M.E. Sharpe.

McCall, G.J. and J.L. Simmons (1966) *Identities and Interactions*, New York: The Free Press.

Maas, A. (1988) *Ongedefinieerde ruimten – sociaal-symbolische configuraties* (*Undefined Spaces – Social-symbolic Configurations*), Delft: Eburon.

Maskell, P. H., Bathelt and A. Malmberg (2004) Temporary Clusters and Knowledge Creation: The Effects of International Trade Fairs, Conventions and Other Professional Gatherings, paper presented at the 100th Annual Meeting of the Association of American Geographers, March 14–19, 2004. Online, available at: www.geographie.unimarburg.de/spaces/click.php?action=go&to=4-04.

Olins, W. (1978) *The Corporate Personality*, London: Design Council.

Parker, M. (2000) *Organizational Culture and Identity*, London: Sage.

People (2002) The restructuring of the Henan animal husbandry proving effective', online, available at: www.people.com.cn/GB/other4788/7900/7913/20020417/711478.html (accessed: 29/8/2004).

People's Daily (2003a) Shanxi opens Yanmenguan Ecological Zone', online, available at: www.people.com.cn/GB/other4583/4593/9324/20030329/957223.html (accessed 25/3/2005).

People's Daily (2003b) 'Yanjing Beer encounters mysterious buy out', online, available at: web.peopledaily.com.cn/zdxw/14/20000302/20000302147.html (accessed 25/3/2005).

Peverelli, P. (2000) *Cognitive Space – A Social Cognitive Approach to Sino-Western Cooperation*, Delft: Eburon.

Peverelli, P. (2001) Negotiating Space', paper presented at Hong Kong Baptist University, May 2001, online, available at: staff.feweb.vu.nl/ppepeverelli.

Peverelli, P.J. (2006) Negotiating space, in: L. Douw and K.B. Chan (eds) *Conflict and Change: An Emergent Transational Management Culture in China*, Leiden: Brill (forthcoming).

Redding, S.G. (1993) *The Spirit of Chinese Capitalism*, Berlin: De Gruyter.

Redland (2003) Wandashan erects an eastern bridge head', online, available at: www.redland.gov.cn/nydt/news.asp?id=1449 (accessed: 20/2/2005).

Riel, C.B.M. van (1996) *Identiteit en imago – grondslagen van corporate communication* (*Identity and Image – Foundations of Corporate Communication*), Schoonhoven: Academic Service.

Rongrong (2005) Rongrong Dairy', online, available at: www.sz.sx.cei.gov.cn/SZQY/rongrongry/index.htm (accessed: 22/2/2005).

Rousseau, D.M. and R. Schalk (2000) *Psychological Contracts in Employment – Cross-National Perspectives*, Thousand Oaks: Sage.

Shanxi Evening News (2005) 'A report on the Shanxi dairy industry: an agreement leads to shock', online, available at: www.xbry.com/news_view.asp?id=2835 (accessed: 20/4/2005).

Shanyin Gov. (2005) Shanyin making progress through reforms', online, available at: www.sz.sx.cei.gov.cn/szgk/SZGK/SYX.HTM (accessed: 19/2/2005).

Shuozhou Gov. (2005) online, available at: www.sz.sx.cei.gov.cn/cpbl/rzp.htm (accessed: 19/2/2005).

SIDDAIR (2004) www.siddair.com (accessed: 29/8/2004).

Sina (2004) 'Yili's Founder: Mr. Zheng Junhuai', online, available at: finance.sina.com.cn/g/20041221/08211238963.shtml (accessed: 2/2/2005).

Skinner, G.W. (1964) Marketing and social structure in rural China Part 1, *Journal of Asian Studies*, 24: 1.

Skinner, G.W. (1977) Cities and the hierarchy of local systems, in: G.W. Skinner (ed.) *The City in Late Imperial China*, Stanford: Stanford University Press, pp. 275–351.

Skinner, G.W. (1977) Urban development in imperial China, in: G.W. Skinner (ed.) *The City in Late Imperial China*, Stanford: Stanford University Press, pp. 9–17.

Skinner, G.W. (1985) The structure of Chinese history, *Journal of Asian Studies*, 44: 2.

Southnet (2005) RMB 200 million investment in Nanhai – Beijing Yanjing Brewing to invest in a large brewery in South China', online, available at: www.southcn.com/news/dishi/foshan/jingji/200411180579.htm (accessed: 21/4/2005).

Steinfeld, E.S. (1998) *Forging Reform in China – the Fate of the State-Owned Industry*, Cambridge: Cambridge University Press.

Studwell, J. (2002) *China Dream*, London: Profile.

Tang, J. and A. Ward (2003) *The Changing Face of Chinese Management*, London: Routledge.

Walsh, J.P. and G.R. Ungson (1997) Organizational Memory, in: L. Prusak (ed.) *Knowledge in Organizations – Resources for the Knowledge Based Economy*, Boston: Butterworth-Heinemann, pp. 177–212.

Wang Haixia (2002) Branded Dairy Industry will invigorate the Citizens', online, available at: news.xinhuanet.com/focus/xiangguan/2002071111.htm (accessed: 29/8/2004).

Webber, M. and M.Y.L. Wang (2003) '*Globalising the Chinese countryside: the case of "Rich Wang's Village"*', Melbourne: Melbourne University Private, School of Development Studies, Working Paper Series Nr 3.

Weick, K. (1979) *The Social Psychology of Organizing*, New York: McGraw Hill.

Weick, K. (1995) *Sensemaking in Organizations*, London: Sage.

Weick, K. (2001) *Making Sense of the Organization*, Oxford: Blackwell.

Wong, J., R. Ma and M. Yang (1995) *China's Rural Entrepreneurs – Ten Case Studies*, Singapore: Times Academic Press.

Wong, G.Y.Y. and R.J. Stone (1998) Chinese and Western negotiator stereotypes, in: J. Selmer (ed.) *International Management in China – Cross-cultural Issues*, London: Routledge, pp. 207–222.

Wu Bohong (2003) *Ni shi nali ren* (*Where are You From*), Beijing: China Theatre Publishing House.

XBRY (2005) *Xibu Ruye* (Western Dairy Industry') is a web site dedicated to the dairy industry of West China, it carries a bulletin board with a long discussion on Mengniu by a number of participants; online, available at: www.xbry.com/forum_view.asp?forum_id=1&view_id=68 (accessed on: 11/1/2005).

Xi (2000) *The Logic of Chinese Actions* (*Zhongguoren xingdong de luoji*), River Edge: Global Publishing Co.

Xing Jianguo (1998) *Study of Foreign Invested Enterprise* (*Sanzi qiye yanjiu*), Beijing: China Construction Materials Industry Publishing House.

Xinhuanet (2004a) Interview with Mengniu's CEO Niu Gensheng', online, available at: www.nmg.xinhuanet.com/xwzx/2004-7/11/content_2471495_I.htm (accessed: 11/2/2005).

Xinhuanet (2004b) Who moved the cheese of the Shanyin Agricultural Commercial Farm?', online, available at: www.sx.xinhuanet.com/qyzx/2004-11/13/content_3212750.htm (accessed: 18/2/2005).

Yan Yanni (2000) *International Joint Ventures in China – Ownership, Control and Performance*, London: Macmillan Press.

Zhengzhou Evening News (2001) Zhengzhou starts new major dairy project', online, available at: www.tjkx.com/resource/42/2001-04-11/000009668C.html (accessed: 4/9/2004).

Zhou Jihu and Yang Xiaomin (2000) *China's Unit System* (*Zhongguo Danwei Zhidu*), China Beijing: Economic Publishing House.

ZYQNW (2003) Zhengzhou Shanmeng Dairy Co.', online, available at: www.zyqnw.com/new/readnews.asp?NewsID=406&BigClassID=45&smallClassID=45&SpecialID=0 (accessed: 4/9/2004).

ZZNET (2004) Henan Animal Husbandry in progress', online, available at: www.zznet.com.cn/xhjh/xhjieshao/js5.htm (accessed: 29/8/2004).

Index

9 780415 546768